UNTOUCHABLE FREEDOM

UNTOUCHABLE FREEDOM

A Social History of a Dalit Community

Vijay Prashad

OXFORD

UNIVERSITY PRESS

OXFORD
UNIVERSITY PRESS

YMCA Library Building, Jai Singh Road, New Delhi 110001

Oxford University Press is a department of the University of Oxford. It furthers the
University's objective of excellence in research, scholarship, and education
by publishing worldwide in

Oxford   New York

Athens   Auckland   Bangkok Bogota Buenos Aires Calcutta
Cape Town   Chennai   Dar es Salaam   Delhi   Florence   Hong Kong   Istanbul
Karachi   Kuala Lumpur   Madrid   Melbourne   Mexico City   Mumbai
Nairobi Paris Sao Paolo Singapore Taipei Tokyo Toronto Warsaw

with associated companies in Berlin Ibàdan

Oxford is a registered trade mark of Oxford University Press
in the UK and in certain other countries

Published in India
By Oxford University Press, New Delhi

ISBN 019 565 075 1

Typeset at Urvashi Press, 49/3 Vaidwara, Meerut 250 002
Printed by Pauls Press, New Delhi 110020
Published by Manzar Khan, Oxford University Press
YMCA Library Building, Jai Singh Road, New Delhi 110 001

Acknowledgements

The debt of scholars is not written up in account books. For us junior scholars, the fellowship of our seniors in the time of our apprenticeship is a token of their selflessness. Of all my teachers, Gyan Pandey provided me with the discipline and the compassion to conduct myself during my research and with the necessity to be sincere as I put my findings down on paper. He guided my thesis, along with Bernard S. Cohn, Ronald B. Inden and Leora Auslander and, in Delhi, he was joined by a phalanx of Marxists who helped keep me honest, people such as Lisa Armstrong, Aijaz Ahmad, Brinda Karat, Dilip Simeon, Prabhu Mohapatra, and Prakash Karat.

When I set out to research this book, I thought that the conventional historical materials would be inadequate. For that reason, I spent a considerable amount of time in the collection of stories and in ethnographic fieldwork (from 1992 to 1994, then again in the summer of 1996). Extensive interactions with the Balmikis of Delhi and Jalandhar (and also of Patiala, Dehra Dun and Meerut) enabled me to explore different ways in which folks conceptualize their histories. I was also able to find a trove of documents held by elders, many of them in plastic bags hidden in cabinets. These allowed for the richness in the latter half of the book. Understandably, few Balmikis felt enthusiastic about letting these papers go to public institutions which they regard as hives of corruption. For letting me into their lives, I want to thank Ranjeet Singh, Raju Kumar, Bimla Devi, Santoshi, Mahesh Kumar, Rakesh Milind, Baru Ram, Madan Lal Parcha, Prem Prakash Ujjainwal, Guruji, Sant Chandrabhan, Maharaj Chena, Babu Krishen, Pradhan Saheb, Madan Lal Saugwan, Sadan Lal Saugwan, Ram Krishen Saugwan, Kamla Saugwan, and other members of the Saugwan clan, Dalbir Singh, Rattan Lal Balmiki, Puran Chand, Khilati Lal, Ravi Chauhan, Krishen Kumar Vidyarthi, R.C. Sangar, Lahori Ram Balley, Rolu Ram, Charanjit Kalyana and Bhagmal 'Pagal' as well as the Delhi unit of the CPI (M) for all manner of kindness. During my research, Bhagwan Das, Manjula Sahdev, Indu Agnihotri and Neeladri Bhattacharya helped me decipher Punjabi history. Materials for this study came from the National Archives of India, Delhi State Archives, Delhi Town Hall Record Room, University of Delhi Library, Arya Sarvadeshik Pratinidhi Sabha, Harijan Sevak Sangh, Nehru Memorial

Museum and Library, Gandhi Memorial Library, Punjabi University Library (Patiala) and National Library (Calcutta). I am thankful to the generosity of the staff at these institutions.

The gestation of this manuscript from an unwieldy dissertation saw the helpful intervention of numerous well-wishers, such as Amitava Kumar, Biju Mathew, Chitra Joshi, David Ludden, Dipesh Chakrabarty, Faisal Devji, Gautam Premnath, Janaki Nair, Kaleem Siddiqi, Karen Leonard, Kasturi Ray, Madhava Prasad, Mala DeAlwis, Mir Ali Hussain, Mir Ali Raza, Pradeep Jeganathan, Raj Chandavarkar, Ram Narayan Singh, Rizwan Ahmad, Sabyasachi Bhattacharya, Sangeeta Kamat, Shonali Bose, Sid Lemelle, Sudhir Venkatesh, Sunaina Maira, Suvritta Khatri and Vrinda Narain. In addition, Trinity College, Cornell University and Syracuse University gave me shelter while I wrote this book and my colleagues at these institutions provided much solace and intellectual stimulation (notably, Ellison Findly, Maurice Wade, Janet Bauer, Dario Euraque, Luis Figueroa, Steve Valocchi, Johnny Williams, Gustavo Remedi, Raymond Baker, Fred Errington, Joan Hedrick, Jerry Watts, Gay Weidlich and Susan Sanders). Parts of this book appeared courtesy of Marcel van der Linden in *International Review of Social History*, Shahid Amin and Dharma Kumar in *Indian Economic and Social History Review*, Marcus Klee in *Left History*, Krishna Raj in *Economic and Political Weekly*, Gautam Bhadra, Gyan Prakash and Susie Tharu in *Subaltern Studies X* and N. Ram in *Frontline*. The book bears the marks of many anonymous readers and of one very supportive and diligent editor at OUP, Bela Malik, to whom I am very grateful. I am also thankful to Gopalakrishnan Nair for three of the photographs appearing in the book, and Thomas J. Mathew for a careful reading of the manuscript.

Much respect to my late grandparents, Dr Baini Prashad (Persian scholar and zoologist), Dr Ram Dass Prashad (Surgeon), Lt Col C.L. Pasricha (School of Tropical Medicine) and Sita Pasricha (author of cookbooks). They produced my parents, Pran and Soni, who in turn support me with love and challenge me to stay rational. Rosy (who taught me the value of labour), my siblings (who are also friends), my in-laws (who heard many of these ideas in an inchoate form) and the Delhi clan (which is an unending source of inspiration) are all in my thoughts for their many acts of generosity and for their vivid love. This book is for Lisa.

Hartford, CT   VIJAY PRASHAD

Contents

List of Illustrations

Introduction

Being an Indian, I am a partisan, and I am afraid I cannot help taking a partisan view. But I have tried, and I should like you to try to consider these questions as a scientist impartially examining facts, and not as a nationalist out to prove one side of the case. Nationalism is good in its place, but it is an unreliable friend and an unsafe historian.

(Jawaharlal Nehru, 14 December 1932).[1]

In the aftermath of the pogrom against the Sikhs in Delhi (1984), in which 2500 people perished in a few days, reports filled the capital of the assailants and their motives. It was clear from the very first that this was no disorganized 'riot' and that the organized violence visited upon Sikhs was engineered by the Congress (I) to avenge the assassination of Indira Gandhi. Of the assailants, we only heard rumours, that they came from the outskirts of the city, from those 'urban villages' inhabited by Jats and Gujjars as well as *dalits* (untouchables) resettled there during the National Emergency (1975–7). The People's Union for Democratic Rights (PUDR) published a pamphlet, just after the carnage, which reported that 'the Bhangis—many of them working as sweepers in the corporation—comprised the bulk of the local miscreants who attacked the Sikhs'.[2] For many middle-class residents of the city, this news simply reaffirmed their stubborn conviction that the 'low castes', being prone to violence and devoid of any promise or potential beyond that required strict control. Nanki Bai, one of the survivors, told her interviewers in the relief camps that the metropolitan councillor in her locality 'had the killing done by the *kanjars* and the *bhangis*', both compensated with liquor and cash, since, in her opinion, 'the educated can't do this sort of thing—only the *neech-log* (derogatory for low-status persons) do things like this'.[3] Such statements of prejudice that

[1] Jawaharlal Nehru, *Glimpses of World History* (Allahabad: Kitabistan, 1939), p. 443.

[2] PUDR, *Who are the Guilty? Report of a Joint Inquiry into the Causes and Impact of the Riots in Delhi from 31 October to 10 November* (New Delhi: PUDR, 2nd edition, December 1984), p. 3.

[3] Uma Chakravarti and Nandita Haksar, *The Delhi Riots: Three Days in the Life of a Nation* (New Delhi: Lancer, 1987), p. 43.

exempt the 'educated' from culpability erase the crime of the councillor and the complicity of the bulk of the middle class which benefits from a political system run by authoritarian parties to maintain economic, social, and political inequality. The screen between the acts of violence and the political structures that work at the behest of certain dominant classes enables the latter to disown responsibility for making violence a means to realize their agenda (as in the 'excesses' of the period of the National Emergency).[4] The sustained exploitation of the working people produces a circumstance wherein some dalits become clients of political strongmen to act on behalf of a status quo that oppresses the bulk of the dalits.

Among the dalits of Delhi, several young men of the Balmiki community seemed to lead the way in the conflagration. If the Balmikis offered fealty to the Congress in the early 1980s, by the end of the decade most indications showed that a set of them had begun to work closely with the Hindutva movement, first in anti-Muslim actions in Delhi and Khurja (among other places) and subsequently as part of the caravan to Ayodhya to participate in the 6 December 1992 destruction of Mir Baqi's mosque.[5] Few realized the gravity of the situation and there are as yet only rudimentary explanations for the anomalous turn taken by this dalit community as it linked its destiny to the political agencies of the established order (particularly the Hindutva ensemble, a markedly conservative, misogynist and communal political bloc). If some young men did the killing, the response of much of the rest of the community ranged from tacit to active support for their actions. There is now sufficient commentary on the assertion of dalits across the country, but this does not address the counter-intuitive alliance between activist dalits (at some level committed to end the order that enforces dalithood) and the forces of Hindutva (which are committed to the defence of that very order).[6] A similar entry of women activists into the Hindu right provoked several useful studies of the phenomenon and we

[4]Vijay Prashad, 'Emergency Assessments', *Social Scientist*, nos. 280–1 (September–October 1996), p. 52.

[5]Pradip K. Datta, *et al.*, 'Understanding Communal Violence: Nizamuddin Riots', *Economic and Political Weekly*, 10 November 1990; Uma Chakravarty, *et al.*, 'Khurja Riots, 1990–91: Understanding the Conjuncture', *Economic and Political Weekly*, 2 May 1992 and my own research during the 1992–4 period.

[6]Achin Vanaik, *The Furies of Indian Communalism* (London: Verso, 1997), pp. 320–1.

are only now getting a glimpse of the reasons why some women ally themselves to a programmatically misogynist political formation.[7] In an ahistorical view of the dalits as a unified entity that *should* be opposed to Hindu supremacy in an unproblematic way, this alliance makes little sense. On the other hand, a social history of the Balmikis reveals the institutional roots of the alliance in the colonial municipality where these dalits were hired as clients of Hindu overseers who exercised inordinate control over their lives. This institutional connection was given an ideological framework in the 1930s when these dalits, hired exclusively into the municipality as sweepers, adopted and refined an anti-Muslim Hindu identity proffered in the first instance by militant Hindus. These dalits, in other words, have a long history within the ensemble of Hindutva, even if it did not inform the politics of many of them until recently. That is, most of the Balmikis, until the emergence of the BJP in 1980 tended to live their political lives within the Congress, even as they remained wedded to a contradictory Hindu faith (with its anti-Muslim undertones and its humanist overtones) in their private domains. The 1980s enabled many Balmikis to commit themselves to the Hindutva project, particularly since it seemed to promise them the emancipation held off for five decades. One of the indications of this emancipation was the Vishwa Hindu Parishad pledge to erect a temple to Valmiki (the sage of the Balmikis) within the Babri Masjid–Ram Janmabhoomi complex (this commitment, like many others made by the Hindutva ensemble to the dalits, comes and goes).

HINDUTVA AND BALMIKI CONSCIOUSNESS

In the Saugwan home in Old Delhi on 28 March 1993, Tara Chand ended an emotional conversation with the plaintive refrain, *hum aur kya kar sakte the* (what else could we have done)? He, his friends, and family had just finished collectively telling me about a fracas of 18 June 1978. In their version, a young Muslim boy from the neighbour-hood urinated in the narrow alleyway that led into their Kalan Mahal locality. Some Balmikis asked the boy not to use the drain as a latrine, since, as Madan Lal emphasized, 'both our women walk on this road'. The 'road' is a tight lane with houses on one side and a high wall on the other, with surface drains along its edge to bear the refuse from the

[7]*Women and the Hindu Right*. Eds Tanika Sarkar and Urvashi Butalia (New Delhi: Kali for Women, 1995).

homes to the sewer. The conflict was less about the urine and more about the affront to the dignity of the women by public urination. The Muslim boy was beaten by several Balmikis as a prelude to an evening of mayhem. Several Muslim families up the lane told me a different story, that the filth of the Balmikis led to a fight rather than the act of one boy. In highly tense times (1993), it was hard not to emphasize one's own innocence in sectarian struggles. Both Balmikis and Muslim families, however, recounted the story with great sadness, since they operated as mutual allies over time. Speaking of her Muslim neighbours, Kamala Devi said that they have *daya* (compassion), 'if you fall in a drain, they will stop and pick you up. A Hindu won't'.

The 1978 incident, in which no lives were lost, marks a change in the relations between working-class Muslims and Balmikis across north India. Their structural and spatial proximity allowed them to entertain some similar views on similar dilemmas. Investigators of the May 1987 riots in Old Delhi met a dalit worker from Churiwalan who said that dalits

used to play cards with their Muslim neighbours. But now, that would be over. Old residents of the area regretted that the past custom of holding occasional meetings of the elders of both the communities in the localities was no longer followed, resulting in widening the distance between the two.[8]

In the aftermath of the 1987 riot, links between Muslims and Balmikis appeared to diminish. Both Balmikis and Muslims complained against each other's violation of their limited space in the old city and these tensions developed 'over private altercations which are inevitable in any crowded locality where the residents always feel threatened by incursions into their tightly bound world of privacy'.[9] Congested and poorly maintained living conditions provide the roots of disenchantment, but these do not in themselves lead people to riot and to murder. The moral basis of neighbourliness remains despite the distrust that has flowered in the past two decades; as Bimla Devi of Karol Bagh told me, the Muslims and the Balmikis are both children of poverty and that makes them treat each other with some measure of respect. These roots of conviviality need to be recalled when we consider the development of conflict between some Balmikis and Muslims.[10]

[8]PUDR, 'Delhi Walled City Riots', *Delhi–Meerut Riots*. Ed. Asghar Ali Engineer (Delhi: Ajanta, 1988), p. 105.

[9]Ibid., p. 87.

[10]At the Aurangabad Depressed Classes Conference, the dalit leader Shyam

Nevertheless, since the 1980s, a number of Balmikis have participated in the anti-Muslim pogroms in Delhi and smaller towns such as Khurja and Meerut. By the 1982 Meerut riot, one investigator noted that the Balmikis 'have now come to find shelter under the broad Hindu umbrella'.[11] The immediate explanation was that the forces of Hindutva purchased the support of the Balmikis with liquor and money. A teacher in Meerut told Asghar Ali Engineer that the Hindutvawadis mobilized the Balmikis 'to fight the Muslims by proxy' and that the dalits received 'Rs. 200 and a bottle of liquor for killing one Muslim'. During the riots, Engineer commented, the Hindus do not come 'directly into the picture'.[12] Certainly, the Balmikis may have taken payment for their actions, but that does not exhaust the reasons for their participation in the bloodshed. People are not driven solely by a thirst for power, but also by social and political visions that provide the rich context within which historical actors make history. These social visions are located in the cultural histories of particular groups. This book will introduce the contradictions of Balmiki life to interpret the turn of a considerable number of them to Hindutva. The Hindutvawadis began to make statements about the dalits in 1981 during the time of the Meenakshipuram conversions, but this was not their first entry into the lives of dalits.[13] From the 1920s, militant Hindus worked amongst the Balmikis. The historical and sociological narratives from the pasts of these Balmikis were now reintegrated into the Hindutva framework (the reader will find that Chapter 4 is analytically central to this argument). Such groundwork remained within the lifeworld of the Balmikis even though they did not find the Hindutva electoral machinery attractive until these dalits rejected the Congress party which, by the 1980s, was no longer able to command their political loyalty. The militant Hindu alliance rekindled its Balmiki links through the promise

---

Sunder noted that 'the time had come when (dalits) should declare an open revolt against caste Hindus and join hands with Muslims for the betterment of their conditions'. *They Burn: The 160,000,000 Untouchables of India* (Bangalore: Dalit Sahitya Akademi, 1987), p. 11.

[11]Rajiv Tiwari, 'After the Riots: Pointers from Meerut', *Communalism: The Razor's Edge (Factsheet #2)* (Bombay, n.d.), p. 37.

[12]Asghar Ali Engineer, 'An Analytical Study of the Meerut Riot', *Communal Riots in Post-Independence India.* Ed. Asghar Ali Engineer (Delhi: Orient Longman, 1984), p. 274.

[13]George Mathew, 'Politicisation of Religion: Conversion to Islam in Tamil Nadu', *Economic and Political Weekly*, 19 and 26 June 1982.

of constructing a Valmiki temple within the future Ram temple site in Ayodhya and through the assurance that a radical anti-Muslim struggle would bring more results than the Mandalist path of state benevolence. The Balmiki youth who participated in militant Hindu politics and those Balmikis who tacitly supported the alliance are driven by the belief that their poverty is the result of Muslims (who are seen by many Balmikis as the cause of their untouchability and their enslavement) and Jatavs or Chamars (whose aggressive neo-Buddhism and support for the Ambedkarite Social Democracy agenda is seen by many of them as the vehicle of Jatav sectoral advancement at their own expense).[14]

Engineer astutely observed after the 1982 Meerut pogrom that only the 'poor and illiterate' Balmikis had 'fallen into the RSS trap. The Chamars who are more educated are nowhere on the scene'.[15] It certainly seems correct that dalits apart from the Balmikis do not share the Hindutva political vision and have not entered its political machinery. Significant numbers of Jatavs form the backbone of the Bahujan Samaj Party and the Samajwadi Party. Further, dalits in Maharashtra, such as the Mahars, stand apart from the kinds of tactics used by the Hindutva machine to incorporate dalits. In fact, many form the heart of the crucial anti-Hindutva political formations.[16] Jatav and Mahar militancy against Hindutva may be traced both to their independent location in the economy (as artisans) and to their vibrant anti-Hindutva ideological traditions (such as Raidas and Chokhamela).[17] The institutional and

[14]Here we might understand something of the current politics of Uttar Pradesh, wherein the 'party of the dalits' (the Bahujan Samaj Party) joins with the 'party of the Brahmins' (the BJP) to combat the 'party of the Other Backward Castes and Muslims' (the Samajwadi Janata Party).

[15]Engineer, 'An Analytical Study', p. 274.

[16]Gopal Guru, 'Understanding Communal Riots in Maharashtra', *Economic and Political Weekly*, vol. 28, no. 19, 8 May 1993 and Jayant Lele, *Hindutva: The Emergence of the Right* (Madras: Earthworm Books, 1995).

[17]On Jatavs, see O. Lynch, *The Politics of Untouchability: Social Mobility and Social Change in a City of India* (New York: Columbia University Press, 1969); S.K. Sharma, *The Chamar Artisans: Industrialisation, Skills and Social Mobility* (Delhi: BR, 1986); R.S. Khare, *The Untouchable as Himself* (Cambridge: Cambridge University Press, 1984). On Mahars, see E. Zelliot, *From Untouchable to Dalit* (Delhi: Mahohar, 1992); Jayashree Gokhale, *From Concessions to Confrontation: The Politics of an Indian Untouchable Community* (Bombay: Popular Prakashan, 1993); Joseph Mathew, *Ideology, Protest and Social Mobility: Case Study of Mahars and Pulayas* (New Delhi: Inter-India, 1986).

ideological independence of these castes, despite the atrocities visited upon them by dominant castes, allows for a certain amount of political flexibility. That the Jatavs, for instance, have at their disposal a reasonable amount of collective capital to finance a political movement is of some significance. The Balmikis, on the other hand, do not enjoy such benefits. This book offers an extended social history of the Balmikis to demonstrate how their space for political manoeuvre was restricted so that the politics of Hindutva can appear to many Balmikis not only as their politics, but as one of the few available avenues for their (often) individual or (sometimes) collective advancement.

CASTE AND BALMIKI CONSCIOUSNESS

Recent scholarship on dalit history shows us that struggles by the oppressed drew myriad responses from native and colonial élites, since both were affected, in different ways, under pressure from these mass developments.[18] The pressure from below was exerted not only through agrarian struggles, but also through demands for social equality in ritual and market terms. This book will focus on the pressures exerted by those dalits of Delhi and its environs who are now known as Balmikis, particularly in the period from the 1860s to the 1960s in terms of the institutional and ideological incorporation of these dalits into the maelstrom of militant Hinduism.

The bulk of the Balmiki community today labours as sweepers hired by the municipalities of Delhi where they work under the close supervision of Hindu overseers and Jamadars. The British hired a set of castes into the sanitation department due to the dominant belief that 'caste', especially for the dalits, had something to do with occupation. 'Special circumstances have combined to preserve in greater integrity and to perpetuate under a more advanced state of society than elsewhere the hereditary nature of occupation', a colonial official noted, 'and thus in a higher degree than in other modern nations to render identical the true principle of community of blood and community of occupation'.[19] Notwithstanding the colonial officials' wisdom the temporal and spatial variations in the regimes of caste render the

[18]Sekhar Bandyopadhyay, *Caste, Politics and the Raj: Bengal 1872–1937* (Calcutta: KP Bagchi, 1990), chapter 3 and Saurabh Dube, *Untouchable Pasts: Religion, Identity and Power among a Central Indian Community, 1780–1950* (Albany: State University of New York Press, 1998).

[19]*Census of India*, Punjab, 1881, vol. 1, p. 334.

postulation of any single, pristine and timeless operative social principle of caste or any one functionalist system of occupational castes, explicable by reference to one, necessarily ahistorical key or another (whether hierarchy or otherwise), virtually impossible.[20] Many factors influence the idea and practice of caste and routinely transform not only the immediate relationship between discrete castes, but also the regime of castes as such.[21] One of the determinants of caste is the misogynist idea that women's menstruation is taboo and that only certain castes experience a second, sacred birth which cleanses them of the first, bloody birth. Even this notion, however, is not shared by all castes in the same way, since some deny the very existence of such a thing as a sacred birth. Certainly, the various forms of caste (*varna, jati, gotra*) are inherited from the past, particularly in their stress on the protection of sexuality of women and of sexual relations across castes. These relations are shaped in the contemporary world by the transformation of marriage laws and other such instruments, but their lineage can be traced to the creative contradictions born in an earlier time.[22] For dalits, such as the Balmikis, questions of sexuality are immensely important given, for example, the retribution visited on them by dominant castes for infringement of the latter's prohibitions on sexual congress across caste. The site of caste of particular importance for the Balmikis, and for the book, is the ascribed link between occupation and caste, one that traps them into work as sweepers. The issue of the labour regime and of a caste's relationship to occupation has a long history as well and, like the issue of sexual taboos, the social matrix of the relationship is fundamentally reconfigured during the penetration of the countryside by the colonial state and the concurrent expansion of urban areas. In this context, certain castes find themselves locked into specific occupations by the state, a procedure justified by the colonial officials as a mark of caste culture when, in fact, there was little connection between the modern occupation and the caste's own work history. For the Balmikis, for instance, most worked as general landless

---

[20]Arjun Appadurai, 'Putting Hierarchy in Its Place', *Cultural Anthropology*, vol. 3 no. 1 (February 1988).

[21]G.S. Ghurye, *Caste and Race in India* (London: K. Paul, 1932) and his revised 1961 edition.

[22]M.N. Srinivas, 'The Changing Position of Indian Women', *Man*, no. 12 (1977); R. Palriwala, 'Production, Reproduction and the Position of Women: A Case Study of a Rajasthan Village' (Delhi: University of Delhi Ph.D., 1990).

field-hands, but by the 1880s those who moved into the cities entered the sanitation workforce and all Balmikis began to bear the taint of being sweepers *in perpetuum*. This fundamental element of the social history of the Balmikis is recounted in detail in Chapter 2.

The stereotype that identifies certain oppressed castes by their occu-pations is not unfamiliar within the world of the dominant castes, many of whom knew that their menials did many other things apart from the ascribed occupation. Nevertheless, they colluded with the colonial officials to associate the Balmikis, for instance, with sanitation work. 'In India, blind people require neither a name nor an occupation', Premchand wrote in 1925, for 'Surdas is their automatic name and begging their occupation. Their nature and attributes are also univer-sally known, a particular aptitude for singing and performing, a particular love in their heart, a particular involvement in spiritualism and devotion'.[23] Indeed, Premchand noted, people often assume that all Pasis sell liquor, all Dhobis wash clothes and all Chamars remove dead animals, all this without any idea where and how these views emerge, since they are so far removed from what appears before one's eyes. Of the Balmikis, there is a dominant caste assumption that they deal in the refuse of other humans and that they are all culturally dysfunctional.[24] The British built upon these reductionist images to hire only the Balmikis into the sanitation departments and to leave them with few other options for their livelihood. Over time, the Balmikis became entrenched in the municipalities (particularly during economic slumps, when at least their jobs remained protected) and they began to rely upon their Hindu overseers who became the colonial state's representa-tives at the local level. The clerks at Town Hall and the Jamadars forged a patron-client relationship with the Balmikis, such that many among these dalits took shelter in the putative benevolence of the petty satraps and relied upon the state and its representatives for succour. This book unravels the social history of the patron-client relationship between the class of municipal administrators (including the Jamadars) and the Balmikis, whose work as manual sweepers enabled the city to remain clean at little cost. The arrangement of modern Delhi relied upon the fact of refuse removal by manual methods and these tech-niques marked the sweepers even more, in the eyes of dominant castes,

[23]Premchand, *Rangbhumi* (Allahabad: Saraswati, 1973), p. 7.

[24]Amritlal Nagar, *Nachyo Bahut Gopal* (Delhi: Rajkamal, 1980).

with the taint of impurity and untouchability.[25] The sight of headbaskets and shoddy brooms reminded the dominant castes of the Balmiki's *inevitable* occupation and of their menial status. 'As long as there will be a metal trash can in Rameshwari's hands', noted one Balmiki poet, 'the democracy of my nation will be an insult'.[26] There was to be no emancipation of the Balmikis from a profession to which they became linked (despite the absence of any living, historical tie with refuse removal), neither was there even relief from the harshness of the manual system and the overlordship of the municipal supervisors, all of which was put in place from the 1860s to the 1930s (and catalogued in Chapters 1–3).

The Balmikis did not accede to their recrafted subordination without a fight. The literature on Balmikis in particular and on dalits in general shows us that there is little evidence of mindless submission to Brahmanical custom.[27] This is not a new pattern, for there is evidence of struggle through the historical record.[28] In 1729, for instance, the shoemakers of Delhi led a revolt against injustice with such simple weapons as the strike, the *gherao* (protest by confinement) and a bombardment of slippers. The city's rulers stopped the revolt by a demonstration of firepower and by the mercurial tongue of the *vizier* (minister) who, when he found the shoemakers somewhat quiet, 'addressed them in modest terms, and by employing, by turns, expressions of severity and consolation, he prevailed upon them to disperse'.[29] Such struggles developed in opposition to the colonial state, and its outcome, detrimental to the sweepers, produced the patron-

[25]Such contradictions between being relied upon and reviled are shown in Robert Deliège, *Les Paraiyars du Tamil Nadu* (Nettetal: Steyler Verlag-Wort und Werk, 1988), p. 117.

[26]Om Prakash Valmiki, 'Jharuwali', *Sadiyon ka Santap* (Dehra Dun: Philhal, 1991), pp. 16–7.

[27]Pauline Kolenda, *Caste, Cult and Hierarchy* (Meerut: Folklore Institute, 1983), part 2; Kathleen Gough, 'Harijans in Thanjavur', *Imperialism and Revolution in South Asia*. Eds H. Sharma and K. Gough (New York: Monthly Review, 1973), p. 234 and J. Freeman, 'The Consciousness of Freedom among India's Untouchables', *Social and Economic Development in India*. Eds D.K. Basu and R. Sisson (New Delhi: Sage, 1986).

[28]Irfan Habib, 'Caste in Indian History', *Essays in Indian History* (New Delhi: Tulika, 1995).

[29]Ghulam Husayn Khan Tabataba'i, *Siyar al-muta'akhkhirin* (Lahore: Sheikh Mubarak Ali, 1975), vol. 1, p. 264.

client relation of Jamadar/Town Hall sweeper. The municipality in Delhi narrowed the space for political work, since the sweepers came to rely inordinately upon the Jamadars and the clerks at Town Hall. Nevertheless, the space did not close as these dalits fought for their emancipation on various fronts (radical nationalism, dalit nationalism, Hindutva fascism, trade unionism, socialism, plebeian forms of theology and justice), most of them allowing the Balmikis to produce a complex rendition of their socio-economic status as well as tasks for both accommodation with the established order and liberation from that very order. The Balmikis fought against the Gandhian reduction of their trials to a problem of their culture (Chapter 5) and of the Hindutva reconstruction of their religious history into an anti-Muslim tradition (Chapter 4). They participated in intense battles, but when the accounts are done, the totality of the community, perhaps, did not gain more than some short-term benefits. A few Balmikis were able to advance as tokens of dominant caste benevolence.

The institutional incorporation of the Balmikis under the shadow of the petty municipal officers was met at each turn by an ideological campaign waged by militant Hindus (some within the Congress) to draw the Balmikis firmly into their politico-cultural camp. Many of these militant Hindus in cities such as Delhi came from families who earned their livelihood from trade and from employment in the lower reaches of urban government. These people formed the cadre of local Congress organizations and they worked amongst the masses on many fronts, either to conduct various kinds of reforms or else to demonstrate against the excesses of colonial rule.[30] From the 1920s onwards the anti-colonial national movement proceeded apace and many of these Congress workers turned to the dalits, following Gandhi's lead, to recruit them into their protests. The entry into the dalit neighbourhoods by these political cadres required that the cadres ideologically mobilize the dalits to either join the demonstrations or else the organization. Many of the stories told to the Balmikis resemble the common anti-colonial one, but frequently the Balmikis heard an anti-Muslim tale from the lips of those who worked both for the Congress and for

---

[30]A colonial report offers us the category of 'Arya Samaj Congressman', a notion that fits many of the characters encountered in this book, people such as Shraddhananda, Sundarananda and Ami Chand Pandit. NAI, Home (Political), no. 41/5-Poll. and KW 193.

militant Hindu organizations.[31] The militant Hindus strongly attacked the old faith of the Balmikis and many of them did so not just with ritual and social power, but notably with professional authority. The Balmikis did join other dalits in such liberation strategies as the Ad-Dharm agitation, but, as we shall see, their institutional binds and their paucity of capital derailed much hope for the constitution of an independent political movement. In a struggle of immense proportions for the Balmikis, militant Hindus trounced their preceptor-based faith and inserted the Balmikis crudely into the 'Hindu family' (but only as inferior country cousins). That is, militant Hindus successfully preached against the Balmiki worship of Bala Shah Nuri and Lal Beg, two figures of an immense dalit-Bahujan pantheon of local spirits and teachers.[32] Rather than these figures, the Balmikis turned to Maharishi Valmiki, the legendary author of the *Ramayana*, as the godhead of the community. The militant Hindus claimed that the earlier faith came to these dalits from Muslim rulers, who, they erroneously claimed, captured and confined the Balmikis. As these dalits increasingly placed culpability for their oppression on the Muslims, they entered willy-nilly into the framework of Hindutva despite the fact that most Hindus refused to sup with them or to marry them. The ideological link, made fast in the 1930s, has a strong legacy. The Balmikis, whatever their tactical and strategic sacrifices, are sustained by the vitality of the social contradictions that continue to oppress them. There is little social advancement despite the claims of Hindutva and there is a fleeting recognition that there can be no gain without sustained political struggle.

[31]Eleanor Zelliot, among others, points out that the Congress' approach to the dalits came in terms of the formation of a 'Hindu' community, but she misses the anti-Muslim dimension of this strategy. 'Congress and the Untouchables, 1917–1950', *Congress and Indian Nationalism*. Eds R. Sisson and S. Wolpert (Berkeley: University of California, 1988), p. 185.

[32]Kancha Ilaiah, *Why I am Not a Hindu* (Calcutta: Samya, 1996), chapter 5 and Harjot Oberoi, *The Construction of Religious Boundaries* (Delhi: Oxford University Press, 1994), chapter 3.

1

Mehtars

In the 1870s, the sweepers of Delhi repeatedly went on strike against the Delhi Municipal Committee (DMC) and the Chief Commissioner of Delhi (CC). For the sweepers, the main issue remained their refusal to submit to the overseers hired by the DMC to bring them under its control. Before the reconstruction of Delhi's urban governance by the British, the sweepers worked as employees of *mohallas* (neighbourhoods) rather than as the servants of the state. The sweepers belonged to a set of menial castes, mainly dalits, a social fact that brought on them the scorn and prejudice of those for whom they cleaned. Nevertheless, for many sweepers the relative independence they enjoyed, such as their freedom to work in bands across the cityscape in accord with rules of their own making, was a matter of considerable importance. This relative independence did not mean that the sweepers lived and worked in conditions of freedom. Many felt the sharp edge of caste prejudice and of feudal violence, stories of which continue to permeate the landscape of dalit history.[1] British rule, for these dalits, while doing little to neutralize, or even mitigate, those aspects of prejudice, snatched from them the few moments of institutional power they enjoyed. This chapter will detail the battle between the sweepers of Delhi and the DMC, one that led to the subordination of these dalits to their Hindu overseers.

TYRANNICAL SWEEPERS

In 1803, the British defeated the remnants of the Maratha army and took possession of Delhi, the erstwhile capital of the Mughal empire. Between 1803 and 1857, the British held Delhi as a curiosity, allowing its administrators (such as David Ochterlony and Charles Metcalfe) the

---

[1]Sant Ram, *Hamara Samaj* (Hoshiarpur: Vishveshwananda-vaidia Sansthan, 1957), pp. 202–20.

luxury of exploration and of diplomacy. The British lived alongside the Mughal sovereign, who continued his tentative rule over a curtailed empire (as a British pensioner he was paid an annual allowance of eleven and a half lakh rupees). When the peasants rebelled in 1857, the studied distance ended. The British terror in the aftermath of the revolt left Delhi with what one historian described as the 'shadow of death'. The legacies of 1857 included poverty and demoralization for the natives.[2] The British removed the Muslim masses from the city, exiled the Emperor to Burma, destroyed many of the buildings of the city, hung a number of rebels on the outskirts of the city and set swine upon their feet, in short, terror memorable for its barbarism.[3]

Anxious to consolidate legitimacy after its reign of terror, the British turned to lesser noblemen and to apolitical merchants for their support. While the regime did not devolve power, it did appoint loyalists to the DMC (founded in 1863). Established families that may have held some small measure of power in the Mughal court entered the DMC as intermediate authorities of the new colonial state. The British rewarded these loyalists with wealth, land, titles, and positions of honour.[4] The task of the new administration was to keep the city loyal, to make the city pay and to keep the city clean.[5] In the tropics, cleanliness was as important to the British as loyalty.

Tropical countries terrified colonial officials, who believed that they harboured malevolent diseases and miasmas. An early task of the newly established DMC was the collection of death rate statistics and a medical survey of the city to find a suitable site for a military camp. Alarmed by the death rate (61 per 1000 in some areas), the British settled themselves in a zone apart from the city.[6] Secluded in such colonial enclaves, the British attempted to secure themselves from the inhospitable biological environment of the native city.[7] Colonial

[2]Narayani Gupta, *Delhi Between Two Empires, 1803–1931* (Delhi: Oxford University Press, 1981), p. 39.
[3]Brijkrishen Chandiwala, *Dilli ki Khoj* (Delhi: Vibhag Prakashan, 1964), pp. 265–6.
[4]Gupta, *Delhi*, p. 73.
[5]Veena Oldenburg, *The Making of Colonial Lucknow* (New Delhi: Oxford University Press, 1989), p. xv.
[6]NAI, Home (Sanitary), A Progs., 7 November 1868, nos. 5–6 and *Paisa Akhbaar*, 26 July 1898.
[7]David Arnold, *Colonizing the Body: State Medicine and Epidemic Disease in Nineteenth-Century India* (Berkeley: University of California Press, 1993), pp. 274–80. In Bharatendu Harishchandra's 'Bharat-Durdasa', the character

officials appreciated the precariousness of their position, since the history of 'Asiatic cholera' illustrated the fallacy of segregation. They tried to both engineer their own enclaves as well as ensure the sanitation of the native parts of Delhi (so as not to produce uncontrollable epidemics within the city walls). The brave sanitary officer, the municipal archive tells us, 'has been unceasing in his exertions for the improvement of the city; and his "pluck" and untiring energy during the cholera epidemic elicited the hearty admiration of all classes'. The officials showed 'a most laudable zeal in this work of sanitary improvement'.[8]

Yet, the city remained in a state of acute distress. Delhi's native èlite (*rais*) vociferously demanded the right to live in a clean city. They argued that after six decades of *de facto* British rule

the arrangements for the cleanliness of the city are day by day less attended to. Some parts of the city are well cleaned and lighted, while others are totally deprived of these benefits, which is highly unjust. As the octroi tax is collected from all the inhabitants alike, there is no reason why the benefits of the municipality should not be equally extended to all.[9]

The rais protested the Manichean logic of colonial development,. wherein the advantages of modernity were wrested by the British, while walled Delhi was abandoned to ruin. The DMC did not argue against the rais' complaint about unequal provision of services. Instead it blamed the poor conditions on the sweepers whose strikes, it argued, prevented the DMC from doing its work.[10] There was no public admission of the DMC's view that the natives did not deserve the amenities of modernity, since, colonial officials argued, the natives' threshold for pain and suffering was greater than that of the colonials.[11]

The sweepers partly controlled their labour process as they came to clean at their own time and cleaned at their own speed. Dirt left the boundary of the home only to enter the public space of the street, to

---

Rog (disease) taunts the white colonials for their futile attempt to hide from a paralyzed and oppressed cityscape. *Bharatendu Granthavali* (Kaashi: Nagari, 1950), vol. 1, p. 478.

[8]NAI, Home (Sanitary), A Progs., 7 November 1868, nos. 5–6.

[9]*Urdu Akhbaar*, 8 July 1871.

[10]William Crooke, *Natives of Northern India* (London: Archibald Constable, 1907), p. 122.

[11]Vijay Prashad, 'Native Dirt/Imperial Ordure: The Cholera of 1832 and the Morbid Resolutions of Modernity', *Journal of Historical Sociology*, vol. 7, no. 3 (September 1994), pp. 252–7.

remain there to putrefy.[12] The task of the sweeper was to remove the accumulated dirt and dispose of it, to remind the residents of their civility and to hide the city's own refuse from itself. Often the sweepers came late. 'Many of the lanes looked as if they had not been swept for several days,' a colonial official reported, 'heaps of rubbish were lying here and there, and I saw several heaps of street sweepings and matter from private houses lying in the smaller streets as late as 10 o'clock.'[13] Officials drew upon discourses of disease and of worker inefficiency to justify their attempt to take charge of the sweepers' labour, the waste that they collected and their own parochial notions of time. In 1873 and 1876, the sweepers went on strike to fend off the DMC's challenge. The sweepers won these early battles and the 'officials had to admit defeat and allow the sweepers to retain their monopoly and did not enroll them as paid servants of the Municipality'.[14] In 1879, the sweepers threatened to strike once more, 'to be followed by legal proceedings if their monopoly over nightsoil was interfered with or their birth rights disturbed. These rights had all along been a very great stumbling block to the improvement of the mohalla,' or, in other words, to the DMC's control over the system.[15]

Each mohalla was serviced by a sweeper whose employment was guaranteed by an unwritten agreement with the other sweepers rather than by the householders. The householders of each mohalla paid their sweepers. Daily dues were given in food, monthly dues in cash. Dues were also paid on certain domestic ritual occasions such as marriages and deaths, and on certain annual festivals. The sweepers also controlled the manure, that waste-as-ore exchanged with the hinterland farmers for cash or kind. Control over this waste was essential, for it provided the sweepers with additional income (including that generated when the sweepers repaired and recycled items deposited in the trash).[16] The bonds between the sweepers, operating as an unregistered guild, prevented householders from the exercise of unrestrained power over the

[12]Dipesh Chakrabarty, 'Of Garbage, Modernity and the Citizen's Gaze', *Economic and Political Weekly*, 7–14 March 1992.

[13]DMC Progs., 19 September 1887.

[14]Gupta, *Delhi*, p. 161.

[15]Rai Sahib Madho Pershad, *The History of the Delhi Municipality, 1863–1921* (Allahabad, 1921), pp. 47–8.

[16]Vallabhaswami, *Safai: Vigyan aur Kala* (Varanasi: Sarva Sewa Sangh, 1957), p. 3.

menial.[17] If the householder mistreated the sweeper or withheld wages, the collective of sweepers refused to work in the mohalla. Given the prejudice against contact with refuse shared by *ashraf* (respectable classes) Muslims and Hindus, the sweepers' refusal to move trash ensured that the householders felt ensnared by both ritual and economic power.[18] Without control over and possession of their means of survival, the sweepers would have neither economic security nor a sense of dignity.[19] Their relative independence, then, was not just a frame of mind, but was principally an aspect of their ability to materially take care of themselves.

The independence of the sweepers frustrated colonial officials. 'If any housekeeper within a certain circle happens to offend the sweeper of that range,' Sleeman wrote in 1844, 'none of his filth will be removed till he pacifies him, because no other sweeper would dare touch it; and the people of the town are more often tyrannized by these people than by any other.'[20] Sleeman exaggerated the power of the sweepers in order to make them look both dangerous and ridiculous. Thus, he portrayed sweepers as tyrants, and yet it is made to appear that this tyranny is provoked only by some petty offence or trivial action (either accidental or perhaps even merely imagined) that offended their sensibilities. The genuine demands of the sweepers were of no concern, since people such as Sleeman argued that sanitary problems in India stemmed from an undisciplined sweeper force.

Until the strike of 1889, the rais provided the sweepers with vital support, perhaps partly as a holdover from their memory of colonial brutality in 1857 and partly due to their distrust of the foreign invader.[21] By the 1880s, the rais' rebelliousness withered, to be substituted by a constitutional nationalism among the emergent bourgeoisie (industrialists, merchants, bankers, traders) and some old princes as well as a gradual communalization of the social domain.[22] In 1871, we gain one

[17]NAI, Home (Public), A Progs., 4 February 1859, nos. 68–71.

[18]E.A.H. Blunt, *The Caste System of North India* (Oxford: Oxford University Press, 1931), p. 240.

[19]Hazari, *Untouchable: The Autobiography of an Indian Outcaste* (London: Bannisdale, 1957), pp. 8–9.

[20]Major General Sir W.H. Sleeman, *Rambles and Recollections of an Indian Official* (Karachi: Oxford University Press, 1973), pp. 49–50.

[21]*Ashraf-ul-Akhbaar*, 1 March 1875 and *Sadadarsh*, 2 July 1875.

[22]Kenneth Jones, 'Organized Hinduism in Delhi and New Delhi', *Delhi Through the Ages*. Ed. R. Frykenberg (Delhi: Oxford University Press, 1986),

early indication of the rais' frustrations with the DMC, misdirected against the sweepers:

> The haughty and overbearing behaviour of the sweepers is another nuisance. In all cities, they have divided mohallas among them, so that each is the sole and hereditary lord of his circle, and troubles poor persons by refusing to remove filth from their houses, and in many cases leaving them uncleaned for several days till his demands are satisfied. The people, knowing that they cannot change their sweepers, and fearing lest they should make false and calumnious reports against them to the police, and thereby involve them in troubles, tamely submit to their oppression. This conduct of sweepers is the cause of the houses of the people constantly remaining in a dirty state.[23]

The rais, in this text, reproduced the prejudices of the colonial officials. They argued, like the DMC, that the city's filth was a consequence of the 'wicked behaviour of the sweepers [which left] the houses of the people in a filthy state, in consequence of which children contract diseases and die in numbers'.[24] For the rais, the immediate association of the sweepers with the collapse of municipal services had more to do with the sweepers' partial control over the neighbourhoods. The rais simultaneously indicated that the city's problems stemmed from its rapid expansion of scale, from the diversion of its funds to the colonial enclaves and from the structural decay of its infrastructure. Nevertheless, the sweepers bore the brunt of their recommendations, since the rais found the colonial rulers obdurate on the other issues.

MUNICIPAL SERVANTS

On 4 September 1882, the DMC decided that 'early action must be taken in view of securing the entire nightsoil of the city with the double object of securing the better sanitation of the city and insuring the sale of the filth collected at the Depots'. The officials noted that 'until the interference of the private sweepers is effectually stopped, neither the sanitation of the city nor the sale of the filth can be ensured'.[25] If the DMC took charge of the nightsoil, it would both undermine the sweepers' independence (their earnings from the sale of manure and other *kabaari* or recyclable trash) and enable the DMC to profit from

---

p. 337.

[23]*Urdu Akhbaar*, 1 December 1871. For more on the police, see Vijay Prashad, 'Marks of Capital: Colonialism and the Sweepers of Delhi', *International Review of Social History*, vol. 40, part 1 (April 1995), pp. 7–8.

[24]Ibid.

[25]DMC Progs., 4 September 1882.

the sale of the manure. Further, the DMC pledged to subordinate the sweepers further by tying them to the DMC through the fixed wage.

Before its thrust against the sweepers, the DMC built up its hardware, such as refuse-removal carts and warehouses to store the nightsoil. Its feint was met by a petition from seventeen sweepers which promised a strike 'in consequence of being deprived of the city's nightsoil'.[26] Nonplussed, the DMC challenged the sweepers to stand up to the empire.[27] In 1884, the DMC passed a resolution to 'enforce their right to the monopoly of all the nightsoil and sweepings of the city proper'.[28] Taking refuge in the right of conquest and the discourse of efficiency, the DMC refused to recognize the customary right of ownership and partial control exercised by the sweepers. The law spoke soon after in the unmistakable tone of the colonial state's emissary, 'on and after 1st December 1884 the removal of nightsoil from the city, except by the servants of the Committee be strictly prohibited'.[29]

With a history of struggles behind them, Delhi's sweepers did not yield to the Town Hall's pompous declaration. Refuse was not surrendered to the authorities, and the DMC called attention to 'the matter of the surreptitious removal of the nightsoil'. The officials asked their subordinate native overseers to 'exercise greater vigilance and control in preventing removal of such other than by Municipal Staff.'.[30] One of the easiest ways to monitor the removal of nightsoil was to have *dalaos* (depots) on each street and to have the mohalla sweepers bring the nightsoil to these sites under the vigilant gaze of the overseer.[31] The dalaos played a crucial role in the struggle to control the movement of nightsoil, so that the DMC passed a resolution to 'prevent mohalla sweepers placing filth anywhere else, or even if placed at the fixed dalaos to compel the sweepers to place the filth inside the receptacles and not outside them'.[32] Once the nightsoil was collected inside the dalaos, the sweepers moved on to the next worksite; other sweepers

[26]DMC Progs., 6 November 1882.

[27]DMC Progs., 7 August 1883.

[28]DMC Progs., 12 February 1884 and 4 September 1884.

[29]DMC Progs., 2 December 1884. By 1 June 1885, the DMC also secured nightsoil from the suburban wards.

[30]DMC Progs., 5 April 1886 and 9 August 1886.

[31]DMC Progs., 5 March 1887 and 2 July 1888.

[32]DMC Progs., 4 September 1889 and Section 127 of Act XIII (1884) of the DMC.

removed the refuse in their 'filth carts'. The work was apportioned out
to various elements, none of whom controlled the entire process (now
effectively united under the aegis of the DMC). Since the DMC
systematized the flow of refuse outside the city and since it kept a
steady eye on the sweepers, furtive removal of refuse became increasingly difficult (although the municipal archive continued to bristle with
stories of petty theft).

Sweepers Outside the Town Hall

From being part of the mohalla's fabric (although living outside it), the
sweepers slowly became municipal employees with little direct link to
the families in the homes along their routes. The DMC delegated
sweepers to mohallas, thereby disrupting the continuous relationship of
clientship and servitude established through the sweepers' negotiation
with the householders on the conditions of their work. The turn to
municipal employment freed the sweepers from the direct bonds of
subordination to Hindu and ashraf Muslim families, but it also deprived
them of even their limited control over the process of work. Instead of
the erstwhile bargain with the householders, the sweepers had now to
contend with the DMC, which would mediate the conflicts of the street.
As municipal employees, however, the sweepers did not even gain

anonymity of labour, since householders knew them as dalits even without any personal familiarity or acquaintance with them. Sweepers became merely dalits, rather than Allarakhi or Bunno, as the minimal courtesy of a long-term relationship was now largely unavailable to sweepers.

Once the DMC centralized the source of sustenance, it effectively controlled the sweepers. The sweepers did not succumb to the wage easily, for many knew that it entailed being *mere* employees of the DMC. The new form of labour was, again, secured through the law. The Town Hall pronounced that because 'the sweepers are permanently employed and in receipt of full wages, the Committee declines to permit them to take private work of any kind'.[33] From 1881 to 1885, mohalla sweepers received one rupee per mensem from the DMC, a sum which they supplemented with neighbourhood emoluments and sale of refuse. In 1885, however, the DMC hired them as 'permanent sweepers' with a total wage of Rs 4 per mensem, a figure even the officials agreed was far lower than the total earnings of the sweeper.[34] The DMC shifted other costs onto the sweepers as well, such as the cost of uniforms and some implements. The Delhi authorities faced an onslaught of criticism from the working people of Delhi, whose actions in the grain riots of 1877 put the administration on notice.[35] The famine of 1898 again revealed to the DMC that the dalits, 'a most miserable looking lot, many diseased and wretchedly poor,' bore the brunt of the new arrangements. Without remorse, the DMC fell upon the sweepers:

If any mohalla sweeper who by custom or hereditary right receives fees from the residents of that mohalla willfully or negligently omits to clean the private privies or premises of any such resident or willfully or negligently omits to remove any nuisance in that mohalla which is his duty to remove he shall be punishable with fines which may extend to ten rupees and with a further fine which may extend to one rupee for every day after the first during which the offence is continued.[36]

The DMC fixed a steep fine of Rs 10 on the sweepers' salaries for rebellious behaviour, a fine that was more than just a threat to one who earned only Rs 4. The unreasonable fine was a sign of the DMC's

[33]DMC Progs., 4 May 1885.

[34]Ibid.

[35]NAI, Home (Police), B Progs., October 1877, nos. 18–19 and December 1877, no. 9.

[36]DMC Progs., 2 July 1888.

anxiety over sweeper militancy. When the DMC halved the Rs 4 salary in November 1888, the culture of militancy allowed the sweepers to risk a strike.[37] It was to break this culture that the DMC reorganized the sweepers' work process.

Before examining this reorganization, a brief glance at the strike of 1889 is important. On previous occasions, the sweepers relied upon some support from the rais, but by 1889, the native elite refused to join hands with the 'tyrannical' sweepers. The sweepers went on strike against a host of regulations, especially with regard to contract labour, under the impression that the DMC did not have the legal power to punish them. This was indeed so, but the DMC changed a bye-law soon after and crushed the workers' protest. When the secretary of the DMC banged his gavel on the meeting table at the Town Hall on 1 February 1892, he effectively signalled the end of the struggle as the sweepers slowly took their places as uniformed municipal servants.[38] Under section 118 of Act XX of 1891, the DMC was now allowed to prosecute mohalla sweepers who neglected their statutory duties. The DMC's punitive action was 'to prove to the public the fact that customary sweepers can now be prosecuted for not doing their work properly'.[39]

CONFIGURATIONS OF POWER

Having wrenched power from the mohalla sweepers, the DMC reorganized its functions under the overall supervision of a sanitation supervisor. This 'responsible person', a Health Officer, was to take charge of a bifurcated structure: part of the city was to be cleaned under his direct supervision (with sweepers under the everyday surveillance of the Jamadar, the jobber and overseer), while the rest of the city was to be cleaned by competitive contract. The DMC took charge of the wards that lay to the north of the city and Subzimandi, all of which either ran adjacent to the Civil Lines (the northern colonial enclave) or to the Military Lines (to the east of the city). Contractors took charge of the rest of the wards, with those on the south of the city (furtherest from the colonials) reduced to 'sinks of filth.' 'It is a mystery,' one journalist wondered, 'how the residents of these *kuchas* [lanes] manage to live.'[40]

---

[37]DMC Progs., 6 November 1888.
[38]Prashad, 'Marks of Capital', p. 12.
[39]DMC Progs., 1 February 1892.
[40]*Gham Khwar-i-Hind* (Lahore), 13 August 1898.

If the legal contractors tried to establish an oligopoly, the DMC was able to break them by its Jamadar system; if the Jamadars got too powerful, the DMC offered more contracts as a means to thwart their power.[41] Either way, the DMC was able to conduct the removal of refuse at low rates with power vested in itself through the grant of contracts and of Jamadarships by patronage. The contractors and the Jamadars, mostly Hindus and ashraf Muslims, became the daily overseers of the sweepers. From 1892 to 1912, the Jamadars and the contractors ran the system under the rather nonchalant eye of the DMC. There was little conflict between these agencies and the DMC since the work appeared to be done without any undue stress on the finances of the DMC and without any disturbance to the colonial enclave north of the city.[42]

In 1912, the creation of the new imperial capital added to the significance of the sanitation of the walled city. 'It does not seem to me that the sanitary policy of Delhi is on the right scale,' wrote the Viceroy's assistant, 'or that it is realized that our object is not to clean up the filthiest place which I have seen in India, but to make old and new Delhi sanitary on the modern European scale. If any part of our work must be sacrificed it must not be Delhi.'[43] To run a sanitary operation on an 'European scale' necessitated an expansion in the DMC's financial resources, but since this was not forthcoming the government hastened to make the operation more efficient. Rather than a 'bazaar sergeant' running the sanitary service, the Viceroy's office urged the DMC to hire a 'missionary of sanitation,' someone with 'technical knowledge'. The current Health Officer was 'a worthy and kindly gentleman, who is liked by the people,' but he 'does not carry sufficient weight to make himself felt or to insist on the carrying out of his recommendations or orders.'[44] The day of the amateur was to give way to that of the technocrat. In July 1912, an Indian Medical Service

[41]DMC Progs., 31 March 1887, 1 March 1888, 5 March 1888 and 2 April 1888.

[42]This despite the panic in Delhi during the 1898–1900 plague, for which see Gupta, *Delhi*, pp. 136–9.

[43]NAI, Education (Sanitary), A Progs., March 1913, nos. 73–75.

[44]NAI, Education (Sanitary), A Progs., September 1912, nos. 9–19; NAI, Education (Sanitary), A Progs., January 1912, nos. 50–65; J.B. Harrison, 'Allahabad: A Sanitary History'. *The City in South Asia.* Eds K. Ballhatchet and J. Harrison (London: Curzon Press, 1980), pp. 173–4.

officer was seconded to Delhi with wide powers to demolish the 'trammels of petty local considerations and parochial ideas' as well as to introduce 'programme and efficiency'.[45] The reconfiguration of power in Delhi occurred between 1912 and the 1930s, wherein the DMC subordinated the sweepers to their immediate bosses, the Jamadars and the contractors.

Contract Labour

Rather than trouble itself with management of all the sweepers and with the enhancement of the physical plant of the sanitation department, the DMC offered contracts on refuse removal of the various wards (this was first done in 1887). Numerous reports in the municipal archive show that the contract system was unsatisfactory in terms of cleanliness and in terms of the treatment of labour. Furthermore, the profitability of the contracts meant that they attained the status of a commodity, so that some contractors transferred them for a small commission. This agitated the DMC especially since it wished to directly control the recipients of contracts. When the DMC tried to revoke all contracts in 1915, the contractors went on strike. The DMC fired them all and in 1916 severely punished the new contractors of two wards for 'these contractors did their work miserably and took very little trouble in removing filth from the dalaos and refuse from the dust bins of their wards.'[46] The DMC eventually dismissed them, confiscated their securities, and found new contractors to take the tenders. The system was far too profitable to allow it to lapse.

The municipal archive informs us that the problem with the system was not its ecological and labour ills, but that the contractors were themselves of the 'sweeper class'. The fines, we are told, do not produce discipline since the contractors 'never carry out the terms of their contract' and the DMC is put through 'continued anxiety'.[47] The colonial officials felt they could not be disciplined due to their culture of insubordination, as demonstrated by the strikes of the 1870s. 'As customary house sweepers are related to one another,' the Health

---

[45]NAI, Education (Municipalities), A Progs., April 1914 and September 1912, nos. 9–19.

[46]K.S. Sethna, *Report on the Administration of Delhi Municipality* (Delhi: GOI, 1917), vol. 2, pp. 32–3.

[47]Sethna, *Report*, vol. 2; DSA, CC (Education), B Progs., 1927, no. 6 (7); Ibid., 1929, no. 4 (11).

Officer wrote in 1935, 'the sweepers owning bullocks are not ready to do the work left over by their kinsmen.'[48] There is no evidence to show that the sweepers controlled these contracts, only that a few who hailed from similar dalit communities as sweepers bid for contracts. These few dalits, we can surmise from the minimal information available, bid in alliance with middle-caste Hindus and Muslims, almost as their surrogates (rather than in pursuance of a strategy of upward mobility). At the auctions for the contracts, the DMC argued, 'cliques are formed' by groups of contractors to bid for all the wards.[49] These contractors may be seen as 'rich sweepers', but there is little indication that the entire body of dalits or sweepers gained from the contract system. The community of sweepers is here disrupted by individual advancement, especially since those who advance now lean upon the rest who must work for the gain of the few. The bulk of the contractors, however, did not come from among the dalits, since the archive shows that most of them were middle-caste Hindus and Muslims.

The details of one contractor's budget allows us a glimpse into the system.[50] The contractor offered the DMC Rs 110 per mensem to clean a ward in 1933. Of this amount, he paid Rs 10 to the local Jamadar, 'the remover of all obstacles', who as petty supervisor turned a blind eye to the overloaded carts and the unhygienic disposal of refuse in watercourses and hollows. The contractor spent Rs 45 on three bullocks which drew the refuse carts from the city three times a day. The carters who led the bullocks earned about Rs 30. If a carter was ill or a bullock was lame, the contractor hired carters or bullocks at a daily rate of Re 1. Leaving some petty cash for such wages of sweepers hired to load the cart, other miscellaneous expenses and bribes, the contractor earned Rs 20 per mensem. To make a larger profit, contractors learned to cut corners. 'The Delhi municipality has found the contract system the cheapest, for bidders bid the lowest and make it up by bribing Jamadars and using *jhuta* [left-over food]. The bullocks are well-fed and can do 12 hours work per day; the Jamadar's palms are well greased, he does not mind how many carts carry or don't carry the refuse of the city.'[51] The carters' and sweepers' wives who worked as domestic servants

[48]DSA, CC (Education), B Progs., 1935, no. 4 (6).

[49]DMC Progs., Sanitation Sub-Committee, 16 August 1929.

[50]N.R. Malkani, 'Sanitation of an Imperial City', *Harijan*, 30 September 1933.

[51]Malkani, 'Sanitation'.

collected left-over food for the bullocks and the sweepers often flouted all regulations to dump garbage into the drains.[52] The DMC frequently caught the contractors breaking these rules and levied large fines upon them. For the last half of 1934, the DMC collected Rs 529 per contractor in fines. By 1935, seven of the contractors were 'in debt, with their salaries attached in court'.[53] The low tenders could only be honoured by such techniques, short of the technological enhancement of the sanitation system. The contractors, however, did not bear the burden of the fines and of the virtuoso mechanism put in place by them. Rather they shifted part of the burden of debt and fines onto the sweepers, whose meagre wages were already affected by inflation, and they relied upon the hard work of the sweepers to cover any technological shortfall.

Both the press and the DMC reports went after individual contractors rather than the system itself. Those individuals came to be seen as replaceable delinquents, while the system was hailed as the best way to get the work done at a low cost. The social costs of the system fell upon the sweepers (who, then, relied upon their links to extended families for survival), the environment and the city's residents (who, perforce, were fed upon by the intestinal parasites let loose by inadequate refuse disposal) and the city's institutions (which fell prey to the institutionalized corruption of the DMC, now reliant upon the contractor's oligopoly).

Jamadars

To monitor the entire system, the DMC appointed Jamadars to each ward. The Jamadar (variously called the Conservancy Daroga, Safai Daroga, Muqaddam, Sardar, etc.) not only monitored the work of the contractors, but also took charge of the sweepers who removed refuse in wards not given out on contract. In those wards, the Jamadars held the absolute power to hire, fire and fine sweepers. To enter municipal service, the sweepers paid *dasturi* (a bribe in the name of a commission) to the Jamadar (in collaboration with the Sanitary Inspector who took his cut). If the sweepers did not pay the Jamadar all sorts of levies to retain their jobs, he reported them to the Sanitary Inspector for negligence or insubordination. In 1933, the dues (or bribes, *rishwat*) ran to Re 1. The sweepers, we are told, dare not 'displease their Daroga by non-payment [of the dues], otherwise, he may throw them out of

[52]DMC Progs., Sanitation Sub-Committee, 12 July 1929.
[53]DMC Progs., Sanitation Sub-Committee, 27 February 1935.

employment on the least pretext'.[54] Given the lack of permanency and the insecurity associated with the Jamadar's capriciousness, the sweepers understood their own frail position. Yet, it was not just the whim of the Jamadar, since the rules gave the Health Officer and his minions power to 'appoint, dismiss or suspend any of the ménial servants of the Sanitation Department drawing a salary of Rs 10 or under'. These 'menials' included sweepers, *beldars* (manual labourers), carters and others. In sum, the sweepers. 'are always at the mercy of their Jamadars and are therefore compelled to bribe them even for small mercies and even for ordinary rights'.[55]

The Jamadar, colonial records indicate, was a 'well-meaning person, but he has received no training, his pay is only Rs 20 per month and his understanding of his duties is little greater than that of the *mehtarani* (sweepress or woman sweeper) who early that morning made her rare offering of fine, sharp sand at the public latrine'.[56] This comment underestimates the shrewdness of the Jamadar, who used his powerful position to command the sweepers. He (all Jamadars seem to be men, unlike in the case of the Bombay textile industry) manifested his power in physical strength, spending hours at the *akharas* (gymnasia) to demonstrate his physical power.[57] He roamed among the homes of the sweepers to ensure his omnipresence and to violate any notions of privacy held by the sweepers. Premchand's fictional Jamadar harassed Allarakhi, a street sweeper, and demanded sexual favours to protect her job.[58] The Jamadars and the contractors joined together in their use of extra-economic violence against the sweepers. There are few overt cases of resistance from the sweepers recorded in the archive, but those

[54]A.V. Thakkar, 'Sweeper by Choice', *Harijan*, 1 April 1933.

[55]A.V. Thakkar, 'The Plight of the Sweepers', *The Hindu* (Delhi), 13 September 1937.

[56]NAI, Education (Sanitary), A Progs., December 1907, nos. 301–3.

[57]A recent study of the akhara did not find many dalits within the ranks of the wrestlers, I imagine, because of the lack of structures for dalit wrestlers, such as a poverty of built spaces (such as gymnasia); most dalits wrestle on patches of open ground. The lack of space compares unfavourably to the built space of Hindu gymnasia, in the main due to the benefactors of such spaces (such as the Birlas who financed the grand Birla Mill Vyayamshala in Old Delhi from 1928 onwards). Joseph Alter, *The Wrestler's Body: Identity and Ideology in North India* (Berkeley: University of California, 1992), pp. 88–89.

[58]Premchand, 'Jurmana', *Kafan* (Allahabad: Hans Prakashan, 1960), pp. 29–34.

that are recorded show us that the sweepers felt a fierce hatred for their overseers. In 1929, for example, Sami Ahmed's sweepers gathered at his house and threatened to kill him and the moneylender Kallu Mal Bania. Their wanton ways with money and the fist angered the sweepers' sense of justice. Police intervention prevented the fracas from going further.[59] Patronage relations are not built simply on force, but also with gestures of kindness. When the Jamadars discharged the DMC's orders, for example, they enhanced the orders to fit their own immediate interests. If a favourable message was to be transmitted, it was done in their name ('I struggled to get you this benefit'); if an unfavourable order was given, it was done in the name of the Sanitary Inspector ('I tried to prevent it, but on this they would not budge'), but in all cases it was done with the intent to aggrandize the Jamadar himself. Proximity to power endows power in itself.

Like most contractors, the Jamadars did not hail from among the dalit communities of the sweepers. In the 1870s, some sweepers became Jamadars, but in 1888 the DMC decided to hire 'some other caste but sweepers'.[60] The DMC appointed 'literate military pensioners' as Jamadars in the belief that the ex-armymen would be able to command the dalits. These Jamadars had to wear a badge to show their distance from the sweepers. The power of these Hindu and Muslim Jamadars over the dalit sweepers was twice as strong, for not only did the Jamadar exert the authority of his office, but he was able to exert the ritualized authority of caste. The Jamadar's patronage network was to be a major determinant in the social lives of the dalits, as we shall see in the second half of this book.

DISTRESS OF THE SWEEPERS

In the 1930s, the Gandhians who went among the Delhi sweepers felt shocked by the conditions of their lives. 'Why should these sweepers be cheated of these elementary rights?' Mahadev Desai wrote, referring to such socialist staples as decent wages, fixed hours of work, cost of living increases, holidays on periodic days, provident fund, and privilege and casual leave.[61] While the colonial archive paid little attention to the lives of the sweepers, the Gandhians wrote extensively

---

[59]DMC Progs., Executive & Finance Sub-Committee, 4 February 1929.
[60]DMC Progs., 5 September 1887 and 1 October 1888.
[61]Mahadev Desai, 'A Quarter in New Delhi', *Harijan*, 15 April 1933.

about them and provide us with more than a glimpse of their distress.

To become a sweeper in 1933, one had to offer two months salary to the Jamadar. Why did the dalits pay such a steep mortgage on their future salary? They paid for coveted full-time jobs, since the DMC was tending towards part-time jobs. One full-time sweeper tended to six lanes in a ward, a task which occupied the sweeper till the afternoon, as a result of which residents complained that their streets remained dirty. Two part-time sweepers, on the other hand, could work three lanes and get the work done in the forenoon. In 1939, two-thirds of the sweepers worked half-time for Rs 6 per mensem, less than half the salary of a full-time worker (Rs 13 per mensem). The half-time sweepers held multiple jobs to secure their livelihood. Even full-time sweepers worried about being released during the slow season. The DMC hired 75 per cent more sweepers in the winter than in the summer (when the bureaucrats went to Shimla).[62] To secure precious full-time work or any work, the sweepers offered the Jamadar the 'commission', that often placed them in debt.

To finance the payment of this commission, the sweepers went to the moneylenders, many of whom moon-lighted as Jamadars or else worked in cahoots with them.[63] Sweepers' debt came more from the rishwat than from expenditure on non-utilitarian or social ceremonies. Kallu and his wife, two representative sweepers, earned Rs 23 per mensem, of which Rs 3 went to the Sanitary Inspector and the Jamadar.[64] Kallu borrowed money to pay for some medical expenses, so he owed an interest payment of Rs 11. Of the remaining Rs 9, the family paid for rent (Rs 3), purchased flour (Rs 4), pulses, meat, vegetables, spices, salt, fuel, oil and soap (Rs 2). One rupee was spent by them on tobacco and two rupees on liquor. In the context of the family's earnings and of the budget, the high price of liquor stands out and consequently 'the liquor shop men have a feeling that the pay of the scavengers stands mortgaged to them'.[65] The family incurred a deficit of Rs 4 per mensem, a debt which we are told 'is handed down from

[62]DMC Progs., Special Meeting, 27 August 1929.

[63]NAI, Education (Sanitary), A Progs., February 1913, nos. 49–50.

[64]Sivanarayan Tandon, 'The Food they take and their way of living', *Harijan*, 26 August 1933.

[65]C. Rajagopalachari, 'Municipal Sweepers', *Young India*, 12 November 1931.

generation to ·generation'.[66] In 1933, no sweeper in Delhi owed less than Rs 300.

The DMC ignored the plight of the sweepers using two arguments. First, the DMC noted that there is 'seldom distress' among the sweepers, for 'true, their incomes are small, but then their wants are few'. Rather than accept responsibility for the sweepers' poverty, the DMC argued that 'the squalor of their surroundings is due far more to ignorance and want of civilisation than to want of means'.[67] The Harijan Sevak Sangh knew this was not quite the case, since they had joined the sweepers in the 1930s to protest the DMC's neglect. 'The cold, callous and criminal negligence of the employees of the munici-palities and other public bodies' accounted for the plight of the sweepers; 'months of irritating and futile correspondence have won a tap or two for some dry and dirty *basti* [habitation]'. Rather than address the problem, the DMC has 'learnt the fine art of transforming the fixing of a water-tap or an electric light into a second class commu-nal question in the heat of which the authorities can bask in comfort and write reports'.[68] In 1992, a dalit man led me into these bastis, pointed to the animal refuse all over the narrow streets and said, 'all this is the *jaydad* [property] of the municipality'.[69] The heirs of the DMC still rely upon 'culture of poverty' arguments to avoid joining the dalits in making their lives more livable.

The DMC's second argument turned on the issue of family wages. Since, men and women worked as sweepers, the DMC felt it did not have to pay either of them a 'family wage'. Sweepers may be op-pressed, one official wrote, but 'they are not in a material sense by any means the poorest part of the population'. That 'they can rely on the assistance of their women and to some extent their children . . . places them in an unusually favourable position as wage earners'.[70] In 1911, 795 women worked as sweepers for every 1000 men (5403 women; 6792 men); in 1921, 667 women worked as sweepers for every 1000 men; in 1931, 642 women worked as sweepers for every 1000 men,

[66]Tandon, 'The Food' and *idem*, 'The Problem of Indebtedness', *Harijan*, 23 September 1933.

[67]*District Gazetteer Delhi* (1912), p. 139.

[68]Harijan Sevak Sangh, *Annual Report* 1932–33 (Delhi: HSS, 1933), p. 10 and 1933–34 (Delhi: HSS, 1934), p. 11.

[69]Raju Kumar, Sau Quarters, Karol Bagh, Delhi, 18 January 1992.

[70]DSA, CC (Home), B Progs., 1916, no. 169.

that is, about three women worked as sweepers for every five men.[71] In 1929, a municipal document tells us, only 228.4 women worked as full-time municipal sweepers for every 1000 men.[72] The bulk of women, then, must have worked as part-time sweepers. In the full-time category, we have the carters, drivers, Jamadars and sewage cleaners, all tasks reserved for men. The full-time jobs reserved for women included those in which husbands and wives lived beside a public convenience and attended to it through the day. The couple would live beside the facility and clean 'the latrine all hours as one of them can stay during the absence of the other'.[73] The women in part-time work cleaned homes and removed refuse to the municipal dump from the houses.[74] The fact of women in the workforce allowed the DMC to justify paying low salaries to all their sweepers, this without an adequate study of the distress of both men and women.[75]

In a 1926 inquiry, the DMC felt that part-time sweepers pose difficulties of discipline and that it was 'essential that (the sweepers) should all be Municipal sweepers otherwise there is no control over them'.[76] The next year, the DMC felt that it was in a quandary. The part-time sweepers allowed the city to be cleaned faster than the full-time sweepers. Nevertheless, they are not 'as well-disciplined and alive to their responsibilities as is practicable in the case of whole time employees'. Given this, the DMC noted that the maintenance of Delhi in a sanitary state 'more than counter-balances any apparent economy

[71]*Census of India*, 1911, vol. XIV part 2, Table XV part A; *Census of India*, 1921, vol. XV part 1, Report, p. 363; *Census of India*, 1931, vol. XVI, chapter VIII.

[72]DMC Progs., Executive and Finance Sub-Committee, 23 March 1929.

[73]DSA, CC (Education), B Progs., 1928, no. 6 (15) and 1931, no. 4 (31); DSA, DC Files, 1938, no. 49.

[74]N.R. Malkani, *Clean People in an Unclean Country* (Delhi: Navajivan, 1965), p. 99.

[75]From the 1970s onwards, women begin to predominate in the DMC's street sweeping squads. Malavika Karlekar, *Poverty and Women's Work: A Study of Sweeper Women in Delhi* (Delhi: Vikas, 1982), p. 49; Mary Searle-Chatterjee, *Reversible Sex-Roles: The Special Case of Benares Sweepers* (Oxford: Pergamon, 1982), p. 35; Andrea Singh, 'Women and the Family: Coping with Poverty in the *Bastis* of Delhi', *The Indian City*. Ed. A. deSouza (New Delhi: Manohar, 1978), p. 78; Shyamlal, *The Bhangis in Transition* (New Delhi: InterIndia, 1984), p. 6.

[76]DSA, CC (Education), B Progs., 1926, no. 5 (7).

that may result' in the use of part-time sweepers.[77] This logic was not
acted upon, since the DMC had already begun to rely upon discipline
being guaranteed by the extra-economic force of the Jamadars and the
contractors and the economic force of debt and unemployment.

THE MEHTARS AND THEIR STRUGGLES

Given the plight of the sweepers, why was there no institutionalization
of resistance alongside the institutional integration of the DMC? From
the sweepers' defeat in 1889 to the formation of the sweepers' union in
the 1930s, there are few examples of collective action. If organization
at the workplace was difficult because of the Jamadars, the contractors,
and the dispersed nature of the occupation, why did the sweepers not
organize in their neighbourhoods? Many studies show us that while
workers formulate the immediate goals of their politics at the work-site
(higher wages, better work and living conditions), the neighbourhoods
allow the workers to get together and politicize each other without the
watchful eye of the overseer.[78] Delhi's sweepers shared neither a shop-
floor nor neighbourhoods nor did they come from one ethnic community.

We have only the barest information about the lives and biographies
of the sweepers. In the early eighteenth century, two writers who wrote
of popular culture and plebeian life in the city concentrated on festivals,
intellectuals, astrologers, *pirs* (saints), singers, courtesans, bazaars,
merchants, artisans, poets, *dastangos* (story-tellers), thieves and other
colourful personages. Nazir Akbarabadi and Dargah Quli Khan inclined
themselves more towards the arts and crafts of Mughal Delhi than to
the inner workings of the city of Shahjahanabad.[79] The only component
of the city's infrastructure which they mentioned was the water-supply,
given the celestial importance of the *Nahr-i-Bihisht* (Canal of Para-

---

[77]DSA, CC (Education), B Progs., 1927, no. 6 (7). The League of Nations
noted 'the danger of employing low-paid and imperfectly trained subordinates
in a matter so closely affecting village life is now generally recognized and
should never be out of mind'. *Health Organization in British India* (Calcutta:
Thacker, for The League of Nations, 1928), p. 47.

[78]Rajnarayan Chandavarkar, *The Origins of Industrial Capitalism in India*
(Cambridge: Cambridge University Press, 1994), ch. 5.

[79]*Kulliyat-e-Nazir Akbarabadi.* Ed. Maulana Abdul Bari Saheb 'Aasi'
(Lucknow: Navalkishore, 1951); Dargah Quli Khan, *Muraqqa'-e-Delhi.* Tr.
Chander Shekar and Shama Mitra Chenoy (Delhi: Deputy, 1990).

dise). The sweepers were nowhere to be seen, despite the fact that Shahjahanabad boasted a permanent sanitation crew which bore the name Shahi or Nawabi *Mehtar* (prince), or, alternatively, *Khakrub* (to sweep the dust) and *Halalkhur* (to whom all food is lawful). In his compendium on life in the reign of Akbar, Shaykh Abul Fazl noted that it was the emperor who made the name Khakrub '*en vogue*', while Halalkhor referred perhaps to the fact that the sweepers' labour made it possible for others to live with the rules of *halal*.[80] There are only the briefest glimpses of the sweepers.[81]

Early European travellers, fascinated by life in India, wrote about many of the things which the natives themselves did not find so noteworthy. In the late eighteenth century, one traveller described the sweepers as 'the refuse of all the Tribes. These are a set of poor unhappy wretches, destined to misery from their birth.'[82] From such scraps we can surmise that the Mehtars were more a community of sweepers than a discrete caste community. The dregs of all caste communities, such as Khatiks, Sansis, Chamars, Chuhras, Reghars, Lodhas, among others, formed the community of sweepers. We have evidence that the Mehtars were divided along lines of habit and custom. For example, among Mehtars there were some 'who will eat of the food which goes from the master's table, whilst others would hold themselves defiled by so doing'.[83] Or again, we hear that 'for the meaner offices' such as sweeping 'we have a Hallalcor or Chandela (one of the most wretched Pariahs)'.[84] Many different caste designations represent those in the phalanx of sweepers, but the occupation itself does not appear to be the preserve of any special caste.[85] The Mehtars were certainly not a community which had endogamous and exogamous

[80]Abul Fazl 'Allami, *Ain-i-Akbari*. Tr. H. Blochmann (Calcutta: Asiatic Society of Bengal, 1927), p. 147.

[81]A fact that became the story 'Kalu Bhangi' in Krishan Chandar's deft hands. *Krishan Chandar ke Numaindah Afsane* (Karachi: Al-Muslim Publishers, 1990).

[82]Luke Scrafton, *Reflexions on the Government of Hindoostan* (London, 1770), pp. 7–8.

[83]Grant Colesworthy, *Anglo-Indian Domestic Life* (Calcutta: Subarnarekha reprint, 1984), p. 111.

[84]Maria Graham, *Journal of a Residence in India* (Edinburgh: J. Murray, 1812), p. 31.

[85]Blunt, *Caste System*, p. 225 and *Census of India*, 1911, vol. 1 part 1, Report, p. 368.

strictures, themselves elements of the theory of jati (i.e. the experiential form of caste). At most, the Mehtars were a community of sweepers who were joined by their menialness, by their dalit status and their fellowship in some dalit neighbourhoods.

Many Mehtars, however, did not live in the vicinity of dalit neighbourhoods either. In 1916, the colonial authorities settled most dalit communities into the easily managed and monitored Western Extension Area, west of the walled city. The justification given for this was that the walled city was congested and the productive trades practised by the dalits needed to be moved out of its environs. Rather than allow many slums to dot the walled city, the DMC provided one area to localize the trades (such as leather-work, lime-burning, pottery and animal slaughter) and the impoverished unemployed.[86] Until the late 1930s, the DMC did not allot sweepers housing in the new development. They lived in neighbourhoods spread out across the cityscape, some having just one family unit and others up to ten units. The logic for this arrangement stemmed from the process of refuse removal, with the sweepers made to live in the locale of their work 'in the interests of efficiency'.[87] In the single family unit, a couple raised a family and tended to the latrines in their zone. In the larger complexes, the sweepers cleaned dumps and refuse works.[88] For the Mehtars there was little possibility to produce the solidarity afforded other workers in their neighbourhoods.

If sweepers did not have the neighbourhoods to give them an indispensable base for politicization, this did not mean that they did not develop any sense of community.[89] *Pahalwani* (wrestling) in akharas was one of the modes of interaction for the male Mehtars, who met at their wrestling pits to test their strength. 'There was a time,' Faqir Chand told me on the roof of his house one evening in 1993, 'when we used to hold our own in Delhi against the other communities'.[90]

[86]NAI, Education (Municipalities), A Progs., March 1916, nos. 17–18 and February 1917, nos. 3–8.

[87]DSA, CC (Education), B Progs., 1936, no. 4 (64).

[88]DSA, CC (Education), B Progs., 1914, no. 40; 1931, no. 4 (31); 1932, no. 4 (114); 1932, no. 4 (139) and DSA, DC Progs., 1930, no. 33.

[89]Because of strict regulations about marrying outside their gotra, one caste that added to the ranks of sweepers retained links with other dalits from far afield. R. S. Sandhu, 'Rites de Passage of some Scheduled Castes: II. Marriage Rites', *Eastern Anthropologist*, vol. 34, no. 2 (April–June 1981).

[90]Faqir Chand, Paharganj, Delhi, 23 March 1993.

Proudly, he declared that his community is a martial *qaum* and that the motto of the young men was '*kasrat karo, aur tagre raho*' (exercise and remain strong). Part of this sentiment comes from the machismo of the akhara, part of it as a response to the Hindu prejudice that dalits are feeble of mind and body, and part of it to indicate the pride of a community now rather disjointed. Names of individual wrestlers are repeated by the elders (Baru Pahalwan, Bunno Pahalwan, Raghu Pahalwan) to maintain a memory of community power. In the story of Keer Singh, the collective memory of the dalit men resonates with the real effect of their strength. Keer Singh's father, Chowdhry Bondhu borrowed between Rs 500 and Rs 1000 from Bhasheswar of Teli Mandi in the early 1930s. The Chowdhry was unable to repay the debt, so the moneylender insulted him and his caste. Incensed, the son, Keer Singh killed the moneylender and was sentenced to death. On the intercession of the judge's sweeper and a group of Mehtar elders, the boy was sent to the penal colony on the Andaman islands. The pleaders, I was told not without pride, did not plead the boy's innocence, since he killed the moneylender and avenged the community's insult.

While the more physical men met in their various akharas to wrestle,. other men, women and children took advantage of wide kinship ties to pay sporadic and inconstant visits to kin across the cityscape. Sunheri Devi remembered her trips into the walled city to meet and eat with kin and friends. 'We were not from one *khandan* [family]', she said, 'but it felt just like we were'.[91] The trips did not come too often, since people mostly took advantage of irregular events such as births, deaths and marriages to meet. Twice a year, the Mehtars gathered for a fair which was also 'an occasion of religious worship to people of low castes, such as sweepers, who carry pendants made of sticks and rags in honour of their pir'.[92] We will hear more of this pir later, but for now it needs to be said that little political activity was conducted at what was essentially a place to pray and to renew ties. These fleeting contacts did provide fellowship, but were too brief for forging sustained solidarity.

Further disruption in the short-term came from the migration of Chuhras to the city into the DMC's sanitation service. Immigration into a tight labour market normally provokes a struggle between communities of labourers, but in the case of Delhi, which was a fairly open labour market after 1912, the Chuhras had little trouble finding work as

[91]Sunheri Devi, Delhi, 28 December 1992.
[92]*District Gazetteer Delhi*, 1883–4, p. 62.

sweepers. The irony of this labour market is that while the DMC actively sought out the Chuhras to work as sweepers, the Jamadars still doled out the coveted full-time jobs only after receipt of a bribe. The Chuhras easily found part-time work (of which a person often took two or more jobs—sweeper in the morning, garbage cart-driver in the afternoon), which were not considered desirable by the Mehtars. Between the Mehtars and the Chuhras there was neither immediate antipathy nor affinity. *Hum pesha*, the same work as sweepers, provided some grounds for empathy between the *shahri* (urban) Mehtars and the *gaoni* (rural) Chuhras. As yet, however, these two groups did not consider themselves as part of one community (*hum qaum*) nor a *khandan*. The Chuhras had no connection to the labour struggles of the 1870s, fights only one generation out of the living memory of the Mehtars. 'It has been found by experience,' the DMC noted, that 'outside sweepers [Chuhras] are better workers than these in the city'.[93] The Chuhras were in awe of the wonder and wages of urban life because they had just escaped from their own struggles in rural Punjab (the subject of the next chapter).

Between the 1850s and the 1930s, the sweepers of Delhi lost two important things: first, their partial control over their labour process and second, their right to claim that their betterment was for the good of the city. On the second point, when the sweepers protested their treatment, their struggle was couched by the DMC as parochial, while the DMC put itself forward as the voice of transcendental reason. The DMC claimed that sanitation was not commercial activity, but a bureaucratic venture, hence it was not to be troubled either by the laws of the market or the desires of the workers. The DMC was the benevolent overlord, the Jamadars and the contractors played the role of the patrons, and the sweepers acted as serfs in a familiar drama. The patronage of the Jamadars and the contractors as well as other low-level Hindu and Muslim bureaucrats in Town Hall is a precondition of the life and struggle of the sweepers for the rest of this book.

[93]*Report on the Administration of Delhi Municipality* (Delhi: DMC, 1927), vol. 2, p. 34 and DSA, CC (Education), B Progs., 1927, no. 6 (7).

2

The Chuhras

In the early years of the twentieth century, a host of Chuhras from rural Punjab travelled to Delhi to work in the sanitation service of the DMC. They joined the Mehtars to help keep an expanding Delhi clean. The East India Railway drew commerce into Delhi, enhancing its position as an entrepôt. The introduction of electricity in 1902 meant that the city did not have to rely entirely upon the immediate hinterland for its fuel. In 1885, only 200 men worked in *karkhanas* (factories), but by 1911, over 23,000 people worked in just the cotton textile trade. The activity in the city was given an additional fillip by the creation of the new imperial capital (1911–31). To keep the city's atmosphere 'salubrious', the sanitation department grew, a growth facilitated by migrants from the turbulent countryside. This chapter leaves the city for the countryside, to follow the trek of the Chuhras, the major component of dalits who would join the Mehtars to become Balmikis in the 1930s.

THE OCCUPATIONS OF THE CHUHRAS

In a colonial anthropological journal in 1887, a missionary criticized the way many writers assumed that the dalits lived a miserable life and, particularly, that the Chuhras are exclusively scavengers or sweepers. 'It would be a mistake', he wrote, 'to suppose either that the Chuhras are nothing but a tribe of scavengers or that their life is a mere burden'. Rather, the Chuhras in rural Punjab worked, in the vocabulary of English feudalism, as the 'villeins of the soil, who do the hardest work for the yeoman landholder'.[1] Local colonial officials concurred with the missionary. They noted that the 'Chuhras are the main agricultural labourers in the province'.[2] Three decades later, another missionary

[1] H.U. Weitbrecht, 'Panjab—The Chuhras—Lal Beg', *Indian Notes and Queries* (August 1887).
[2] DSA, DC Progs., 1890, no. 14.

was emboldened by the prevalence of a countervailing stereotype to note that the Chuhras and Chamars 'are little more than serfs; they are the hired labourers who follow the plough, drive the bullocks and sow the seeds of both the tenants and landlord . . . [they] perform most of the menial offices of the village'.[3] The general stereotype was that the Chuhras worked simply as sweepers or as scavengers and that their caste, in an absolute sense, determined their occupation. In the influential 1901 Punjab Census, for instance, Rose wrote that census enumerators 'recorded a Chura or "Khak-rob" as a sweeper by occupation without ado, because it is obviously the business of a sweeper to sweep, and further questions as to his occupation would have been superfluous'.[4] Those who worked amongst the rural Chuhras knew better, for most of them were expert reapers (*lawis*) and winnowers (*urawas*), makers of the winnowing pan (*chhaj*) and cart covers (*sikri*), magicians, potters, leather workers, midwives, musicians (particularly at weddings, funerals, dances and festivals), village messengers (during betrothals) and, general labourers on the fields. In their everyday lives, few Chuhras worked as sweepers.

Although Punjab boasts a rural ethos of self-cultivation, dominant caste cultivators deem certain tasks to be defiling and demeaning, tasks for which they hire menial, dalit labour. The agrarian history of the dalits from the ancient period to colonial times is a major project that needs to be undertaken. For now, we only have some suggestions, many of them not more subtle than those proposed by Kosambi decades ago. We know, from the Buddhist canon, that dominant castes of the time disallowed the Chandalas and the Nisadas, assumed to be early dalits, from being agriculturalists and that these people 'became a reservoir of unfree, servile landless labour available for work at the lowest cost to peasants as well as superior landholders'.[5] That there was a vast landless class prior to British rule is by now undeniable, but we know little of the contours of the lives and labour of this large number

[3]G.W. Briggs, *The Chamars* (Calcutta: YMCA, 1920), p. 57.

[4]*Census of India*, 1901, Punjab, vol. 1 part 1, p. 301. The general principle for this was laid out in the 1891 Census, which argued that 'the occupation to which the caste in question was to be credited was not necessarily that actually exercised by the caste in the present day but that which was assigned to it by tradition, and generally implied in its current appellation'. J.A. Baines, *General Report on the Census of India* (London, 1893), pp. 188–9.

[5]Irfan Habib, *Essays*, p. 166; D.D. Kosambi, *An Introduction to the Study of Indian Civilisation* (Bombay: Asia, 1956), p. 176.

of people.[6] We know that by the 1890s colonial officials saw Chuhras as the 'indispensable servants of the zamindar' who performed all the 'most disagreeable work which the zamindar would otherwise have to do himself'.[7] In Kangra, for instance, Rajput zamindars would not handle the plough, but those who did become plough drivers (*Hal Bah*), 'to avoid the indignity of exclusion, never appear at public assemblies'.[8] In Karnal, Rajputs 'look upon manual labour as derogatory, much preferring the care of cattle, whether their own or other people's'. Where Rajputs had to break the soil out of economic necessity, 'they will seldom, if ever, do the actual work of ploughing with their own hands'. Dalit men and women came to work on these farms, facing labour scarcity due to the Rajput prejudice against working the soil.[9] If Hindus worked the fields in other districts, they refused to manure, winnow and harvest.[10] In either case, the dalits entered the workforce as generic labourers, much like those called *balahars* centuries before.

The genealogies (*kursinamas*) of the Chuhras provide ample documentation of the dalits' self-consciousness of subordination. Like other dalits, the Chuhras narrate the myth of their descent into untouchability. The historical narrative of their oppression reveals that there is little sense of being inherently menial, since their condition is historical and can therefore be overcome. These same myths, it needs to be said, draw many notions from the Brahmanic universe which they otherwise contest.[11] In the Chuhra songs, the origin of untouchability is attributed to an act of betrayal by a brother. An object of pollution, a dead animal, is discovered in the midst of their living space. Someone in the family is urged to pollute himself by removing the carcass so that the living area could regain its purity. A pact is made between the volunteer, the community and the divine figure not to render him permanently

[6]Dharma Kumar, *Land and Caste in South India* (Delhi: Manohar reprint, 1992), p. 193 and Habib, *Essays*, pp. 360–1.

[7]*District Gazetteer* (1894–5), pp. 98–9.

[8]Himadri Bannerjee, 'Agricultural Labourers of the Punjab during the Second half of the Nineteenth Century', *Punjab Past and Present*, vol. 11 (1977), p. 98.

[9]*District Gazetteer Karnal* (1872–1880), para. 191.

[10]NAI, Rev. & Agri. (Land Revenue), A Progs., October 1913, no. 45, *District Gazetteer Hoshiarpur* (1883–4), p. 70 and *District Gazetteer Karnal* (1872–80), paras. 418–20.

[11]Robert Deliége, 'The Myths of Origin of the Indian Untouchables', *Man* (n.s.), vol. 18 (1993).

unclean. Once the taboo is removed, the community betrays the volunteer who is not seen as momentarily, but as ontologically unclean. In the future, we are told, there is some hope that the community will be reunited at a resurrection.[12] In some stories, the community is traced back to the Pandavas, in yet others to Brahma's four sons, but in all of them they are generally Hindus, who must deal with the most supreme taboo, a dead cow. The songs consistently undermine the notion that there are inherently dirty things, since, in one dramatic moment, the divine intervenes to tell us that since he created everything, all things are divine.[13] The betrayed volunteer, at one stage, trembles with anger and declares, 'I wish to make a community (jati) of my own' and thus, a separate jati of Chuhras arose.[14] The carcass in these stories is a metaphor for tasks seen to be defiling or difficult, but these are also seen as tasks not inherent to the Chuhras, only a temporary dilemma that will be sorted out with the intervention of the divine.

The local officials knew that the Chuhras did not work as sweepers, so many tried to resolve the discrepancy between the census classification and the diversity of their occupations by resorting to a local distinction. There are some Chuhras, one official wrote, who are 'agricultural menials' (*vadee kamins* or *athri Chuhras*) and are 'employed entirely in the fields'. There are other Chuhras who work as 'house menials' (*khangi kamins* or *sepi Chuhras*) and serve 'two or more families' by scavenging, making dung cakes, assisting with the cattle as well as working on the farms. Besides this, the sepi Chuhra is expected 'to run messages and make himself generally useful'.[15] Even the description of the sepi Chuhra varies from that made by Rose in the census, but the local official could not even countenance this since he noted that the Chuhra is 'both a scavenger and an agriculturalist and for this reason it is impossible to give an exact idea of how many should properly be classed as agriculturalist and non-agriculturalist'.[16] In the late 1890s, this question was far from being a benign one, for on its answer depended the future of the Chuhras in the countryside.

[12] Reverend J. Youngson, 'The Chuhras', *Indian Antiquary*, March 1906 to May 1907.

[13] Ibid. (December 1906), pp. 350–2.

[14] Ibid. (December 1906), pp. 345–52 and (January 1907), p. 23.

[15] *Settlement Report Sialkot* (1894–5), pp. 98–9.

[16] Ibid., p. 126.

COMMERCIALIZATION AND THE CHUHRAS

The late nineteenth century was a time of troubles for the Punjabi dalits, as much as it was a period of agrarian expansion. Punjab's agricultural commodities gained access to the world market. Shiftless Punjabi men went into the army and travelled the seas to stand sentinel for the British empire. Irrigation canals opened up barren land in western Punjab and drew many Hindu and Muslim families to self-cultivation. From 1849 to 1901, the commercialization of agriculture resulted in the expropriation of land from significant numbers of poor peasants (who now joined the landless sharecroppers and agricultural menials in dispossession) as well as the consolidation of land in the hands of rich peasants, the gentry and urban moneylenders. The fluctuations of world grain prices, famines and imperial taxes passed on by the rich peasants to their wage labourers compounded the agrarian distress.[17] Of this, the dalits bore the brunt.

The dalits faced problems from the outset, when the colonial officials began to codify the rights accorded to each person on a farm. Sikh and Mughal officials did measure the land for its productivity so that they might derive a revenue scheme, but they did not record the dues owed to menials. The colonial settlement officers noted such details as the productivity of the land, the type of soil in the revenue circles, the average yield of land per acre, the average price of the crops, the trend of prices, gross produce, gross profits, costs of production (including menials' dues) and from all these numbers they calculated the net profits out of which they drew revenue. By recording dues, the colonial officials intervened in the conflict between landlords and wage workers over what is often called 'custom'. To the land revenue officials the landlords exaggerated their dues to the menials to reduce the burden of tax upon themselves.[18] Settlement officers knew that the 'framing of the record of rights was a more important matter than the assessment', since the former was permanent while the latter was temporary. 'When a body of loose and varying local custom is poured into the mould of

[17]Naveed Hamid, 'Dispossession and Differentiation of the peasantry in the Punjab during colonial rule', *Journal of Peasant Studies*, vol. 10 (1982); Himadri Banerjee, *Agrarian Society of the Punjab, 1849–1901* (Delhi: Manohar, 1982); Imran Ali, *The Punjab Under Imperialism, 1885–1947* (Princeton: Princeton University Press, 1988); M. Mufakharul Islam, *Irrigation, Agriculture and the Raj: Punjab, 1887–1947* (Delhi: Manohar, 1997).

[18]*Settlement Report Jullunder* (1892), p. 157.

rigid definition', an official warned, 'it is certain to be changed in the process', so the record of custom needed to be delayed until 'the customs have been fully ascertained'.[19] Colonial officials did not 'invent' caste nor did they 'invent' the relations between the landlords and the wage workers, but they certainly intervened in clear and specific ways to set certain 'customs' above others as the legal norm.[20] In some circles, the records produced by the colonial officials stood as timeless charters of popular wisdom, a conception that produced a severe history for the dalits.

Recording Rights

Village officials used the village administration paper, the *wajib-ul-'arz*, to record various rights such as village cesses, rights to common land, rights to water sources, customs regarding habitations and royal property. The *iqrar-nama*, the text of the 1840s, did not pay any attention to the waged menials, but the wajib of the 1850s onwards took note of them and recorded their dues and the customary service to be rendered by them, including forced labour (*begar*).[21] The degree of state intrusion increased with the consolidation of conquest. Much that is of interest for a dalit history is at the information gathering stage, for many colonial officials relied not on the dalits but on landholders and local elites for their information. Many dalit peasants did not know Persian or Urdu, few followed the pronouncements of 'some learned Hindustani *munshi*', and many 'did not know their customs very well', which shows us that 'custom', for them, was a practice and not a codified right.[22]

The Privy Council called the wajib 'the proprietor's document' since much of what these texts contained revealed the will of the landholders who used every means to influence the collection of informa-

---

[19]J. Douie, *Punjab Settlement Manual* (Lahore: Daya reprint, 1985), pp. 52, 93.

[20]Rosalind O'Hanlon, 'Cultures of Rule, Communities of Resistance', *Social Analysis*, no. 25 (1989), p. 99; Aijaz Ahmad, 'Between Orientalism and Historicism', *Studies in History*, vol. 7, no. 1 (1991), p. 150; Neeladri Bhattacharya, 'Colonial State and Agrarian Society', *Situating Indian History*. Eds. S. Bhattacharya and Romila Thapar (Delhi: Oxford University Press, 1986), p. 144.

[21]Richard Saumarez Smith, 'Rule–by-records and rule-by-reports', *Contributions to Indian Sociology*, vol. 19 (1985), pp. 167–70.

[22]NAI, Rev. & Agri. (Rev.), A Progs., February 1892, no. 37 and November 1893, no. 42.

tion to 'close every door against future encroachment and intrigue'.[23] In 1887, one landholder, Fatteh Kanwar appeared in court to fight for her land on the basis of the wajib from her village, a text hitherto considered the 'official record' and used as 'important evidence, as a document of weight'. Some scrupulous justices investigated the wajib and found that it was 'the concoction of Fatteh Kanwar herself', since the colonial official received her views, 'which she had a right to enter upon the village records, because she was a proprietor of the estate', and entered them as fact in the wajib.[24] Begum Kanwar's story was typical. A settlement officer, often young and inexperienced, entered a village and made an outline of its customs and of ownership patterns. A *patwari* [accountant] followed the outline with a preliminary survey, checked by the Deputy Superintendent of the district and re-evaluated by the settlement officer to see that the papers 'really correspond with the custom of the village'. In numerous cases, the landholders told the officers what to record.[25] Despite evidence of the wajib's inaccuracy and hence inadequacy; as a record, the government held onto the idea that these documents recorded customs in a manner not 'contrary to justice, equality or good conscience'.[26] Furthermore, the colonial state tended, in general, to favour people such as Begum Kanwar who would provide a steady revenue with the minimum political fuss (since, the landholder would ensure 'law and order' amongst the landless).[27] The dalits, on the sidelines, could not but know that these documents would close the door to their agrarian hopes.

Recording Strife

In the late-nineteenth century, three famines left a lasting imprint on the grain market as prices doubled overnight, as a reaction to the decline of the international price of silver.[28] Rising prices did not necessarily

[23]Douie, *Punjab Settlement Manual*, p. 153 and p. 135.

[24]NAI, Rev. & Agri. (Rev.), A Progs., May 1889, nos. 36–40.

[25]*Settlement Report Karnal* (1872–80), para. 626; *Settlement Report Meerut* (1865–70), paras 18–19; *Settlement Report Amritsar* (1888–93), p. 22; NAI, Rev. & Agri. (Rev.), A Progs., January 1895, nos. 14–16.

[26]NAI, Rev. & Agri. (Rev.), A Progs., May 1889, nos. 36–40.

[27]J. Rosselli, 'Theory and Practice in North India', *Indian Economic and Social History Review*, vol. 8, no. 2 (June 1971).

[28]T.W. Holderness, *Narrative of the Famine in India* (Simla: GOI, 1897), p. 10; *Punjab Report in Reply to Inquiries Issued by the Famine Commission* [hereafter *PFRC*] (Lahore: GOI, 1878–9), vol. 1, pp. 41–3; Neeladri Bhattacharya, 'Agrarian Change in Punjab, 1880–1940' (New Delhi: Jawaharlal

benefit the landholders, but it certainly worked to the benefit of grain dealers, many of whom lent their surplus capital to beleaguered landholders who mortgaged their land.[29] The rising value of land and the relaxation of the usury laws in 1854 made this use of capital possible and profitable. A wide range of peasants borrowed not only for such conventional purposes as ceremonies, but increasingly to pay revenue dues, ground rent and for the extensive capitalization of their farms. A consequence of the turn to credit was the growing indebtedness of a number of landholders, who were dispossesed either by urban moneylenders (many of whom rack-rented the land) or by rich and middle peasants (who expanded their own farms). Given the pressures of debt, the rich and middle peasants struggled against their wage labourers to secure their profits by reducing the wagebill. The conflict hinged on the nature of recompense, so that when the prices rose the landholders tried to pay their labourers in cash and when prices fell they sought to compensate them in kind. The landless labourers, mostly dalits, fought for the right to collect fuelwood, to draw water from the wells, to take the carcasses of dead animals, to manure, to get a share of the crop, to graze cattle on the commons, to the barley sown in a strip around the wheat field (*pir de dané*), to the wheat sown along the watercourses, to food on workdays, to clothes and to tobacco. At harvest time, the landholders offered wages in kind, but in times of scarcity, this was not profitable for them. During the famine years, almost a third of the cattle in Karnal and Gurgaon perished. The 'cultivators are beginning', an official wrote in 1887, 'to deprive the Chuhras of their valuable perquisite', the skin of dead animals.[30] Landholders wished to benefit from the value of the skins, so that if they did not withhold them from the labourers, they demanded such things as more shoes and belts per carcass (an obligation factored into the relationship between landholder and waged worker).[31] The dalits resisted the landholders at every step,

---

Nehru University PhD, 1985). There is evidence that the famines influenced the prices until the Depression. Abdur Rab, *Acreage, Production and Prices of Major Agricultural Crops of West Pakistan (Punjab), 1931–59* (Karachi: Institute of Development Economics, 1961).

[29]NAI, Rev. & Agri. (Famine), A Progs., December 1888, nos. 1–24; *Siraj-ul-Akhbaar* (Jhelum), 21 June 1901; *PFRC*, vol. 1, p. 62.

[30]*Indian Notes & Queries* (August 1887); *Settlement Report Karnal* (1880), para. 63; NAI, Rev. & Agri. (Rev.), A Progs., November 1889, nos. 30–34.

[31]*Settlement Report Karnal* (1880), para. 284–5; H. G. Walton, *A Monograph on Tanning and Working in Leather in the United Provinces of Agra and*

including by resort to sabotage.[32]

Entrance to Valmiki Basti

In the last decades of the nineteenth century, the dalits lost access to many of the customary rights they had secured through struggle. In Jalandhar, for instance, 'in many cases Chamars and Chuhras are not retained as village servants (sepi), but are employed when needed, and paid by the job. In such cases, they have, of course, no right to dead cattle or anything except the wages agreed on'.[33] The revocation of the rights of the landless wage labourers meant only that the landholders refused their end of the bargain, since there is adequate evidence to suggest that the landholders continued to demand services from the dalits. Despite Lord Hastings' proclamation in 1820 to abolish begar, the practice continued, even in the form of the notorious *sarkari begar*,

---

Oudh (Allahabad: GOI, 1903), p. 25; *District Gazetteer Hoshiarpur* (1883–4), p. 70; *District Gazetteer Sialkot* (1894–5), pp. 98–9.

[32]T.G. Kessinger, 'The Peasant Farm in North India, 1848–1968', *Explorations in Economic History*, vol. 12 (1975).

[33]*Settlement Report Jullunder* (1892), p. 87.

services performed free by the dalits for the state officials. In 1848, a group of Chuhras confronted a mounted colonial official to complain about begar, but the official remained wedded to the practice that allowed his luggage to traverse the countryside without payment to the dalits.[34] In villages across the Punjab, the dalits performed begar to earn the right to their homesite, a payment demånded by *thikar* banias who called the dalits to work in rotation.[35] Dalit women not only carried the official's luggage, worked the landholders' fields and tended their children, but they had to struggle against and sometimes concede to the widespread rape of the women by Hindu men. In 1881, a colonial official noted that Chamar women 'are celebrated for their beauty, and loss of caste is often attributed to too great a partiality for a Chamarni'.[36] The proverb *beeran ki kai jaat* (women have no caste) protected Hindu men from excommunication for their violence against dalit women. The children born of this union were known as *churni ki* or *chamaran ki* and proverbs tell us of the social disregard they faced.[37] F.L. Brayne and Malcolm Darling, advocates of the middle peasant, shunned the dalits as 'an inferior and semi-slave race' cohabitation with whom, despite their innocence, was held responsible for the 'ruin of the Gurgaon peasant' and his 'magnificent physique'.[38] The dalits held their own view of this violence, for one of their proverbs tells us that a Hindu man gives many carcasses to his dalit mistress, but she is not allowed to touch his household vessels (*bahauriyan ke bahar duar, handi basan chunne na pawa*).[39]

The commercialization of land worked to the detriment of the dalits, many of whom accumulated little other than misery. The rich and middle peasants used the recurrent costs, such as dues to the landless dalits, as a means to retain their incomes despite the crisis of the agrarian economy. The colonial state did not sit back as an idle

[34]*Political Diaries of the Residents of Lahore and his Assistants* (Allahabad: Punjab Government Records, 1911), vol. IV, p. 341.

[35]*Settlement Report Karnal* (1880), para. 283 and 297.

[36]*Census of India* (1881), Punjab, para. 604.

[37]*Settlement Report Sialkot* (1894–5), p. 190 and Prem Chowdhury, 'Customs in a Peasant Economy', Recasting Women. Eds Kumkum Sangari and Sudesh Vaid (New Delhi: Kali for Women, 1989), pp. 324–5.

[38]Prem Chowdhury, *Punjab Politics: The Role of Sir Chottu Ram* (Delhi: Vikas, 1984), p. 65.

[39]*Census of India*, 1911, vol. XV part 1, p. 328.

spectator, but it intervened in specific forms to circumvent the mobility of the dalits and to bolster the aspirations of certain castes and class fractions in the Punjabi countryside. The mechanism for colonial intervention was to be the law, specifically the Punjab Alienation of Land Act of 1901 (hereafter PALA).[40]

"NON-AGRICULTURALISTS"

After the British capture of Punjab (1849), colonial officials went among the people to write settlement reports and to codify land relations. They collected several proverbs that encapsulate a folk wisdom in favour of self-cultivation, one that allowed the English to equate certain castes (Jats, Gujars, Arains) with the yeoman of Virgilian romanticism. John Lawrence, for instance, visualized 'a country thickly cultivated by fat, contented yeomanry, each man riding his own horse, sitting under his own fig-tree, and enjoying his rude family comforts'.[41] Colonial officials distinguished between those whom they saw as 'agriculturalists' (these yeomen, whose own proverbs provided sufficient evidence for the English claim) and the 'non-agriculturalists' (such as non-agrarian moneylenders and landless labourers, all of whom the English saw as parasites). As the yeoman became the emblem of Punjab in the colonial mentalité, certain castes reaped significant benefits in the land revenue reports, a process that inaugurated the categorical emergence of these castes as Punjab's contemporary rich peasantry.[42]

Jats and other 'agriculturalists' enjoyed the full beneficence of colonial policy as the state sought to protect these figures from the predations of 'outsiders'. Of course, 'agriculturalist' is not a descriptive but a legal term, since the dalits who toiled on the land did practise the agrarian profession. When the colonial documents wrote of 'non-agriculturalists', in most cases, they referred less to the dalits and more to the urban moneylenders. In the overheated land market, the capital of

[40]D.A. Washbrook, 'Law, State and Agrarian Society in Colonial India', *Modern Asian Studies*, vol. 15, no. 3 (1981), p. 681.

[41]Eric Stokes, *The English Utilitarians in India* (Oxford: Clarendon Press, 1959), p. 244 and P.H.M. Van den Dungen, *The Punjab Tradition* (London: Allen & Unwin, 1972).

[42]Satish Chandra Mishra, 'Commercialisation, Peasant Differentiation and Merchant Capital in Late Nineteenth Century Bombay and Punjab', *Journal of Peasant Studies*, vol. 10 (1982), pp. 37–41.

many urban and rural moneylenders went towards speculation or (in the case of usufructuary mortgages) to rent. The moneylenders preferred to claim the land as security against loans to peasants, an easy strategy to increase their own landholdings. Many of these moneylenders did not come from the city, as suggested by the colonial officials, but they came from amongst the rich peasants and some middle peasants who wished to increase their own holdings and to invest their surplus capital.[43] There is some dispute in the literature over the actual debt of the peasantry, but there was certainly an anxiety amongst the colonial officials which produced the laws to forbid dalits from the land. One official noted that the roots of rebellion lay in land alienation and that 'we dare not wait for agrarian disturbances before we remove the cause of agrarian distress', particularly not in the recruiting ground for the army.[44] Thorburn described the 'gradual transfer of ownership of the soil from its natural lords', the landed aristocrats in the western districts and the yeomen of the Doab, to the 'traders and bankers' (castes such as Khatris, Aroras and Marwaris). These financiers used chicanery to defraud the simple peasant, he suggested, so the government must rapidly produce an 'Act of Bunniah spoilation' to stem their tide.[45]

The literature on PALA, that 'Act of Bunniah spoilation' of 1901, assumes that its effects lay mostly on the fortunes of the 'agrarian castes'.[46] However, the Act forbade dalits from access to landholding, a right that they had begun to exert from at least the days of Ranjit Singh and his diwan Sawan Mull (1821–44). The diwan allowed dalits to break the soil and extend cultivation and he deployed them as a means to undermine old landed tribes.[47] Until PALA, Chuhras held small plots of land, purchased, in some cases, from meagre savings that attracted

[43]Neeladri Bhattacharya, 'Lenders and Debtors: Punjab Countryside, 1880–1940', *Studies in History,* vol. 1 (1985).

[44]NAI, Rev. & Agri. (Rev.), A Progs., October 1895, nos. 72–3.

[45]Septimus Smet Thorburn, *Musalmans and Moneylenders in the Punjab* (Edinburgh: W. Blackwood, 1886), p. 1 and pp. 39–40; NAI, Home (Judicial), A Progs., December 1891, nos. 234–300; NAI, Rev. & Agri. (Rev.), A Progs., May 1891, nos. 1–8.

[46]N.G. Barrier, *The Punjab Alienation of Land Bill of 1900* (Durham: Duke University, 1966) and Richard G. Fox, 'Urban Class and Communal Consciousness in Colonial Punjab', *Modern Asian Studies,* vol. 18, no. 3 (1984), pp. 477–8.

[47]*Annual Report Punjab* (1849–50), *Annual Report Punjab* (1850–1) and Douie, *Punjab,* p. 21.

farmers during the famines.[48] By the 1880s, the colonial state in Punjab politically relied upon a fragile coalition of dominant castes, rural gentry and the emergent bourgeoisie, a compact that made the emancipation of the dalits an unlikely affair. To make natural the dalits' destitution, one official remarked that 'nothing was sacred to Sawan Mull. Chuhras and *kamins* (waged workers) were in his eyes just as good proprietors, probably better than Syals and Beloches'.[49] Driven by this sanctified notion of the yeoman, colonial officials sought some way to exclude the 'non-agriculturalists' from the soil:

It may be considered unfair (and a similar plea has been put forward by Christian missionaries in Madras) to impede the accrual of property in the hands of the village menials, but the increasing power of that class and the disturbance thereby threatened in the village system of upper India is a danger which requires special consideration from an administrative point of view, and it might be advisable in certain districts to go to the length proposed.[50]

The measure proposed was to exclude the dalits.

The revenue department asked local officials in 1900 to proffer a comment on the agrarian status of dalits in their various regions, although the secretary prejudiced the question with the comment that 'ordinarily, it is believed they should not be so classed'.[51] Replies flooded in from the districts, with most officials in concurrence with the secretary. Hoshiarpur's note clinched the case:

Our decision as to any particular tribe must turn largely on political considerations. The whole Act itself is confessedly an attempt to check results which naturally flow from the educational, legal and fiscal systems which we have established in this country. The main pretext for such action is the political danger of the expropriation of the agricultural tribes, and therefore before a tribe is declared agricultural and brought within the direct scope of the Act, it seems proper to consider whether its numbers, position, & c., render it of sufficient political or social importance to be considered an agricultural tribe for the purposes of the Act. If it is not so, interference with it seems needless. Political and social importance I should gauge by (i) numbers and (ii)

[48]*Annual Report Gurgaon* (1883); NAI, Rev. & Agri. (Rev.), A Progs., May 1891, nos. 1–8; NAI, Rev. & Agri. (Rev.), A Progs., October 1895, nos. 72–3; NAI, Rev. & Agri. (Land Revenue), A Progs., August 1896, nos. 28–29.

[49]Chhanda Chattopadhyay, 'The Growth of the 'Punjab Tradition': Emergence and Consolidation of Small Peasant Tenures in Nineteenth Century Punjab', *Bengal Past and Present* (1985), p. 43.

[50]NAI, Rev. & Agri. (Rev.), A Progs., October 1895, para. 318.

[51]NAI, Rev. & Agri. (Rev.), A Progs., May 1901, nos. 11–12.

agricultural aptitude and industry, (iii) past history and social rank.[52]

Based on this logic, the note argued that if a caste is 'socially, politically and agriculturally of little consequence its expropriation in the natural order of development can be contemplated with equanimity'. While section 25 of PALA let local officials exercise their judgement, the Act was itself unambiguous: 'the artisan and menial classes, such as blacksmiths, carriers, weavers, Chamars, Mochis, Chuhras, Musallis, Mazhabis, etc., should certainly be excluded'. The Act protected certain 'agricultural' castes from alienation, a situation familiar across the subcontinent.[53] An Act designed to protect the cultivators from the avariciousness of the financiers ended up preventing the dalits from access to land ownership, from, in sum, the ability to satisfy their land hunger. Freedom, for the Chuhras, had to be sought in other registers.

STRATEGIES FOR FREEDOM

'Old Thakur landlords have often complained bitterly to me of the insolence of the (landless dalits)', William Crooke wrote in 1885, 'the fact being that they are no longer inclined to submit to bullying and drudgery. They know their rights, and they are determined to assert them'.[54] A few decades later, a missionary noted that the Chuhras 'are filled with a deep, passionate resentment against their servile condition. It is not their poverty which they resent, but their slavery'.[55] Such statements do not accord with the Wisers' claim that the Bhangis of their western UP village 'accepted the situation (of their oppression) complacently'.[56] Despite the instances of Chuhra rebelliousness, however, there seemed to be few avenues for their freedom and there seemed to be limitations as well in their political vision. Freedom, in their songs, was both resurrection in the future and it was immanent in the present. The Chuhras waited for the divine to lift them into a realm of joy. Resurrection in the future took the place of insurrection in the

[52]Ibid.

[53]Anand Yang, 'An Institutional Shelter', *Modern Asian Studies*, vol. 13 (1979).

[54]NAI, Rev. & Agri. (Famine), A Progs., December 1888, nos. 1–24.

[55]Henry Whitehead, 'The Mass Movement towards Christianity in the Punjab', *International Review of Missions*, vol. 5 (July 1913).

[56]William and Charlotte Wiser, *Behind Mud Walls* (New York: R.R. Smith, 1930), p. 62.

present, for the general notion was that the divinity must rescue them, they cannot rescue themselves. Part of the difficulty for the dalits was the limited career of the language of class in the Punjab at this time. The industrial labour force was tiny compared to Bombay and Bengal, a lack that meant that the workers had á harder time to organize themselves than those who worked in the dense site of the workshop.[57] Punjab's lack of industrialization left it open to a politics dominated by the agrarian elites who configured the region as a 'peasant society' and put themselves forward as its populist leaders. The Unionist Party, founded in 1923, was known as the 'government of the peasantry' and it relied upon a crude racialism (*Raj karega Jat* [The Jat will rule]) to forge a cross-class alliance that obscured the trials of certain rural folk. At the 1928 Punjab Provincial Conference, the secretary of the Punjab Achutuchdar Mandal moved a resolution to revoke PALA:

This conference, while extremely deploring the arbitrary decision of the Punjab Government in classifying about 3 million village kamins among the non-agriculturalists, in complete disregard of the fact that they are found practising agriculture as tenants, field labourers and farm servants throughout the Province, earnestly appeals to all patriotic citizens of the Punjab to render them all the needful help to their agitation, for getting themselves notified as agriculturalists.[58]

The 'party of the peasantry' failed to consider this mild resolution and the disorganized Chuhras, without an elaborated language of class, could not proceed against both the landholders and the colonial state. The power blocs instituted from above squelched the formation of a socialist party until the emergence of the Kirti Kisan Party in the 1930s, by which time, for our purposes, a large section of Chuhras had already moved to Delhi and assimilated themselves into its labour market.[59] While in the countryside and prior to the entry of the Left in their lives, most Chuhras took their rebellion down two paths, conversion to Christianity and migration.

[57]A.K. Bagchi, *Private Investment in India, 1900–1930* (Cambridge: Cambridge University Press, 1975), p. 436.

[58]Bhagwan Josh, *Communist Movement in Punjab* (Delhi: Anupama, 1979), p. 79.

[59]Ian Talbot, *The Punjab Unionist Party and the Partition of India* (Richmond: Curzon, 1996) and Mridula Mukherjee, 'Communists and Peasants in Punjab', *The Indian Left*. Ed. Bipan Chandra (New Delhi: Vikas, 1983).

Conversion

In June 1878, a dalit man named Ditt walked into a United Presbyterian Church in Sialkot and delivered himself to Christianity. He was followed by a vast number of dalits, with the district registering a six-hundred-and-sixty per cent increase in Christians from 1881 to 1891 (11,669 by 1891). During this period, Christians in Punjab increased by four hundred per cent.[60] By 1911, Indian Christians in Punjab numbered 168,944, the bulk of whom came from the Chuhra community. The numbers mask a story of immense courage as the dalits challenged both the landholders and the colonial authorities to treat them as humans and not as beasts of burden. 'I am not afraid of you now', a convert told a British chief of police, 'and I can go around among these villages with freedom, and people do not take me for a thief or rascal, as they used to do when we were heathen Chuhras. They take me for a man now'.[61] Or as another said, 'Christ gave me a *pagri* (turban, a mark of respect) in place of dust'.[62]

The landholders fought the conversions. Many of them disallowed the converts to bury their dead, they spread rumours that the sacrament was tantamount to cannibalism whereby the Church made the converts drink the blood of cows, pigs and hares (the Chuhras revered the hare). The missionaries felt the landholders dreaded 'the loss of their power and influence over (the Chuhras), they have very much the same feeling as that which one may suppose animated the slave holder in America at the prospect of the liberation of the negro hence they annoy and persecute them in every way possible to prevent their becoming Christian'.[63] In Sialkot, a proverb bemoaned the fate of the landholder, for 'all the Meghs are Aryas, all the Chuhras Christians, and God looks after the zamindar'.[64] Despite the pro-landholder PALA, one landholder newspaper complained that the government had reduced landholders to 'the position of menials while sweepers, chamars, & c., are appropriating the place once occupied by them'. It remarked that the dalits converted to 'develop into "sahibs" and one day will over-

[60] *District Gazetteer Sialkot* (1894–5), p. 66; *Census of India,* 1891, Punjab, p. 97.

[61] Reverend G.E. Phillips, *The Outcastes' Hope or Work among the Depressed Classes in India* (London, 1912), p. 83.

[62] J.C.B. Webster, *The Dalit Christians* (Delhi: ISPCK, 1992), p. 56.

[63] *The 61st Annual Report of the Lodiana Mission* (Lodiana, 1896), pp. 62–3.

[64] NAI, Rev. & Agri. (Land Rev.), A Progs., March 1915, no. 10.

throw British rule in India'.[65] Landholders, we may surmise, wished simply to remain underlings of the empire. The landholders had much to fear, for while the 'new converts are quite willing to retain their old employment, they are asking for a more definite remuneration'. The assertion of the dalits scared the state, who worried about its alliance with 'the natural heads of the people'.[66] 'The emancipation of the kamins is inevitable', wrote the District Commissioner of Delhi, 'but it is not convenient and we should do nothing to expedite it'.[67] In fact, the colonial officials did everything to prevent it.

The missionaries, for the most part, did not go along with the dalits. From Meerut we hear that 'the missionaries do all in their power to induce their converts to work for the zamindar as before, but the latter are unable to compel them to work without pay to the same extent as before their conversion. Unfortunately the independence inculcated by the Christian teaching not infrequently develops into insolence'.[68] Colonial missionary policy was generally wedded to the hope that if the 'natural heads' convert, then the working people may follow suit; they feared that the conversion of dalits may discourage Hindus and ashraf Muslims from making the switch. The story of the Chuhras validates Webster's claim that 'the mass movements were Dalit movements, initiated and led by Dalits; missionaries did not lead Dalits, but responded to them'.[69] The missionary hierarchy remained suspicious of these converts, certain that they came only for the material benefits ('Rice Christians'). But, as one missionary wrote in the context of the 1877 famine in Delhi, given 'the tyranny of caste people over poor degraded outcastes, the moral effect of a great famine, the desire for education and social advancement, it would be unfair to stigmatise these motives as altogether low and unworthy'.[70] Reverend Robert Clark, however, took the influential position that the 'genius of Christianity is liberty. If the Son makes men free, they become free indeed, even when they are living as serfs'.[71] The act of conversion, for such missionaries, the

---

[65]*Zamindar* (Karmabad), 24 September 1906.

[66]*District Gazetteer Sialkot* (1894–5), p. 66.

[67]Chowdhry, *Punjab Politics*, p. 65.

[68]*District Gazetteer Meerut* (1922), p. 81.

[69]Webster, *Dalit Christians*, p. 71.

[70]Society for the Propagation of the Gospel in Foreign Parts, *The Story of the Delhi Mission* (Westminster: SPGFP, 1908), p. 43.

[71]Robert Clark, *Thirty Years of Christian Missionary Society Work in the Punjab and Sindh, 1852–82* (Lahore: CMS, 1883), p. 123.

union with Christ is freedom, even if only spiritual freedom. The freedom sought by the dalits, the freedom to own land and control their lives, still eluded them as the missionaries, for the most part, bowed to the demands of the colonial state. To make marginal amends, the state allotted small farms in the new canal colonies for the missions. Early farms, such as the Clarkabad settlement in Lahore district (named after Robert Clark), failed due to the agrarian inexperience of the converts. With the mass movements from the dalits, the missions now had experienced fieldworkers who revived these settlements, but again the converts worked as mere serfs, but as serfs of Christ no less.[72] The mission farms on the canal colonies failed for the most part because the state charged them higher rates than they charged the 'agricultural castes'.[73] By 1914, the state decided not to offer land grants to dalits, since this would make it hard for the 'agricultural castes' to get landless labour, which could 'upset the existing social and economic order'.[74]

Migration

The turbulence of the countryside wore heavily upon the dalits and their livelihood. During famines, the Chuhras 'generally took to thieving, and satisfied their hunger by eating stolen cattle'.[75] Dietary taboos vanished during the famines, as did the Chuhras' reluctance to steal from the merchants or from the state.[76] Desperate Chuhras turned to the moneylenders, many of whom offered them loans only against the security of their labour (*sarir-ka-karza*), now bonded to the financier.[77] Rather than be bound for their measly debt, many Chuhras took to flight and 'itinerate in quest of charity'.[78] During the 1860–1

---

[72]Rev. & Agri. (Land Rev.), A Progs., March 1896, nos. 5–6; R. Maconachie, *Rowland Bateman: Nineteenth Century Apostle* (London: CMS, 1917) and *61st Annual Report*, p. 106.

[73]Indu Agnihotri, 'Agrarian Change in the Canal Colonies, Punjab 1890–1935' (New Delhi: Jawaharlal Nehru University PhD, 1987), pp. 115, 141 and 454–7; NAI, Rev. & Agri. (Rev.), A Progs., June 1890, nos. 102–3 and August 1902, no. 21.

[74]Ali, *The Punjab*, pp. 95–8 and 112.

[75]*PRFC*, vol. 1, p. 778 and *District Gazetteer Hissar* (1907), p. 181.

[76]*Census of India*, 1891, vol. XIX, part 1, p. 202; Indian Famine Commission, *Evidence of Witnesses from the Punjab* (Calcutta: GOI, 1898), vol. IV, pp. 59–60.

[77]Bhattacharya, 'Lenders and Debtors', p. 320 and *PRFC*, vol. 2, p. 712.

[78]*PRFC*, vol. 2, p. 792–7.

famine, colonial officials watched the dalits move across Punjab, 'a great many of them much emaciated by want of food', in search of work and rain.[79] At times, landholders stretched by inflation and famine could not afford to hire waged landless labourers, who had to then move on.

Most Chuhras went towards the cities of the Punjab (Delhi, Shimla, Jalandhar, Amritsar, Lahore), many of which began to expand and demand labour at this time. Chuhras migrated in families, since few could afford to manage two homes simultaneously and the landholders refused to let them retain their homes without the labour of the entire family. 'My love', one Chuhra song goes, 'if you go for employment [*chakri*], take me with you, my life'.[80] As indentured labourers and armymen, some Chuhras travelled the world, but most went along well-worn furrows into the main cities in search of land and fortune. 'At the gates of Delhi', the Chuhras sang, 'gold is sold'.[81] The gate that most Chuhras visited was not the treasury, but the sanitation department. The city did need more and more workers, but not in highly remunerative positions. The Chuhras, long accustomed to agrarian work, entered the cities where the British, Hindu and ashraf Muslim officials saw them as sweepers (a legacy of certain legends of the Chuhra past). 'Had not the caste system of our country condemned a certain class of people for (sanitation work) on the score of birth alone', one Gandhian wrote in 1937, 'it would have been difficult to procure the growing army of sweepers required for new towns growing in our midst'.[82] There was little interest in the work experiences of the Chuhras, in the textual validity of the stereotype regarding caste and occupation, in the rebellious consciousness of the dalits who preferred freedom rather than assimilation into an imputed hierarchy (with all the Brahmanic virtues it entailed). The strictures of *varnavyavastha* (social organization of the four varnas) emerged from the sanitation departments which sent out recruiters to hire the dalits before they gained much urban

---

[79]*PRFC*, vol. 2, p. 823.

[80]Youngson, 'The Chuhras' (November 1906), p. 304–8.

[81]Youngson, 'The Chuhras' (November 1906), p. 306.

[82]Thakkar, 'The Plight of the Sweepers'; R.V. Russell and Rai Bahadur Hira Lal, *The Tribes and Castes of the Central Provinces of India* (London: MacMillan, 1916), vol. 4, p. 215; *Indian Notes & Queries*, vol. 4, no. 47 (August 1887), p. 204; Stephen Fuchs, *At the Bottom of Indian Society: The Harijan and Other Low Castes* (New Delhi: Munshiram Manoharlal, 1980), p. 236.

experience. 'One day, as it used to happen occasionally', Bholi said of the early 1930s, 'the Jamadar of the sweepers stood on a pedestal before the municipal office, pointed to a pile of uniforms stacked near a store and shouted, "Who amongst you will join our forces? Put on the uniform and take a *jharu* (broom) from that store and join us! Come on everybody!" '[83] 'When I came to Delhi from Punjab with my family', Puran Chand recalled of the same period, 'I was small. I took a job in the municipality. The Jamadar was not of our caste. All of us *safai karamcharis* [sanitation workers] were Chuhras. They would only take us. Jamadars used to come into our mohalla and announce openings (in the DMC). Our people would jump at the Jamadars and beg for work. We are proud people. We had pride. In Delhi, who knows?'[84]

Oppressed people fashion a story of the origin of their bondage. Frequently these tales entail an act of betrayal by a wily middle-man who acts on behalf of the powerful. The recruiter, in many tales, is the exemplary mediator who engenders their capture. While these legends are exaggerated, the colonial archive shows us that there is a hint of truth to them. The sanitation departments did indeed aggressively go after what it called the 'sweeper castes', for the most part Chuhras.[85] The Chief Commissioner of Delhi rebuked the nationalist demand for education for the dalits, since he claimed there was plenty of work for their 'hereditary calling of sweeper'. 'Where a class enjoys a fair amount of material prosperity and is not subjected to any actual oppression by its neighbours', he wrote pompously, 'it seems not unreasonable to leave it to work out its future by its own resources and by such facilities as private enterprise is prepared to extend it'.[86] The state inserted itself into the Chuhras' lives to adversely refashion their destiny; when the nationalists spoke on their behalf, the state claimed to be a detached arbiter. The statutory identification of the Chuhras with sanitation had grave consequences for them, since this was the principle job available to them and they went into it in large numbers. In 1921, almost 82 per cent of the sweepers hailed from the Chuhra community,

---

[83]Prasanta and Ila Mazumdar, *Rural Migrants in an Urban Setting* (Delhi: Hindustan, 1978), p. 49.

[84]Puran Chand, Sau Quarters, Karol Bagh, 26 January 1992.

[85]DMC Progs., 1 October 1888, 20 February 1893 and 3 July 1893; *Census of India*, 1921, vol. XV part 1, p. 344.

[86]DSA, CC (Home), B Progs., 1916, no. 169.

while ten years later the percentage increased to 89.4.[87] By the 1950s, few non-Chuhras worked as sweepers. For them, 'the question regarding "prospects" is not understood', one official wrote, since they join the DMC and 'remain as menials through their service'.[88] 'We came to Delhi to find work', one dalit told me in 1992. 'We stayed not as any workers, but as sweepers'.[89]

Tied to an occupation, the Chuhras found it hard to get jobs in other spheres of life, least of all things that paid more than the glorified skills of refuse removal. While the British hired certain oppressed castes into the railways and into the construction trades, the Chuhras and allied dalits had to perforce work in the municipality as refuse removers.[90] In times of unemployment, they held fast to these municipal jobs which, over the years, began to have a gloss of their own. Chuhras competed to prevent the entry of other castes into *their* occupation, one that was steady despite its other problems. Over time, the link between the caste and its occupation became far more pervasive then it ever was in the past. In the late 1950s, M. N. Srinivas recognized that 'there is a tendency for a specialized task in a factory to become a monopoly of a caste or regional group. It is fairly well-known that in appointment to jobs in factories considerations of kinship, caste and region are still relevant'.[91] At the same time, Jagjivan Ram (as Labour Minister of newly-independent India) argued that dalits 'did not take up their present callings out of a consideration that all work was noble but because society forced them to menial jobs'. By the 1950s, the link between caste and occupation (fostered during colonial rule) was in jeopardy, but not for the sweepers. 'The real salvation of sweepers', Ram argued, 'lay in building up a society where there are no mehtars', that is, where technology removes social prejudices against refuse removal.[92] While this chapter showed how the Chuhras leave the countryside to enter the town as sweepers, the next chapter will show how the technology of sanitation was structured to rely upon these manual sweepers rather than to emancipate the Chuhras from the sole task of sweeping.

[87]*Census of India*, 1931, vol. XVI, p. 98.

[88]DSA, CC (Home), B Progs., 1927, no. 128.

[89]Baru Ram, Mandir Marg, New Delhi, 10 March 1992.

[90]Shyamlal, *The Bhangis*, p. 46.

[91]M.N. Srinivas, *Caste in Modern India* (Bombay: Asia, 1962), p. 95.

[92]Jagjivan Ram, *On Labour Problems*. Ed. S.R. Gurtu (Delhi: Atma Ram, 1951), pp. 162–3.

3

Sweepers

In the 1850s, the German scientist Justus von Liebig wrote that the 'preservation of the wealth and welfare of nations, and advances in culture and civilization depend on how the sewage question is resolved'.[1] He wrote these wry words in the aftermath of two major cholera epidemics (1832 and 1848), episodes that recalled for many the tales of the Black Plague and of the Tartar invasions. The virulence of cholera revived stories of the plague, but the origin of the disease in Bengal produced images of Ghengis Khan's invading hordes. The recurrence of disease led to a major reconstruction of urban and domestic space both in Europe, and in the colonies. Before John Snow and Louis Pasteur made their discoveries, Euro-American governments inaugurated a public health reform movement that valorized cleanliness (including regular bathing and prompt refuse removal) towards the transformation of the everyday practices of the population. While elements of the European working-class were reviled as a 'savage race', the muncipalities evinced hope that they too could benefit from the general fruits of modern plumbing. To assist this pedagogy of habit, Euro-American municipalities funded the construction of sewage and water lines as well as poured capital into the apparatus of refuse removal. A few years after the first outbreak of cholera in London, Edwin Chadwick announced that 'the exclusive use of hand-labour in street sweeping is pronounced by competent judges to be a mere barbarism, and several machines have been invented which demonstrate that by mechanical power, moved by horses, the cleansing can be effected in a far shorter time'.[2] Euro-American cities continued to rely

[1] Karl Kautsky, *The Agrarian Question* (London: Swan, 1988), p. 54.

[2] Edwin Chadwick, *Report on an Inquiry into the Sanitary Conditions of the Labouring Populations of Great Britain* (London: W. Clowes and Son, 1842), p. 54.

upon street sweepers, but they gradually became technicians, a far cry from their earlier identification with dirt itself.[3]

In the colonies, the Europeans developed an alternative solution to the sewage question. There was, first, a widespread belief that the Indians did not have the capacity to learn cleanliness (a view disputed by some missionaries and by such stalwarts of local administration as F. L. Brayne).[4] The officials ignored the demands of the Indians for better sanitary care and for consideration of their various modes of sanitary conduct (most of which required fresh water).[5] If the modern state wished to transform the totality of European society into civility, there was only a shadow of this agenda in the colonies. Here, the colonial officials saw the natives as people who needed to be monitored and not provided with the facilities of modernity ('the habits of the natives are such', wrote an official in 1863, 'that, unless they are closely watched, they cover the entire neighbouring surface with filth').[6] 'The prospect of improved systems of sewage disposal being introduced into oriental towns', one manual on sewage disposal tells us, 'depends largely upon a general education of the inhabitants and the elected representatives in the economic value of the works'.[7] There was no need to expend finances on these natives until the colonial officials themselves deemed the natives worthy of sanitation and hygiene. In 1888, Lord Dufferin ordered a general inquiry on hygienic habits of the natives. His officials reported that the natives are 'inoculated by time and habit'. To 'the masses of the people', an official wrote, 'sanitation is foolishness', this in contradiction to earlier representations of the natives as highly sanitary peoples. William Crooke responded to the

[3]Donald Reid, *Paris Sewers and Sewermen* (Cambridge: Harvard University Press, 1991), pp. 113–20 and Suellen Hoy, *Chasing Dirt: The American Pursuit of Cleanliness* (New York: Oxford University Press, 1995), pp. 66–72.

[4]Florence Nightingale, *Life or Death in India* (London: Spottiswoode, 1874) and F. L. Brayne, *Socrates in an Indian Village (Dehati Socrates)* (London: H. Milford, 1929).

[5]The Delhi papers carried frequent denunciations, such as one that echoed John Snow's discoveries to condemn the drainage of sewage into well-water. *Urdu Akhbaar*, 16 April 1871.

[6]Prashad, 'Native Dirt', p. 255.

[7]G. B. Williams, *Sewage Disposal in India and the East: A Manual of the Latest Practices Applied to Tropical Conditions* (Calcutta, 1924), p. 215 and C. C. James, *Oriental Drainage: A Guide to the Collection, Removal and Disposal of Sewage in Eastern Cities* (Bombay, 1902).

Viceroy's request with the hope that 'the time will come when they *will* comprehend the laws of hygiene, just as at some time or other they will get rid of the abject superstitition which leads them now, where they will learn to treat their women properly, to discontinue infant marriage, and emerge from the comparative barbarism in which they are plunged at present'.[8] There was to be no official revision of this view.

Due to this representation of the native, the colonial state was relieved of any obligation to produce a technological modernity. The municipality was to be 'guided not by what is the best system of sanitation', an official wrote in 1912, 'but by what is the best system which the Municipal funds can afford'.[9] For the sanitation department, however, there was not to be much money, since three-quarters of the municipal revenue went to the police, a policy derived from a viceregal declaration of 1864 that 'the cost of the Municipal Police shall be the first charge on all [municipal] funds'.[10] Spaces inhabited by the colonial officials and by unofficial Europeans enjoyed the fruits of modernity; those who financed this modernity, the natives, remained in the sloth of another kind of colonial modernity, one that relied upon manual labour and outdated technology. When a colonial official noted that 'the importance of efficient scavenging with speedy and complete removal of all nightsoil and rubbish from the vicinity of habitations and its satisfactory disposal can hardly be exaggerated',[11] he pledged the colonial state towards the creation of a modern city on the backs of what Chadwick called 'a mere barbarism'. The sanitation system relied upon the hard work of the sweepers, who themselves remained more or less trapped in a patronage system (sweeper-Jamadar) nurtured by the colonial municipality for its own pecuniary benefit.

The sanitation system of Delhi is a vast enterprise that underwent major changes from the 1860s to the 1940s. By 1947, the DMC set in place a form of refuse removal that exists, in most part, till today.[12] To make this ensemble intelligible, we will divide it into three parts (transport of refuse, recycling of refuse and destruction of refuse).

[8]Prashad, 'Native Dirt', pp. 254–5.

[9]NAI, Education (Sanitary), A Progs., September 1912, nos. 1–18.

[10]Gupta, *Delhi*, p. 70 and p. 83.

[11]DSA, CC (Education), B Progs., 1914, no. 183.

[12]M.N. Buch, *The Environmental Impact of Urbanization* (Pune: Parisar Annual Lecture on World Environmental Day, 1989), pp. 6–7.

TRANSPORTING REFUSE

Refuse left the city by two ways, either in drains or else in the carts borne by the sweepers. The Dilliwalas threw their solid refuse into the streets each morning or else they deposited their nightsoil in *sandas* [pit-latrine] toilets and into the drains. The sweepers gathered the solid refuse into jute sacks and placed them in dalaos and they swept the liquid refuse along surface drains to the sub-soil conduits.[13] In the 1870s, Delhi newspapers put on record the DMC's failure to solve the sewage question. 'Beyond the making of gutters of a cylindrical form, of the widening of a few of the drains, little else has been done by the municipality. Some of the mohallas are in such a state that in the rainy season water remains collected in them knee deep which makes it difficult for passengers to pass through them'.[14] The filth in the drains and on the street, we are told, 'is allowed to grow putrid, and emits deadly effluvia which are highly offensive to the brain'. These drains, a colonial official lamented, are 'merely extended cesspools' from which a 'black semi-liquid deposit' exuded a terrible smell and 'concentrated sewer gases', perhaps 'one of the principle causes of the excessive death rate of the city of Delhi'. Further, we are told, the garbage sits in 'untidy heaps, very offensive to the eyes and nose'.[15] When the garbage left the city, one senior official noted that 'I shall never forget the sight of a stream of these carts going to the trenching grounds, meeting another stream of meat carts coming from the slaughter house, with myraid of flies passing from one to the other'.[16] Despite their own vigorous protests, the DMC and city officials recognized that without a capital outlay there was little that they could do, particularly since, as one of them wrote in 1912, 'it is only a few years since this branch of sanitation was overhauled and the present system of sanitation was evolved to replace the system then existing'.[17]

When the British took Delhi in 1803, they inherited a city with an abandoned sanitation system. Without a doubt, Mughal Delhi was famous for its canals which blessed the city with gardens, fresh drinking water and a drainage system, of which the *Nahr-i-Bihist* (the

[13]*Urdu Akhbaar*, 1 August 1874.
[14]*Urdu Akhbaar*, 8 July 1871.
[15]DMC Progs., 19 September 1887 and 5 March 1887.
[16]NAI, Education (Sanitary), A Progs., September 1912, nos. 1–18.
[17]Ibid.

Canal of Paradise), the *Nahr-i-Shibab* (the Canal of Shibah al-Din Khan) and the Ali Mardan canal are the most famous.[18] During Shah Jahan's reign, an elaborate subsoil drainage system was built, in which the masonary conduits had flat stone sides and unplastered beds, as functional as anything of its day and the Jamuna's regular supply of water enabled steady drainage of this hydraulic system. During the mid-eighteenth century, the Jamuna's levels began to drop, the canals slowly desiccated and the drains became cesspools. In 1820, the British tried to repair the Jamuna Canal, in 1821-22 they reopened the Ali Mardan channel and they spent the next several decades tinkering with what lay below the surface rather than doing an overhaul of it.[19] Of the drains, a 1852 report noted that 'without constant and unremitting care even the most perfect system of under-drainage must be ineffective' and without this care, 'their uselessness will become a by-word or their existence a myth'.[20] By the late nineteenth century, British engineers routinely felt that the subsoil conduits in Delhi were 'rotten and more apt to soak in drainage than conduct it off'.[21] Nevertheless, the city discharged its refuse into that derelict system.

Until the creation of New Delhi between 1912 and 1931, the DMC did little to tackle the sewage question, so that by the 1890s, the local press routinely complained that the DMC 'does not discharge its duties in a manner befitting the position of the famous city'.[22] The refuse from the city was collected by the sweepers and transported into the ditch that ringed the walled city, 'an arrangement which cannot fail to be productive of sickness'.[23] The Public Works Department (PWD) filled-in and abandoned the Shahjahani drains and built a set of surface drains to carry liquid refuse into the Jamuna or else into the city ditch.[24] The surface drains drew angry response from the city's residents who complained that the lanes 'are too narrow and lined with open privies,

---

[18]Stephen P. Blake, *Shahjahanabad: the Sovereign City in Mughal India, 1639–1739* (Cambridge: Cambridge University Press, 1991), pp. 64–5.

[19]Gupta, *Delhi*, pp. 18–20.

[20] W. H. Greathed, *Report on the Drainage of the City of Delhi and the Means of Improving it* (Agra: GOI, 1852), p. 10.

[21]Clem G. Parsons, *Delhi Administrative Dictionary* (Lahore, 1906), p. 50.

[22]*Rahbar-i-Hind*, 19 April 1894, *Akmal-ul-Akhbaar*, 20 April 1894 and *Akhbaar-i-'Am*, 19 May 1894.

[23]NAI, Home (Sanitary), A Progs., 7 November 1888, nos. 5–6.

[24]*Notes on the Administration of Delhi Province* (Calcutta, 1926).

the dirty water from which either collects in basins dug for the purpose, or flows through the lanes, which accordingly are always full of exceedingly foul smells'.[25] There was also justifiable anger that the DMC spent more funds to build 'drains of minor importance' in the Civil Lines at the expense of the densely populated walled city.[26] When the DMC opened the Salimgarh channel to draw off drainage from the colonials' homes, it noted that 'no drainage from any native quarter will be allowed to enter Salimgarh channel'.[27] Colonial racism informed the sewage question in Delhi. For the PWD engineers, the surface drains in the admittedly narrow streets became the only way to do something given the DMC's limited budget.

The question of funds was, on the surface, the major obstacle to reform. In 1881, the PWD accelerated the drainage and waterworks project and it turned to the DMC for money. The municipality reluctantly drew a bank loan of Rs 900,000 for the project, but it used most of this money to build a waterworks scheme (mainly for the Civil Lines).[28] When the project exceeded its budget (even before completion), the DMC decided against the use of loans and hoped for grants-in-aid from the Government of India. The DMC, one sanitary official rued, 'have no funds available and they are not prepared to consider even the preparation of a scheme until their water supply and drainage scheme are complete, and until the loans raised to finance these schemes are paid off'.[29] The government, however, was burdened by large-scale investments on its military, railways, and irrigation, yet it still found some small funds for the DMC, but mainly as relief, as a financial adjustment rather than as a financial instrument. Delhi, the most lightly taxed municipality in north India, drew praise from Curzon in 1899, who said that the DMC 'knew when to tax and when to spare'.[30] While this may have been so, the DMC also knew that it could rely upon the social relations between Jamadars and sweepers to maintain a clean city rather than to enhance the physical plant of the city. Frustrated with the lack of technological improvement, some

[25]*Mayo Memorial Gazette*, 19 February 1874 and *Anjuman-i-Panjab*, 24 March 1883.

[26]*Urdu Akhbaar*, 16 December 1871.

[27]Gupta, *Delhi*, p. 162.

[28]Parsons, *Delhi*, p. 51.

[29]NAI, Education (Sanitary), A Progs., September 1912, nos. 1–8.

[30]Gupta, *Delhi*, p. 168.

colonial officials went so far as to suggest that in the tropics it was acceptable for the sweepers to dump solid refuse into the almost dry subsoil sewers, a process that blocked them and left a putrid mass under the city.[31]

New Delhi was constructed on modern lines, but its presence did not do much for the older, neglected walled city. In 1913, the project scheme for the sanitation system of the new city provided 'for the construction of a water-borne system not only in the New Delhi area, but throughout the walled city and the existing suburbs'. This suggestion was not acted upon, since the engineers and accountants agreed that while the improvements must be enacted in the Civil Lines and the new city as a matter of policy, it would be 'many years before all the better Indian houses' could be fitted with water-borne sewage systems.[32] There was a hope that 'as many houses of a good class as possible' should be connected to the new sewage system, perhaps both to reward the emergent native bourgeoisie as well as to ensure that they did not share a common complaint with the masses of the people (who, we are already told, think that sanitation is foolishness).[33] While merchants, such as Chunna Mal, hired a private sanitary force, the resourceless population was left to its own rudimentary devices. 'City funds have not yet permitted the creation of a system of water-borne sewage', one city official reported, but the DMC 'have every intention of introducing an improved system which is hoped will take the form of water-borne sewage but much depends on the funds available, the possibilities of raising a further loan for this special purpose, and the attitude of the Government towards proposals for a special grant'.[34] By 1915, the DMC's water scheme was bankrupt and part of the city's main water supply (the Najafgarh Jhil) was diverted to irrigate crops in neighbouring provinces.[35] The condition of the old sewers and the shortage of water confronted the engineers as palpable limits to their technological resources, which could only be surmounted by an exertion of will and a cannibalization of matériel.

[31]Major W. W. Clemsha, *Sewage Disposal in the Tropics* (Calcutta, 1910).

[32]*New Imperial Capital Delhi. Project Estimate for Works* (Delhi, 1913), vol. 1, pp. 38–40.

[33]DSA, CC (Education), B Progs., 1915, no. 219.

[34]NAI, Education (Sanitary), A Progs., September 1912, nos. 1–18.

[35]NAI, Education (Sanitary), A Progs., March 1915, nos. 31–44; DSA, CC (Education), B Progs., 1927, no. 6 (7).

With the construction of New Delhi south of the walled city, there was now a tide of criticism of the latter's practice of secreting its refuse outside Delhi Gate (closest to the new city). There was no way to move the refuse farther than the walls, since the old carts would not bear the transit on the dirt roads. The New Delhi Municipal Committee (NDMC) could be nonchalant about the DMC's dumping, since it had at its disposal motor lorries for the removal of its waste (of six one-ton lorries, the viceregal estates used three).[36] The cost of the lorries prevented the DMC from making the transition to mechanized removal.[37] 'Conditions in Delhi City are such that the substitution of modern sanitary lorries for carts can never be complete', wrote the Chief Commissioner in 1937, 'and that so far as can be forseen the use of the slow moving sanitary bullock carts will always be necessary'. 'Carts for the transport of refuse are inevitable in any system in any town', the government commented, 'though with improvements in lay-out [etc.] it may be possible to replace them gradually by lorries'.[38]

If there was a consensus that sweepers and bullock carts had to service the walled city, there was also a lingering fantasy that some inexpensive technological device would solve the sewage question. In the 1880s, the DMC built a tramway to conduct refuse out of the city, but the expense of the scheme prevented its continuance.[39] In the 1930s, the DMC revisited the train scheme and by 1940 it built, after intra-departmental struggles, a refuse train to run to the outskirts of the city with some of its garbage.[40] The scheme was a substitute for some of the carts, but it did not significantly dilute the reliance of the DMC upon the sweepers. The web of practices based on the exploitation of manual labour was not undermined by expensive and labour-saving devices as long as the refuse was removed speedily and inexpensively. Colonial officers certainly demonstrated ingenuity in their task, such as the method tried by one officer amongst his sewage cleaners, 'to make each man, before going to work [in the sewage pits], step into a vessel

[36]DSA, CC (Education), B. Progs., 1928, no. 4 (136); Ibid., 1930, no. 6 (26) and Ibid., 1931, no. 4 (8).

[37]DSA, CC (Education), B. Progs., 1930, no. 6 (25).

[38]NAI, Education, Health and Lands (Health), 1937, no. 23-37/A/37-H.

[39]Parsons, *Delhi*, p. 178; NAI, Home (Municipalities), A Progs., January 1891, nos. 10–19; DMC Progs., 10 July 1894 and 12 October 1896.

[40]Vijay Prashad, 'The Technology of Sanitation in Colonial Delhi', *Modern Asian Studies* (forthcoming, 2000).

containing tar, so that his legs are coated with tar to the knees'.[41] While this appears to be the Kurtzian exception, it is not the only harebrained scheme to attempt to overcome the lack of resources provided to sanitary officers. The rais of the walled city protested that the 'New Delhi people have not descended from the heavens. When the Government can spend millions [on New Delhi] why should it treat the Delhi people as untouchables?'[42] The 'untouchables' themselves, of course, remained in a state of distress far more acute than that of the rais. There was to be little improvement of their work lives, now seen as integral to the system and managed by the unregulated power of the Jamadars. Emily Eden, on her travels in 1838, may well have been onto something when she wrote that 'Delhi is a very suggestive and moralizing place—such stupendous remains of power and wealth passed and passing away—and somehow I feel that we horrid English have just 'gone and done it', merchandized it, revenued it, and spoiled it all'.[43] She was wrong to 'blame' the English, for much of the culpability of this, as I have shown, lies in the economic logic that defeated sanitary reform in the city. But there is also something in her imputation of 'blame', since the racist exclusion of the walled city was constitutive of the problems that all of Delhi faces till today.

RECYCLING REFUSE

The hinterland of Delhi until the early 1800s enjoyed the beneficience of sturdy agriculture and the city benefitted from the bounty of its markets.[44] In 1636, 45,000 villages surrounded Shah Jahan's city, but by 1844 the number dwindled to 400 and by 1880, only 288 villages remained in the environs of the expansive city.[45] Those villages that maintained melon and sugarcane production (among other crops) absorbed much of the urban refuse as fertilizer. *Dal raja, mal kheti,* went one Punjabi proverb (what an army is to a king, manure is to a

---

[41]*McNally's Sanitary Handbook for India* (Madras, 1887), p. 147.

[42]DSA, CC (Education), B Progs., 1935, no. 6 (23).

[43]Emily Eden, *Up the Country: Letters from India* (London: Virago, 1984), p. 98.

[44]Sayyid Wazir Hasaan Dihlavi, *Dilli ka Akhiri Didar* (Delhi: Urdu Akademi, 1986) and A. S. Kalsi, '*Pariksaguru* (1882): the first Hindi novel and the Hindu èlite', *Modern Asian Studies*, vol. 26, no. 4 (1992).

[45]Narayani Gupta, 'Delhi and Its Hinterland', *Delhi through the Ages*, p. 251.

farmer). Manure, it is said, is worth a field ploughed a thousand times (*sau wah, ik pah*). These rural values illustrate an ecological concern for the farms' relationship with manure, for as humans remove nutrients from the soil, these must be returned to it. While there is no universal peasant culture, it is certainly true that peasants within different cultural domains recognize the centrality of manure, including human refuse, to their practice. If there are too few humans to provide manure, Quesnay's fourteenth maxim advised farmers to keep livestock. The word 'manure', in the French, comes from the word to work by hand, reminding us that manure was that agrarian value that had to be worked gently into the soil with one's hand. In Punjab, there was an alternative use for manure, as cooking fuel. As most peasants did not have brass pots, their unglazed utensils could not stand 'any fire fiercer than the smouldering one given by dung'. While the peasants worked on the fields, the 'fire will smoulder on and gently simmer the food', often something akin to a mess of pottage (*khichri*).[46] The rural values that cherished manure and fertile soil confronted an emerging law of value; land markets overheated near the city, without heed to the soil's fertility. With the expansion of the city, land under the tiller decreased and the city's refuse could not be absorbed by agriculture in its vicinity. In this small corner of the empire, colonialism was an ecological watershed.[47]

As in Delhi, the sewage of Edinburgh was run-off just outside the city, a tract of 400 acres (Craigentinny Meadows) that had 'long been notorious as the most filthy and offensive plots of cultivated land in Great Britain'.[48] The farmers who worked the land knew that the sewage needed treatment (the finding of a 1821 Royal Commission) and that they required a process to speed-up the absorption of the sullage. The volume of the refuse was far too much for them to be able to find a solution. Drawing from this experience, Edwin Chadwick started the Metropolitan Sewage Manure Company, but it failed due to the vast capital outlay needed to create techniques to treat the sewage.[49]

[46]*Settlement Report Karnal*, 1872–80, para. 420.

[47]M. Gadgil and R. Guha, *This Fissured Land: An Ecological History of India* (Delhi: Oxford University Press, 1992), p. 116.

[48]Williams, *Sewage Disposal*, p. 6 and G. R. Redgraves, *Sewage Utilization* (London: W. Clowes, 1876).

[49]Christopher Hamlin, 'What Becomes of Pollution? Adversary Science and the Controversy on the Self-Purification of Rivers in Britain, 1850–1900'

Chadwick's enterprise was driven by epidemiological, ecological, and financial concerns. On the final score, he worried that the incineration of refuse meant the loss of energy, a concern that was shared by colonial officials in India who berated peasants for the 'custom of burning pats [of dung] for fuel', since the manure could be better used in the fields.[50] By 1882, however, the Royal Commission on Sewage Disposal declared that the manurial content of sewage was too low for municipalities to bother with its use. The Commission made its declaration after von Liebig's artificial phosphate manure came on the market and as Sir John Lawes' Rothamsted Estate demonstrated the utility of artificial nitrates, potash, and phosphates. Agricultural production was on the threshold of intensification, now removed from the rural values of the past and wedded firmly to the production of values for the chemical industry.[51] The relationship to manure also changed at this time, as sanitarians promoted the idea that excreta is inherently bad and that it must be shunned, even as fertilizer.[52] This did not mean that urban refuse was to be treated before being dumped into watercourses. A popular theory of the nineteenth century called 'biological utilization' held that since god made all things, even refuse was divine and it was made for a reason. The refuse of animals, it was argued, was the food of plants and vice versa, so that human refuse was 'eaten' by rivers. The 1882–3 Royal Commission on Metropolitan Sewage held, therefore, that sewage dumped in the Thames had no effect on the health of humans, since the river digested the refuse in a complementary relationship with the city.[53] If a monetary saving could be justified by a scientific principle, so much the better. In the colonies, the license to dump was used even more liberally, although some care was taken not to place the dumps too close to the residences of the colonials.

(Madison: University of Wisconsin PhD, 1982), p. 36; Benjamin Ward Richardson, *The Health of Nations* (London: Longmans, Green, 1887) and his *Hygeia: A City of Health* (London: MacMillan, 1876).

[50]*Settlement Report Delhi*, 1882, p. 43.

[51]J.D. Bernal, *Science in History* (Cambridge: MIT Press, 1971), vol. 2, p. 655.

[52]Reginald Reynolds, *Cleanliness and Godliness* (New York: Harvest, 1974), pp. 291–2 and Mary Douglas, *Purity and Danger* (London: Ark, 1985), p. 121.

[53]Hamlin, 'What Becomes of Pollution', pp. 540–2.

If there was a concern about the utilization of untreated sewage in farms within the boundaries of Europe (although not in watercourses), colonial officials attempted to show that this was not the case in India. For one, colonial officials argued that the diet in India made the sewage less toxic (vegetarian diets have low nitrogen and sulphur contents) and easier to break the compounds for disposal. This 'Indian sewage', it was held, did not need treatment (as suggested by the 1821 Royal Commission) and it could be directly run-off onto the soil to make 'considerable profits'.[54] By 1947, when Hallam Tennyson wrote his novel *The Dark Goddess*, a character offers us a picture of what ensued from this scientific judgement: 'Yes, Miss Joan, we turn India into a sewage farm. Not one nice hygienic English sewage farm where children can be sailing model yachts, but a stinking, crawling, gaping pit of horror'.[55] The farms in the outskirts of Delhi resemble Tennyson's farm, mainly due to the lack of sewage treatment.

The DMC started an experimental farm at Khandrat Kalan in 1894 that drew some of the refuse from the southern wards of the walled city with the refuse to be carried by carts and driven by sweepers. Since the region was rather dry, the DMC opened another 197 acre farm at Firozpur Khadar, closer to the city, but which was prone to become a 'filthy swamp'.[56] In 1926, the DMC constructed a sewage farm at Kilokri on a more firmly scientific basis, but this too was closed in the aftermath of a major enquiry in 1936. The following year, the Kilokri farm was converted into the Okhla bioaeration plant, where the sewage is agitated to assist and accelerate oxidation. The new process (activated sludge) halved the nitrogen content and the less offensive effluent was run-off into the Jamuna.[57] The sewage farms were a strain on the DMC, which learnt three lessons from this experience: first, that the farms ran for profit and not for the purpose of reuse of the nutrients in refuse; second, that the farms could not earn a profit because they

---

[54]Williams, *Sewage Disposal*, p. 101 and Clemsha, *Sewage Disposal*.

[55]Suhash Chakravarty, *The Raj Syndrome* (New Delhi: Penguin, 1991), p. 83.

[56]Parsons, *Delhi*, p. 173 and DMC Progs., 11 May 1896.

[57]NAI, Home (Public), 31/23/40, 1940. Delhi continues to rely upon similar plants and it is estimated that of the 2000 million litres that flow into the Jamuna each day, about 200 tonnes of BOD (biological oxygen demand—the measure of organic pollutants, such as faecal matter) and 160 tonnes of suspended solids flow out of the 11 *monitored* drains, *Sunday*, 27 June 1998.

remained strapped with start-up costs; and third, that the entire process was run on sub-standard technological devices.

On the first point, it was evident by the 1890s that manure was a thing of value and the hinterland farmers drew much satisfaction from their easy access to the city's manure. 'The villagers', one colonial official noted, 'know that the Committee have only a choice between letting the sullage run to waste, or delivering it to them at such rates as they (the villagers) may agree to'.[58] Given the poor municipal pipes, the peasants illegally dug holes into them and siphoned off manurial water for their farms. When the DMC fixed the pipes and drew extended lines closer to the farms, they raised the rates to cover the cost. At Khandrat Kalan, for instance, the DMC felt that the farmers 'would pay anything for the filth rather than go short of supply'. The DMC, to keep the farmers in 'proper check', hoarded the manure to prevent 'promiscuous sales' and enhanced the price of the manure.[59] The peasantry refused to pay those rates, preferring instead to find alternate fertilizers (such as cow-dung). The DMC recognized that the peasants remained 'masters of the situation', so they decided to 'utilize the sullage discharge at the drain end for a municipal purpose, which has yet to be determined'. One such purpose was a municipal sullage farm, owned and run by the DMC, that would compete with hinterland farmers in the Delhi market. The approach would give the DMC 'that whip-hand which they require'.[60] For its farm the DMC turned twice to the Bela, a depression beside the river south-east of the walled city in which some peasants grew melons and sugarcane. In 1892, the DMC declared it malarious (notably since the army had its barracks beside the Bela), but after a brief hiatus, the DMC renewed its use of the area as a sullage farm.[61] Most of the city's semi-processed sullage went to the Firozpur farm, but half a cusec was directly drained into the river. To save this amount, the DMC reopened the Bela farm in 1912 to absorb the almost raw sewage, a policy that was validated by the government, which felt that 'the treatment of sullage water is therefore a secondary considera- tion compared with the interests of the crops'.[62] When the profits from sullage water declined, the DMC tried to turn manure into Poudrette or

[58]Parsons, *Delhi*, p. 173.
[59]Ibid., p. 131.
[60]Ibid., p. 172.
[61]DMC Progs., 4 January 1892.
[62]*New Imperial Capital Delhi*, vol. 1, p. 38.

manure bricks, but this was not a success since most kilns refused to purchase them (perhaps part of the orthodox Hindu prejudice against refuse).[63]

If the entire scheme was driven by the desire for profits, the farms could not deliver this due to the burden of capital inputs. At Khandrat Kalan, for instance, the farm earned an income of Rs 6685 in 1906, but it paid out Rs 7685 due to its payments on the initial loan of Rs 10,600 (for an irrigation system). The running costs of the farm remained at Rs 4800, but the profit could not be counted because of the DMC's discriminatory accounting.[64] Due to this accounting scheme, one official reported in 1914, 'many original works had to remain unexecuted and many desirable improvements were starved or adandoned owing to lack of funds'.[65] The paucity of funds meant that when a project was begun it relied upon anachronistic technology, an impediment that became policy, for, as one official noted, 'in the land of the ox-cart one must not expect the pace of the motor car'.[66]

Of the Kilokri experiment, advertised as a technological wonder when it opened in 1926, an early report in 1933 declared that its equipment was 'no longer adequate'. The DMC's rules prevented the growth of foods with thin skin (such as melons), since these easily absorb parasites, as well as foods eaten uncooked. Therefore, the peasants grew cattle fodder, tobacco and wheat, all crops that could not absorb the vast flow of sullage water.[67] That surplus water was run-off into the Jamuna, a process that poisoned large numbers of fish.[68] Or else, the water was allowed to flood the fallow fields, a situation that led to concentrations of harmful metallic and organic substances in the soil and, from there, in the ground water. The polluted wells raised spleen rates and produced a cholera epidemic just two years after the sewage farm opened. Since the 1890s, techniques to clean sewage had been developed, such as the anaerobic reaction chambers to reduce suspended matter by Mancrieff in 1891; septic tanks to digest organic solid matter by Cameron in 1896; and tanks to force the physical or electro-chemical digestion of sludge (Hampton, Imhoff and Dortmund).

[63]DMC Progs., Sanitation Sub-Committee Meeting, 16 August 1929.
[64]Parsons, *Delhi*, pp. 179–80.
[65]*Annual Report DMC (1913–14)* (Delhi: DMC, 1914), p. 3.
[66]DSA, CC (Education), B Progs., 1914, no. 183.
[67]DSA, CC (Education), B Progs., 1926, no. 4 (28).
[68]DSA, CC (Rev. and Agri.), B Progs., 1931, no. 70.

In 1930, the DMC installed sedimentation tanks and they began to use chemical precipitants (such as milk of lime and aluminoferric) to remove solids in the sludge. The farm did not have a tank to remove colloidal matter nor did it try to oxidize nitrogeneous and carbonaceous residue into stable nitrates and carbonic acid gases. Only in 1931 did the DMC install filters for the irrigation channels, but they spent most of their funds on an elaborate network of trickling filters (originally constructed to supply water to condense engine exhaust systems) to prevent flooding of the fields.[69] An additional method to make the farm sanitary was only used idiosyncratically and that was to grow castor and other aromatic bushes on the fringe of the farm.

The PWD justified these costs 'for health and sanitary reasons for the New City', but the city did not bear these costs at all. In 1935–6, Kilokri earned Rs 29,000 compared to its running costs of Rs 140,500, a vast deficit. To be effective, a 1936 study argued, the farm needed an additional 15,000 acres (to absorb the sullage at a 2:1 dilution of the nitrogen content), an expense of Rs 25 lakhs. The farm would need an impossible additional 36 million gallons of water a day.[70] 'With the evidence of Kilokri before our eyes', wrote the DMC's committee to investigate the farm, 'the Committee have considered very carefully possible disposal by this method and have concluded that on public health as on general grounds of practicability, it is undesirable in the case of Delhi, whatever it may be for smaller areas'.[71] In passing, the Report did not forget the associated problem of finance, since it noted that 'any Government grant should be an out and out payment'.[72] Nevertheless, the Report was anxious to put on record its resolution that 'in a country where manure is deficient and where such as exists is too frequently used for fuel or other purposes it is essential to preserve all elements of manurial value and consequently so valuable a fertilizer as sewage should not be allowed to go to waste but should be fed to the land'.[73] By the late 1920s, the DMC was already of a mind to abandon the pursuit of nutrients and money from the manure and move towards

[69]DSA, CC (Rev. and Agri.), B Progs., 1932, no. 100.

[70]NAI, Education, Health and Lands (Health), 1936, 24-16/36-H and *Report on the Delhi Sewage Disposal Enquiry Committee* (New Delhi, 1936), p. 13.

[71]*Delhi Sewage Disposal*, p. 9.

[72]Ibid., p. 13.

[73]Ibid., p. 8.

incineration and landfills. In 1928, an officer of the Indian Medical Service wondered if it was 'sound economically to destroy this value by means of destructors', but by then there seemed to be few alternatives before a municipality wedded to profit before people.[74]

DESTROYING REFUSE

The DMC's first major project for the disposal of refuse was the dump at Malkagunj, a device that was known as a 'sanitary landfill', in the 1920s. The sweepers gathered the refuse in a pit, filled it with ashes and dry sweepings and packed it as tightly as possible. As in a compost heap, they lay leaves on the surface and waited for the refuse to molt. For the walled city, such dumps around it seemed a reasonable way to deal with refuse, but this was to change as the city expanded beyond its walls. The colonial presence in the city further circumscribed the use of landfills, since the DMC was clear that these must stay far from the Military and Civil Lines.[75] In 1893, therefore, the DMC found the Malkagunj site to be objectionable (it exuded a stench that made its way to the homes and clubs of the colonials), so it was removed south of the city, near Delhi Gate.[76] When the new city was built, the Delhi Gate Dump became the main problem, situated as it was in the buffer between the walled city and the new imperial capital. 'A menace to the health of the New City', the Dump was also the cause of small outbreaks of cholera in the Delhi jail (situated just beside it).[77] The DMC tried to ram more earth on the top of the dump and to use pesterine and zonde to kill the colonies of flies, but little mattered to the authorities of the new city.[78] They wanted to use the space of the Dump as a sanitary corridor, a green lung, to separate the walled city from the new city. The Dump, however, could not be moved, since the river to the east, the new city to the south and the Civil Lines to the north hemmed in Delhi's refuse. 'It is all very well for the New Capital authorities to say that dumping in that particular area should be stopped forthwith', wrote the Chief Engineer of the DMC, 'but the Delhi

[74]DSA, CC (Education), B Progs., 1928, no. 6 (18). An alternative approach was suggested by J. J. Mieldazis, 'Organic Manure from Street Refuse and Nightsoil at Mysore City', *Indian Medical Gazette* (February 1934).

[75]NAI, Rev. and Agri. (Land Rev.), B Progs., April 1904, no. 31.

[76]Parsons, *Delhi*, p. 130 and DMC Progs., 10 July 1894.

[77]DSA, DC File no. 58, 1929.

[78]DSA, CC (Education), B Progs., 1922, no. 6 (3).

Municipality and Deputy Commissioner have found it impossible to choose another site'.[79] In fact, the Jandewalan site had to be abandoned in the late 1930s because of the civil servants' homes nearby, for whose admittedly exaggerated fears the PWD engineer felt he had 'a certain amount of sympathy'.[80] There was even a suggestion to build a ropeway across the river, but this was considered financially impractical; some suggested using lorries to cart the refuse further away still, but the expense was again forbidding.[81] 'We must get our refuse and nightsoil further away', the Deputy Commissioner wrote in 1927, 'however much it may cost us'.[82] Unfortunately, the question of the cost was indeed at the centre of things.

'The health of the Jail, the residents of the neighbourhood, and the employees of the Power House, is constantly menaced', an official wrote of the Delhi Gate Dump, 'and every passerby is assailed by the horrible odours and flies from this area'.[83] The smells and the flies bothered the colonial administrators, many of whom held fast to the miasmatic theory of disease. For them, disease was spread by a miasma of foul odours from the earth that entered and polluted the body to block the essential life flows, thereby causing illness.[84] The dumps acted as the gateway to the poisonous organic smells that lay beneath the surface. Beside this notion, those who held to the germ theory of disease were also worried about the dumps, since the flies acted as vectors for germs. Fly epidemics, then, acted as an 'unmistakable index of insanitary conditions'. During any fly epidemic, an official noted, 'all eyes and thoughts are turned to the nightsoil and refuse disposal grounds at Delhi Gate and Motia Khan'.[85] The Delhi rais objected to the Dump as well, noting that anything was better than its place just outside their homes.[86] By 1935, the DMC noted that it strove hard 'to remove the most insanitary, unhygienic and objectionable practice of

[79]DSA, CC (Education), B Progs., 1928, no. 6 (18).

[80]DSA, CC (Education), B Progs., 1927, no. 28.

[81]DSA, CC (Education), B Progs., 1922, no. 6 (3).

[82]DSA, CC (Education), B Progs., 1927, no. 28.

[83]DSA, CC (Education), B Progs., 1928, no. 6 (18) and no. 6 (5).

[84]Carlo Cipolla, *Miasmas and Disease: Public Health and the Environment in the Pre-industrial Age* (New Haven: Yale University Press, 1992).

[85]DSA, CC (Education), B Progs., 1935, no. 4 (6), DMC Progs., 20 February 1935.

[86]*Hindustan Times*, 16 August 1929.

dumping nightsoil and refuse within our own grossly congested city area'. The 'admitted evil' of the dump, however, could not be closed 'on account of financial and other obstacles'.[87] The refuse train scheme allowed some of the garbage to be removed to the outskirts of the city, to be tended by the sweepers in those dumps. By 1939, then, the DMC closed the Delhi Gate and Motia Khan Dumps, but in the 1950s it took to this practice once again with terrific results for contemporary Delhi.[88]

In the 1880s, European engineers investigated the possibility of a technical solution to the sewage question and they opted for incineration of the waste at high temperatures (to reduce the volume of the waste and to reduce disease; they did not, at the time, recognize the respiratory cancers produced by incineration). Alfred Fryer's refuse destructor demonstrated its efficacy in 1874 and in the next decade, cities across Europe began to install such machines.[89] In 1913, New Delhi's authorities introduced incinerators to the city, but on a trial basis.[90] When some officials suggested that more of these 'garbage crematoria' be installed in the city, one official noted that the tale was 'as old as a dak bungalow chicken', since it was often served, but rarely eaten. He argued that 'refuse destructors had been tried and proved to be costly failures', a judgement accepted by the government which was chary of the capital costs in the first place.[91] Others continued to argue that pulverizers and incinerators reduced the volume of the refuse by ninety per cent and they produced, what was considered at the time, a harmless residue.[92] The high initial outlay forstalled a general mobilization of resources towards incinerators and, as early as 1927, the Delhi officials realized that 'no practicable scheme regarding

[87]NAI, Education, Lands and Health (Health), 1935, 24-19/35-H.

[88]H. U. Bijlani, *Solid Waste Management* (New Delhi: IIPA, 1987).

[89]W.H. Maxwell, *The Removal and Disposal of Town Refuse* (London: Sanitary Publishers., 1898).

[90]*New Imperial Capital*, vol. 3.

[91]DSA, CC (Education), B Progs., 1928, no. 6 (18).

[92]DSA, CC (Education), B Progs., 1926, no. 4 (48) and 1927, no. 4 (130); NAI, Education, Health and Lands (Health), 1936, 45-38/36-H. For some contemporary words on the issue, *Don't Burn It Here: Grassroots Challenges to Trash Incinerators*. Eds E. J. Walsh and D. C. Smith (University Park: Penn State Press, 1997).

incinerators seems likely to materialize'.[93] The mechanization introduced into the city was more sporadic than systematic.

For all this, the sweepers remained the mainstay of the refuse removal system in Delhi. Since the officials relied upon a haphazard technological plant, they banked upon the cheap procedures of the Jamadar and the sweeper. The sweepers removed the refuse in carts and some lorries and they buried it in landfills or dumped it in water courses. As money became available, the DMC created such devices as an activated sludge plant at Okhla, but this was erratic and uneven. The system, such as it was, was able to survive through a great intensification of labour and a creative use of the environment. The labour process, far from holding back the city's modernity, actually enabled it to exist. There was little question of emancipation for the sweepers, since their subjugation allowed the DMC to run the city on the cheap; there was also little question of regulation of the Jamadar by the DMC, since it relied fundamentally on that figure to manage the system. For the sweeper, the tyranny of the Jamadar was sanctioned by the DMC's inability to adequately address the sewage question. In 1872, John Law noted that 'caste is unpleasantly strong in Delhi' and for the sweepers this was a commonplace statement as they felt the burden of their caste in novel ways.[94] Caste in this case, far from being a feudal relic, was the backbone of an unequally structured municipal system.

---

[93]DSA, CC (Education), B Progs., 1930, no. 29.

[94]John Law, *Glimpses of Hidden India* (Calcutta: Thacker, 1872), p. 192.

4

Balmikis

Dalits, like other oppressed people, take refuge in the shadow of the divine in their quest for social justice. Dalit songs are full of references to a divinity who was to enter human history to liberate the dalits from their bondage. For instance, one Chuhra song trenchantly noted that 'the Hindus will not allow me near' and 'the Muslims will not read the burial service', so that there was little salvation from these agents. Therefore, the song pledged, 'at resurrection [*qayamat*], you will get bliss' and 'I wish to make a community of my own'.[1] Religion, to the oppressed, is a means to articulate their dreams for freedom. God is the congealed will of the people who cannot afford to exert their own sovereignty against those who monopolize the forces of repression. Most religious traditions emerged from the experience of the bedraggled people whose struggle for freedom kept alive some of the most powerful urges of the spirit. Whether in the slums of Jerusalem, the bazaars of Mecca or the countryside of Magadha, the main religious prophets spoke a language of ecumenical egalitarianism. All those who joined the society of the new faith would stand together without rank and without pride. Social protest was cloaked in the idiom of religion and the demand for change was legitimized by a claim to godliness. Even the most formally hierarchical religious communities harbour a contradictory urge to erase all differences in the service of a collective salvation. Impatient with the promizes of the guardians of religious orders, oppressed peoples forced salvation into the world in such forms as the Buddhist Sangha and the *Ummah*. These mundane forms of collective salvation collapsed either at the hands of military force or as a result of their own institutionalization or as a result of the gradual transformation of the critique of poverty into the ritual of charity. The

---

[1]Youngson, 'The Chuhras' (December 1906), pp. 350–1.

worldly effects of the ideas of salvation (*qayamat, nirvana*) and of the dissolution of .the human being into oneness (Brahman, Heaven, Paradise) risked the idea that the oppressive present need not retain its shape. Messianism provides us with one generic example of the struggles by the oppressed to transform their world with the assistance of an emblem of the divine.

Until the twentieth century, the dalits found their mundane salvation in the arms of various powerful religious traditions. The Chuhras organized their dreams of freedom around the figure of Bala Shah Nuri, who came from heaven for the sake of the Truth (*'Arshan thin latha Bala, Din de chah'*).[2] Bala was the prophet of the Chuhras who taught them to honour neither secular nor theological intermediaries. The songs to Bala insist that landlords, Brahmans, Mullahs, kings and other agents of repression should not be trusted since they are mortal and therefore cannot be equal to the omnipresent God. 'All the priests and prophets go', one song noted, 'none has escaped death. But one name of Allah is true. In your house there is no want'.[3] Bala came to remind the Chuhras of the omnipotence of God and of the ephemeral power of their social oppressors. Rejection of the comprador was cloaked in the theological idea that mortals can commune directly with the divine; this idea enjoined a maximalist notion of equality upon its adherents. Both Sufism (in the idea of *fana* or nothingness) and the Bhakti tradition (personal devotion) offer this powerful device which was well-developed in the collective lore of the dalits. This chapter will move us from the social history of the processes of sanitation and the role of the sweeper to the place of the Chuhras and Mehtars in the ambit of Hindu militancy during the vibrant explosion of nationalism in the subconti-nent. While the countryside and towns rocked with nationalist energy, Congress leaders vacated the bastis of the dalits in favour of the Hindu militants from 1917 to 1933.

The traditions of Bala Shah Nuri allowed the Chuhras to retain some dignity despite their hard lives and their immoral overlords. Cultural autonomy does not mean that the dalits' cultural universe was not made from the fabric of the ideas which surrounded them, but it drew from such traditions in creative ways. The autonomy of Bala lay in the realm of values and in the theory of emancipation which was embedded in these stories. The normative elements at the core of dalit ideology set

[2]Youngson, 'The Chuhras', p. 347.
[3]Ibid., p. 353.

them apart from the èlite (at least in the world of their hidden transcript), but it was this core that was destabilized during the 1920s and
1930s when the dalits had a confrontation with the Hindu militant. The
votaries of Hindutva mobilized the Chuhras and Mehtars into the
unformed Hindu community at the price of their own cultural traditions
which at least offered them the means to struggle against their material
exploitation. The mobilization of the Hindus drew the dalits into a
horizontal cultural community, but the mobilization left the dalits
without the means to combat the vertical socio-economic world in
which they continue to survive. The tales of Bala Shah offer a clear
vision of contemporary Punjabi reality as the social antagonisms
between the Chuhras and the èlites are represented in unmistakable
terms. The reconfiguration of these tales muted the antagonism at their
core and shifted the Chuhras' acute sense of power relations. This
chapter examines the disruption of the Chuhras' cultural traditions and
their complex incorporation into this amorphous Hindu community.

Bala Shah in the Colonial Imagination

Modern Indian historiography returns repeatedly to the colonial state
principally because the colonial project by its very presumption of
universality transformed the categories by which we can know Indian
society. Eager to know everything about those whom it governed, the
colonial state intervened in every aspect of its subjects' lives. This
knowledge was to enable the colonial régime to make the colonized
more productive and more pliable to the will of the state, for, as
Bernard Cohn argues, 'the conquest of India was a conquest of
knowledge'.[4] The decennial census was the nodal point of information
and it provided the basis for governance, for patronage, and for political
representation and legitimacy. In the census, such infrequently
documented folk as the Chuhras found themselves in the midst of a
crisis of categories. How to represent dalits? Were dalits Hindus?
Could dalits have their own religion? 'In the case of depressed classes,
such as Chuhras, Sansis, etc.', the census held, 'it was laid down that
they should be returned as Hindus if they did not profess to belong to
any recognized religion, and . . . the claims of Chuhras to be registered
as belonging to a separate religion were not allowed to override these

---

[4]Bernard Cohn, *Colonialism and Its Form of Knowledge* (Princeton:
Princeton University Press, 1996), p. 16.

instructions'.[5] In this remarkable injunction, colonial officials declared that Chuhras and other dalits had to be returned in the census as one of a set of stipulated religions (Hinduism, Islam, Sikhism, Zoroastrianism, Jainism, Buddhism, Christianity and Animism). In a frank explanation, a census official declared that 'the Census is not concerned with personal religion, but is an attempt to record religion in its communal aspect, merely distinguishing those who lay claim to one or other of the recognized sectional labels without looking too closely into the validity of their claims'. In this respect, he pointed out, there is 'no difference between the supereducated and westernized Bengali who may be a Hindu by courtesy only and a Chuhra of the Punjab who may be described as a Hindu by discourtesy'.[6] If the Chuhra in question professed faith in Islam (as Musallis), in Sikhism (as Mazhabis) or in Christianity (as Indian Christians), then that Chuhra was to be returned as such. If the Chuhra wished to be returned as professing faith in their 'tribal religion', as Bala Shahis or Lalbegis, that was not to be permitted. The reason, in administrative terms, is simple enough as such local religions did not count for much and they made the census tables unmanageable. Each district, each village would return such a vast number of religions that the entire project of simplification and classification would be squandered. The subtle distinctions in the dalits' practices of worship did not count for much in the colonial imagination. Colonial officials and ethnographers knew of the complexity of dalit religion, a faith based on worship of local deities, preceptors, goddess figures and animals. In Punjab, the landscape was dotted with shrines to blessed figures such as Dadu, Gorakh, Guga, Baba Farid, and Sakhi Sawar, all of whom provided succour to local residents and pilgrims. 'Whole villages of nominal Hindus or Musalmans are sometimes adherents of a sect which practically eclipses the parent religion', a colonial official noted. 'It will generally be found that the peasantry worship minor village deities and local saints far more than the recognized gods of the Hindu pantheon'.[7] Despite this knowledge, from the standpoint of the census the Chuhras remained the

---

[5]*Census of India*, 1921, vol. 15 part 1, Punjab and Delhi, Report, p. 171; NAI, Home (Census) Deposit, November 1910, no. 1.

[6]*Census of India*, 1921, vol. 1 part 1, India, Report, p. 108.

[7]DSA, DC Files, 1904, no. 3 and Lt. Gen. F. R. S. Briggs, 'Two Lectures on the Aboriginal Races of India, as distinguished from the Sanskritic or Hindu Race', *Journal of the Royal Asiatic Society*, vol. 13 (1854), p. 287.

'chief disturbing element in the return of religion'.[8]

In 1881, one official made a plea for more 'information regarding the religion and worship of the outcast and vagrant castes, such as sweepers and the various kinds of gypsies', a project already initiated by Richard Temple some decades prior.[9] In the first of three volumes published in 1884, Temple included a section, 'the Genealogies of Lal Beg' to introduce us to the religion of the Chuhras, 'a religion of their own, neither Hindu nor Musalman, but with a priesthood and a ritual peculiar to itself'.[10] Temple found that the faith was a jumble of notions inherited from 'the tenets of the Hindus, the Musalmans and the Sikhs . . . thrown together in the most hopeless confusion [with] the mono-theism taught by the medieval reformers [underlying] all their supersti-tions'.[11] In the Chuhras' songs, one can hear distinct echoes of the *Japji* (prayers) to Nanak, *suras* (verses) from the Quran and the Punjabi *kafis* (stanzas) of Baba Farid and Bulle Shah. '*Bi Khuda, bi Khuda, Khuda ki baari raza/ Ik Nam such paun dhani, Shah mahan Bala*' (O God, O God, God's grace will be done / There is one true name, the great Shah Bala), sings the Bala Shahi in one invocation to the divine.[12] Bala Shah Nuri is the one name, the only name which leads to resurrection, towards the paradise which rightfully awaits the Chuhras, much like the Japji—'*Ik omkar, sat Nam*'. The songs of the Balas include characters such as Baba Nanak, Dadu, Mardana, Kabir, Loi, Brahman, Ram, Allah, the Pandavas, Krishna, Pir Khwaja, Joseph, Moses, Ranjana, Majnun, Jastri and fragments from a variety of folk stories. We have an indication of the complex cultural resources of the Chuhras which interact with the dominant social forces in order to absorb uncritically some of the practices as well as to challenge those very practices. The Chuhras did not live outside the world of their Hindu and Muslim masters. 'In their songs and customs', a colonial ethnographer noted, 'the Chuhras are much governed by the cult of the people in the midst of whom they live. Among a Hindu population they burn, and among

---

[8]*Punjab Census*, 1901, vol. 1 part 1, Punjab, p. 113.

[9]Denzil Ibbetson, *Memorandum on Ethnological Inquiry in the Punjab* (Lahore: GOI, 1882), p. 5.

[10]Richard C. Temple, *The Legends of the Punjab* (Bombay: Education Society's Press, 1884), vol. 1, chapter 17.

[11]Ibid.

[12]Youngson, 'The Chuhras' (December 1906), p. 340.

Musalmans bury, their dead'.[13] They shared a world which they interpreted in various ways.

The heritage of the Balas is not a syncretic tradition, for syncretism already assumes the existence of discrete traditions which are blended in creative ways. Religion in Punjab was not syncretic, but diverse, popular and formed historically out of the inventory of traces which are found in the songs and stories which travelled the landscape in memory and by bards (*mirasis*). These elements are then merged to make a point about the superiority of the faith of the Balas. Syncretism assumes love for all, a legacy of our national movement's interpretation of Bhakti-kavya and Sufism as all loving rather than militant. One of Bala Shah's songs depicts the end of time when the followers of Ram and Rahim will hide themselves ('*Ram te Rahim kian chhap chhap jana*') in fear and when the sun dips down, Bala will send them to hell ('*sava neze te din avega, hade dosakh pana*'). Meanwhile, for the followers of Bala, paradise (*bihisht*) will be offered.[14] In the law of the Shahis the followers of Bala will not fast on Ashtami, nor will they go to Mecca ('*Shahi nun farmana, na mein vartan Ashtimi, na tur Makhe jana*'). All other traditions fall short of the perfect faith of Kalak Das, an exemplary Chuhra ('*Chuhre Kalak Das da mazhab hai tamam*').[15]

In gatherings at the shrines to Bala, the Chuhras sang these songs, but when colonial officials went amongst them to collect these ballads, the Chuhras refused to part with them. 'There is always some guru or spiritual guide, who lives at some town at a distance from the examinee, who has "the whole book" ', Temple wrote, 'but I have never been able yet to unearth any such person'.[16] Greeven begins his 1894 monograph on the religion of Lal Beg with his own admission at being 'nettled at the jealous mystery with which the scavengers have hitherto guarded their secrets, and we determined, as far as possible, to lift the veil of Isis, by taking the trouble of seeing the ceremonies for our-

---

[13] DSA, DC Files, 1904, no. 3.

[14] The parallels with Bulle Shah are remarkable. '*Musalman sarne to darde hindu darde gor/ dove ese vich mard eho duha di khor*', (the Muslims fear the flame and the Hindus the tomb, both die in this fright, such is their hatred). *Kulliyat-i-Bulle Shah*. Ed. Faqir Mohammed Faqir (Lahore: Panjabi Academy, 1963), Kafi 118.

[15] Youngson, 'The Chuhras' (December 1906), pp. 350–1 and (January 1907), p. 29.

[16] Temple, *Legends*, vol. 1, p. 530.

selves, and of having them explained by the sweeper-priests'. No doubt, Greeven succeeded, as he informs us that 'it is of no interest to others, by what means we overcame the scruples of the high-priest of the scavengers', who then sat and explained the texts to him for hours.[17] Why did the followers of Lal Beg want to protect their traditions from their new masters? The Chuhras may have feared that the officials would use the songs 'to their disadvantage', misconstrue the songs or, indeed, reveal the Chuhra belief in their superiority over the Hindus and Muslims, a certain way to invite retribution from their local èlites.[18] What the Chuhras had to hide was their notion of immanent freedom, a notion that was not permissible without drawing the penalty of death upon the community.

Colonial officials appreciated the differences in the faith, indeed in the very practices of the Hindus and the dalits. Yet, they laboured under a theory made popular by Alfred Lyall which remains popular to this day, the theory of gradual Brahmanization, which we know today as Sanskritization. Lyall wrote that on the 'ethical frontier . . . an ever-breaking shore of primitive beliefs . . . tumble constantly into the ocean of Brahmanism'. In time, a 'tribe or individual becomes Brahmanized by adapting what are held to be respectable, high-bred manners and prejudices of Brahmanism, and afterwards by desire to propitiate gods of a more refined and aristocratic stamp, as well as more powerful than their rough-hewn jungle deities'.[19] In this sort of moral evolution, dalits move towards Hinduism as a natural course, a theory that erases entire centuries of religious innovation. If the Chuhras are not Hindus now, they will be Hindus soon enough, a notion frequently played out in the notes which census officials sent to each other, as well as in the circulars they sent to the native enumerators. 'The practical difficulty is to say at what stage a man ceases to become an Animist and becomes a Hindu', the census reflected. 'The Hinduizing process, however, is a

[17]Richard Greeven, *The Knights of the Broom: An Attempt to Collect and Explain some of the Ceremonies of the Sweepers of the Benares Division* (Benares: Medical Hall Press, 1894), preface.

[18]*A Glossary of the Tribes and Castes of the Punjab and North-West Frontier Province, Based on the Census Report for the Punjab, 1883, by the late Sir Denzil Ibbetson, K.C.S.I, and the Census Report for the Punjab, 1892, by the Hon. Mr. E. D. MacLagan, C.S.I., and compiled by H. A. Rose* (Lahore: Civil and Military Gazette, 1911), vol. 2, p. 210.

[19]Alfred Lyall, *Asiatic Studies* (London: J. Murray, 1899), vol. 1, pp. 136–48.

very gradual one, and it is extremely difficult to say at what stage a man should be regarded as having become a Hindu'.[20]

In order to actualize this belief in the gradual Brahmanization of the dalits, colonial officials documented the traces of Hinduism in their cultural kit. In a number of the genealogies of Bala Shah, the colonial ethnographers marked out four of the ten incarnations to establish a link between the Chuhras and Hinduism. Bala Rikhi (4th), Bir Bamrik (5th), Ishwar Bala (6th) and Balmik (7th) were the four, although it must be noted that the genealogies do not simply point to the men as the incarnations. Sham Rup is equally the fourth incarnation, Rajwanti the fifth, Mansa the sixth, and Mahen the seventh; since they are the called the wives of the preceptors and not the preceptors themselves, they are discounted—this puts into question the easy assimilation of Chuhra tradition into Hinduism. The assumption which is made from taking the four men as representative of the dominant strand in the worship of Bala Shah is that the Chuhras have misdirected their worship, for their real deity, we are told, is none other than the Rishi Valmiki, the author of the *Ramayana*. Temple lists the various names of the incarnations which sound like Valmiki (including Bala Shah), and then points out that they are not incarnations but 'variations of the name of a sacred personage in the scavengers' hagiography'. That sacred personage is 'without difficulty and beyond all doubt to be identified with Valmiki, the low-caste author of the Sanskrit *Ramayana*'.[21] Once the determination was made that the Chuhras are actually worshipping Valmiki without their conscious knowledge, all the stories which relate to the Rishi are now made consonant with this assumption. The Chuhras do have stories of Balmiki, stories which claim him as one of their own and we will relate some of them to get a sense of the complexity of Chuhra traditions.[22]

Valmiki, in one story, is a servant in the court of Bhagwan, the supreme deity. Bhagwan gave Balmiki a coat, which the servant did not wear, but buried in a pit. When Bhagwan asked him about the coat, he went to fetch it and found a boy in it. '*Nikal auo, Lal, beg*', come out quickly, my love—and so, he was named Lal Beg (*lal* being loved one and *beg* being quickly). Another tale tells us that Valmiki was a Bhil (a tribal) and that he was a robber. In this story, he confronts seven *Rishis*

---

[20]*Census of India*, 1911, vol. 1 part 1, India, Report, pp. 129–30.

[21]Temple, *Legends*, vol. 1, p. 529.

[22]*A Glossary*, vol. 2, pp. 185–8 and vol. 3, pp. 20–2.

(holy men) who tell him that they have nothing to give him. They ask him if he has any friends, if his relatives will help him if captured. He asks his relatives, but they say that they will not help him. Distraught, Valmiki returns to the Rishis, who ask him to sit and meditate upon his evil ways. An ant-hill forms around him, and he recites 'mra, mra', which sounds like 'Ram, Ram'. When the ant-hill was broken, his bones were found in a serpents' hole, hence his name Balmiki (from *balni*, serpents' hole). A third tale takes us to the stories of the *Mahabharata*. Yudisthira attempted to perform the Ashwamedha Yagna, but after the ritual eating, the ritual bell did not ring on its own accord, thereby indicating that the rites had not been done to the divinities' satisfaction. It was found that Valmiki was not invited, so he was brought and served thirty-six dishes by Draupadi. He mixed all the food together, for which Draupadi momentarily marked him as dalit.

The stories summarized above are but a few from the collective folklore of the Chuhras. A notable fragment without a story points us in an informative direction. Lal Beg, born of a barren woman through the intercession of Valmiki, retired to Thaneshwar after a glorious military career in Kabul and Kashmir. At Thaneshwar, near Karnal, Valmiki died and his tomb was built there.[23] Manjula Sahdev, in an important study, points out that there are a number of different Valmikis in the folklore of the subcontinent, and one of these Valmikis was indeed at Thaneshwar. He is known as *shwapach* (perhaps, 'one who eats dogs') Valmiki, and he is linked to the dalits. Sahdev notes that he appears in Raidas' *Bani* and that in all likelihood he hailed from a dalit caste. Under pressure from Brahmanism, she suggests, dalits might have adopted him as the Maharishi, especially given Raidas' own conflation of this man with the author of the *Ramayana*. A tradition of revering Balmiki did exist among the Chuhras of the Punjab, but this worship did not include reading the *Ramayana*, nor did it assume an acceptance of the dominant Brahmanical codes inscribed in the epic. The name Valmiki, after all, need not be reserved for the Maharishi who is said to have composed the *Ramayana*. Others, such as the man at Thaneshwar who was clearly outside the Brahmanical tradition, might have borne that name.[24]

---

[23] *Punjab Notes and Queries*, vol. 1, 1883, p. 837.

[24] Manjula Sahdev, *Maharishi Valmiki: Ek Samikshatamak Adhyan* (Patiala: Punjabi University Press, 1980), p. 100, p. 112 and pp. 120–2.

The Chuhras did not consider themselves Hindus because of the labour of colonial ethnographers and the census. The Hinduization of the Chuhras was to take decades and much sweat on the part of Hindu militants and dalit activists. The significance of the colonial context is that its ethnographers and officials unearthed the hidden transcript of the Chuhras and elaborated their autonomous traditions in the vocabulary and cultural history of Brahmanism. The ethnographers did not accept the Chuhras' articulation of their dreams on their own terms; they constantly translated these desires into the traditions of the oppressors, who would shortly use them to their own ends. The autonomy of Bala Shah was shaken; in time, his memory would be virtually killed.

BLAME IT ON THE MUSLIMS

In 1934, Munshi Premchand chided his nationalist friends for merely shouting 'nation, nation [while] our hearts are still plunged in the dark shadow of caste distinctions'. 'Who does not know', he asked, 'that caste distinctions [*jati-bhed*] and nationhood [*rashtriyata*] are opposed to each other like nectar and poison?'[25] Premchand's equation of nationalism with equality draws hope that the nationalist movement would be a sufficient mechanism to eradicate the inequality of caste, a notion shared by many nationalists of the time. There was something fundamentally important about this imputation of equality within the movement, something that a young dalit indicated when he said it made him feel like a 'child of India. If I wore a Gandhi cap, no one would ask who I was'. Of course, the cap did not transmogrify the dalit into an abstract citizen, for the trials of being a dalit continued in his life, either as everyday prejudice or as structural disenfranchisement. Nevertheless, the normative horizon of Indian nationalism allowed the dalit to take some hope for the future. 'What I saw in the movement', he wrote, 'were the seeds of change that sooner or later had to germinate'.[26] Gandhi's 1930s tussles, for another dalit, tried to wake the country from its 'deep sleep' and redeem the dalits' freedom.[27] Nationalism, from this point of view, congealed the general hope and its language

[25]Premchand, *Vividh Prasang*. Ed. Amrit Rai (Allahabad: Hans Prakashan, 1962), vol. 2, p. 471.

[26]Hazari, *Untouchable*, p. 127.

[27]Vishnu Prabhakar, *Mein Achut Hun* (Delhi: Atmaram and Sons, 1968), p. 55.

spoke for the multitudes, who used its vocabulary to fashion their own political visions. The Congress' rentier leadership drew upon the political strength from the concentrated energy of the national movement, but upon it they cast their parochial agenda. The fear of the masses led to the movement's inability to allow the dalits, for instance, to participate in the leadership even if the leaders wanted the dalits to participate in its actions. There was more interest in being the representatives of the masses, than in allowing the masses to represent themselves. The problem of political representation produced a communalized polity in which the dalits became the preserve of the Hindus; militant Hindus, in turn, used the dalits in an ideological war against Muslims. 'Friends', Mohammed Ali honestly told the Congress in 1923, 'let us befriend the suppressed classes for their own injured selves and not for the sake of injuring others or even avenging our own injuries'. In a jaundiced vein, Ali noted that the leadership of the Hindu Mahasabha and the Congress worked among the dalits 'with an eye much more on the next decennial census than on heaven itself, and I frankly confess that it is on such occasions that I sigh for the days when our forefathers settled things by cutting heads rather than counting them'.[28] After the Indian Councils Act (1909), numbers did become the medium of political struggle and in particular the form of the communal electorate turned enumeration into an anti-Muslim project.

The Indian Councils Act opened the question of the franchise which, in terms of representational democracy, proved to be an anxiety over numbers. Colonial officials produced a franchise designed to segment the people along communal lines, to divert the popular energy for freedom, and to produce a 'stable' leadership that accepted the communal framework. These Morley–Minto reforms allowed the British to claim a heritage of liberalism as they consolidated with what John Morley called 'constitutional autocracy'. With the British in complete power of the electoral process, they chose not to allow the nationalist leaders the right to prove their representability in solely territorial constituencies, for, as Sir William Lee-Warner put it, 'national division of India is not territorial, but sectional [communal]'.[29] The nationalist parties, then, perforce planned for the elections

[28] *Selected Writings and Speeches of Maulana Mohammed Ali.* Ed. Afzal Iqbal (Lahore: Sh. Mohammed Ashraf, 1969), vol. 2, pp. 176–81.

[29] Stanley Wolpert, *Morley and Minto, 1906–1910* (Berkeley: University of California Press, 1967), p. 191.

on the basis of sectional or communal ties. Given the colonial representation of the social as political constituencies, the Congress was
enjoined to take these communal divisions as political divisions, a
theory that meshed with that of the militant Hindus.

Just after the publication of the 1909 Act, Lieutenant-Colonel U.N.
Mukerji of the Indian Medical Service published a series of idiosyncratic articles in *Bengalee* under the umbrella title 'A Dying Race'.
Mukerji used census reports (1872–1901) to show that in Bengal the
Muslim population increased by a third, while the Hindu population
increased by less than a fifth, a series of faulty calculations that did not
take into consideration such things as migration, the reassessment of
the region, or of survey methods. His articles fuelled the paranoia of
militant Hindus who sought to undermine what they saw as the
dominance of the Muslims in society.[30] The militant Hindu apprehen-
sion was compounded when E.A. Gait of the census department wrote
that the 'Census returns of Hindus are misleading as they include
millions of people who are not really Hindus at all, who are denied the
ministrations of Brahmans and are forbidden to enter Hindu temples,
and who, in many cases, are regarded as so unclean that their touch, or
even their proximity, causes pollution'.[31] Gait's point was that dalits
are not Hindus, therefore they must not be added to the category
'Hindu' in the census and thereby afford the latter additional political
strength. He suggested that the dalits be counted independently. The
shuddi (purification-conversion) and *sangathan* (consolidation) movement of the militant Hindus and the *tabligh* (conversion) and *tanzim*
(consolidation) of the reactive Muslim orthodoxy emerge partly as a
means to draw more numbers into each 'camp' and to denude the
notion of dalit independence. Srinivas Ayengar, the head of the Bharat
Shuddhi Sabha, told listeners in Delhi's Chawri Bazaar on 29 January
1920 that both Hindus and Muslims must do their own consolidation so
that the political questions can be solved with factual accuracy. Those
who did not wish to line up in either camp found no place else to go.[32]
That shuddhi, etc. are theological and not political weapons was

[30]Gyanendra Pandey, 'Hindus and Others: The Militant Hindu Construction', *Economic and Political Weekly*, vol. 26, no. 52, 2 December 1991, p.
3008.

[31]NAI, Home (Census), Deposit, November 1910, no. 10.

[32]Kantimohan, *Premchand aur Achut Samasyain* (Delhi: Jansulabh Sahitya
Prakashan, 1982), p. 96.

recognized, such as by an editor who wrote that 'it is true that Shuddhi should be for religious purposes alone, but the Hindus have been obliged by other considerations as well as to embrace their other brothers. If the Hindus do not wake up now, they will be finished'.[33] Hindu militancy's drive to incorporate the 'other brothers' included the dalits, who became the object of their politics in the 1920s. The incorporation, however, simply meant that the dalits would be counted as Hindus in the census to bolster the Hindu majoritarian claims made by the militants on the emergent nation and on the colonial state. Of dalit interests, we hear little.

The leadership was clear that the dalits did not have the capacity to articulate their rights with decorum and with clarity. Gandhi, for instance, urged dalits to secure their rights by 'sweet persuasion and not by Satyagraha which becomes Duragraha when it is intended to give rude shock to the deep-rooted prejudices of the people'.[34] If dalits make an appeal on what they consider to be the basis of truth (*satyagraha*), why should it of necessity be an appeal on the basis of falsehood (*duragraha*)? Gandhi was loath to let dalits be represented by one of their own, Ambedkar, at the Round Table Conference and his obstinacy prior to the Poona Pact of 1932 also illustrates the leadership's insistence upon seeing the dalits as pre-political and unable to articulate their rights. During the 1932 deliberations, Gandhi wrote a confidential note to his associates with the worry that if dalits did not fall into the camp of the Hindu, it will 'lead to bloodshed. Untouchable hooligans will make common cause with Muslim hooligans and kill caste Hindus'.[35] With great confidence, the national leadership refused to acknowledge the will of the dalits. The leaders, then, occluded political representation in favour of a representation of dalits as socially inferior and in need of social change from above.

To include the dalits into the community of Hindus, militant Hindus invoked a reading of history as it produced a narrative of the origins of untouchability that charged Muslims with its parentage while it simultaneously exculpated both the colonial state and Hindus. Swami Shraddhananda, pontiff of the Arya Samaj, blamed the 'cruel bigotry of

[33]*Pratap*, 10 January 1921.

[34]*Punjab Achut Udhar Mandal Report, 1926–31* (Lahore: Lajpat Rai Bhawan, 1931), p. 18.

[35]Note of 21 August 1932, *Collected Works of Mahatma Gandhi* (New Delhi: GOI, 1958 onwards), vol. 50, p. 469.

Muslim Emperors' for the creation of the dalits.[36] The militant Hindus drew upon a long-standing narrative of a pristine Vedic Golden Age disrupted by the entry of what they considered 'foreign' Muslims who established a period of 'Muslim Tyranny' (a narrative available in both Tod's 1829 *Annals and Antiquities of Rajasthan* and Bankim's 1882 *Anandamath*). Unwilling to engage in a fundamental and radical critique of the premises of colonialism, the sluggishness of Hindu militancy accepted the Muslim as the Other of the subcontinent's history at the same time as it accepted the British as either benign or cruel redeemers of the golden past.[37] In 1924 a militant Hindu preacher told Delhi dalits that they must turn their ire against Muslims and they must adopt Hindus as their leaders and friends:

There were no sweepers before. They came into existence when the Muslims entered this land. As Muslim women observed seclusion, the Muslims needed sweepers. Therefore, they made others into sweepers. Many of them were Brahmins originally. Some were Rajputs and there were men of other castes. It is obvious that the Muslims forced them to become sweepers and to do such menial work. Now it is the duty of the Hindus to uplift them and to include them in other castes.[38]

Why did the dalits not disregard the militant Hindus who came into their mohallas to disturb their fraternal relations with *razil* Muslims who lived alongside them? The most insidious aspect of the history narrated to the dalits was that it resembled efforts of Kshatriyaization amongst north Indian dalits from the 1880s (the dalits elevated themselves by adopting forbidden customs, such as, for men, the sacred thread and, for women, certain kinds of jewellery). This 'manufacturing of Chattris' took the form of meetings at which, for example, the dissenters declared that the 'practice of poisoning cattle was sinful and must be abandoned'.[39] In the fabricated stories, the dalits recounted acts

[36]Swami Shraddhananda, *Hindu Sangathan: Saviour of the Dying Race* (Delhi, 1927), p. 4.

[37]Sumit Sarkar, 'The Complexities of Young India', *A Critique of Colonial India* (Calcutta: Papyrus, 1985).

[38]*Tej*, 5 May 1924 and Vijay Prashad, 'The Untouchable Question', *Economic and Political Weekly*, vol. 31, no. 9, 2 March 1996, pp. 555–6.

[39]J. C. Nesfield, *Brief View of the Caste System of North-West Provinces and Oudh* (Allahabad: GOI, 1885), p. 71; NAI, Home (Census) A Progs., August 1900, nos. 6–8. The broad context is provided in Gyanendra Pandey, 'Rallying Around the Cow: Sectarian Strife in the Bhojpuri Region, c. 1888–1917', *Subaltern Studies II*. Ed. R. Guha (Delhi: Oxford University Press, 1983), pp. 73–8 and Saurabh Dube, 'Myths, Symbols and Community:

of betrayal or of misfortune that turned bonafide Rajputs and Kshatri-yas into oppressed castes. In the new age, they suggested, the dalits must claim their exaulted status. The militant Hindu narratives simply inserted Muslims into the tale, so that the act of misfortune is the war with Muslims after which, one Gandhian wrote, 'defeated persons were forced into this work [sweeping] and their respect was taken from them'.[40] Another Gandhian and militant Hindu noted that 'no definite conclusions have been drawn by research scholars, but it is likely that the Balmikis [Chuhras/Mehtars] were Rajputs in those days who fought against the Mohammedan invaders and fell captive'.[41]

Although these texts by militant Hindus and some Gandhians make all sorts of gestures towards a historical record of some sort ('research scholars' and 'evidence hitherto collected'), there is not one shred of verifiable historical evidence offered. Instead, we have a discourse imbued with stereotypes, a mythical resolution to historical inquiry. Myth 'does not deny things, on the contrary, its function is to talk about them; simply, it purifies them, it makes them innocent, it gives them a natural and eternal justification, it gives them a clarity which is not that of an explanation, but that of a statement of fact'.[42] A story is being told, one that portrays the Muslim as the villain, the Hindu as the saviour and the dalit as the character who waits off the stage of history, caught between good and evil, waiting for a judgment that is beyond the dalit's control. In such tales, the notion of time which is employed ignores the secular and linear time that enables the creation of a disjuncture between the present and the past. This form of narrative, as Dilip Simeon notes, is 'neither wholly modern nor simply archaic—it represents a schizophrenic experience of historical time by people living in the present'. Hindu militancy opposes the linear notion of time with 'its own ideal time which is an amalgam of the past and the future'.[43] Hindu militants offer a fantasy time in which the chosen

---

Satnampanth of Chhattisgarh', *Subaltern Studies VII*. Eds P. Chatterjee and G. Pandey (Delhi: Oxford University Press, 1992), pp. 151–4.

[40]Vallabswami, *Safai*, p. 33, a position available in Bindeshwar Pathak's *Road to Freedom* (Delhi: Motilal Banarsidas, 1991), p. 39.

[41]Jiwanlal Jairamdas, *Bhangi ksht Mukti aur Bhangi Mukti* (Delhi: Gandhi Smarak Nidhi, 1969), p. 4 and D. S. Chaturvedi, *Patit Prabhakar: Mehtar Jati ka Itihasa* (Ghazipur, 1925) quoted in Amritlal Nagar, *Nachyo Bahut Gopal* (Delhi: Rajpal, 1980), p. 9.

[42]Roland Barthes, *Mythologies* (New York: Noonday, 1972), p. 143.

[43]Dilip Simeon, 'Communalism in Modern India: A Theoretical Examina-

(Hindus) will move into a beloved kingdom (*Ram Rajya*) in which an ancient Hindu sociology will be allowed to come into its own. The reappearance of this sociology is seen to have nothing to do with the extant systems of social production and there is no suggestion how the social order will be fundamentally reconceptualized given the techno-logical leap from Vedic times to the present (but more on this in the following chapter).

Until early in the twentieth century, Hindus did not betray an inter-est in their fraternal ties with dalits. From the 1870s, Hindu èlites in Punjab turned their eyes towards what they saw as an unnecessary fragmentation among their own. Disunity amongst subcastes led to animosity towards each other. Further, Hindu intellectuals looked back at the long span of the subcontinent's history and counted the many people who had left the Hindu pantheon for Islam and Christianity. Eager to claim these people to their flock, Hindu organizations attempted to garner some individual rais Muslims and Christians into the newly-organized Hindu community. The Arya Samaj was at the forefront of the Shuddhi movement and its various periodicals (*Arya Patrika* and *Arya Magazine*) recorded the cases with muted enthusi-asm.[44] In 1893, members of the Samaj joined with the Singh Sabha to form the Shuddhi Sabha at Lahore. Three years later, the Arya Samaj and its confrères conducted a mass reconversion to Hinduism. By 1896, the Samaj was fully equipped with an ensemble for conversion, such as missionaries (*updeshaks* and *pracharaks*) and institutions (orphanages, clinics, and community centres). The Samaj directed all its energy to the consolidation of the èlite; even at this late date, it was not enthusi-astic about the conversion of dalits.

In 1899, the Arya Samaj orphanages made it very clear that they would accept any 'destitute minor ... of castes other than sweeper'.[45] The Arya Samaj schools taught Hindu boys because of the assumption that 'Bhangi and Chamar boys could not possibly attend the same schools in which caste Hindu boys were reading'.[46] From 1886, one faction of the Arya Samaj conducted shuddhi amongst dalits such as the Ods, Meghs, Rahityas, Kabirpanthis and Dumnas, but their activities

---

tion', *Mainstream*, 13 December 1986, p. 10.

[44]R.K. Ghai, *Shuddhi Movement in India* (New Delhi: Commonwealth, 1990), pp. 45–6.

[45]DMC Progs., 28 November 1899.

[46]Jugal Kishore Khanna, Oral History Transcripts no. 177, NMML.

did not please the Arya Samaj hierarchy.[47] In 1895, the Shuddhi Sabha declared that 'the time has not yet come for admitting *Mazhabi, Chamars* and Muhammadans' into the Hindu community.[48] Even these custodians of the Hindu order worried that without the shuddhi of dalits their 'Vedic cosmopolitianism' would be meaningless. In 1907, the admirable militancy of the Hindu Sudhar Sabha drove them to promote the wearing of the *janeau*, the sacred thread, by dalit-Bahujans. They argued that Brahmanhood is earned by good works and these dalit-Bahujans earned their slender threads with their hard work.[49] The Arya hierarchy was furious. Èlite Hindus, Muslims and Sikhs found that their ideals of the *biradari* (brotherhood), *qaum* (community) and *khalsa* (order of Sikhs) could not be realized without great cost. Contradictions within the major religious groups prevented them from smoothly creating social and political communities.

The first attempt among those who tried to construct a Hindu community was to invite the dalit-Bahujans to join their èlite brothers and sisters in well-funded organizations such as the Lok Sevak Mandal and the All-India Achutuddhar Committee which were run by prominent reformers such as Lajpat Rai and Swami Shraddhananda. Preachers from these groups travelled the countryside and offered many incentives to dalit-Bahujans entrants, such as subsidized education, if they joined the Hindus and transformed their social customs. What was it about the way dalits lived that worried the Hindus? The Shraddhananda Dalitudhar Sabha (SDS) founded in 1921 claimed to work 'for the spiritual well-being, religious protection, social and economic uplift and educational betterment of the so-called depressed classes'.[50] This very general charter tells us that the Hindus found that the dalits needed to be lifted from their bedraggled state, which was not just material, but deeply spiritual and religious. The nature of this uplift needs to be explored more closely in order to clarify the limitations of the organs of Hindu reformation.

---

[47]Bhimsena Vidyalankar, *Arya Pratinidhi Sabha Punjab ka Sachitar Itihas* (Lahore: Arya Pratinidhi Sabha, 1935), p. 210; Ramchandra Javed, *Punjab Ka Arya Samaj* (Jalandhar: Arya Pratinidhi Sabha, 1964), pp. 35–6; Indra Vidyawachaspati, *Arya Samaj ka Itihas* (Delhi: Arya Pratinidhi Sabha, 1957), vol. 2, pp. 117–25 and pp. 259–64; Khushal Chand, *Jati Rakhak* (Lahore).

[48]Ghai, *Shuddhi*, p. 68.

[49]NAI, Home (Political), B Progs., October 1907, nos. 80–7.

[50]NAI, Home (Public), 585/1927-Public; *Vir Arjun*, 17 February 1963.

B.S. Moonje of the Hindu Mahasabha, in a speech to the Provincial Balmiki Conference in Amritsar in 1927, declared that the dalits must abandon 'evil habits and customs in the interest of their self-purification and ultimate fusion on terms of equality with the so-called touchable classes'.[51] Liberation would come only if the dalits abandoned a set of 'evil habits'. First, 'uncleanliness because it breeds disease and is against religion and the laws of hygiene'. The laws of hygiene (modernity) and religion (tradition) came together to enjoin cleanliness as they do in much of the reformation's ideology. Second, the 'use of leavings of food' should be avoided 'because it indicates loss of self-respect and carries several diseases to the persons eating them'. Third, eating of carrion should be stopped 'because they are a veritable cause of perpetuating untouchability and forbidden from medical standpoint as well'. Fourth, the dalits were urged to 'practise the rigidest economy in the performance of marriage, death and other ceremonies'. Fifth, the Chuhras were enjoined to give up their 'drink habits because they make a person a physical wreck as misery and destruction comes along with it'.

Many of the issues adopted by Hindus first emerged in dalit neighbourhoods as local concerns. For example, the anti-liquor campaign began in dalit neighbourhoods by residents fed up with the consumption of wine among their brethren and by the self-destruction which ate into the very fibre of the young. The dalits' notion of reform was centreed around their campaign to build power. Nanak Chand's motto, '*sachaie, safai*' (truth and cleanliness), was introduced to produce dalits who would be effective in the struggle for freedom. A number of the issues taken up by the Hindu reformers were already in popular consciousness, and so the èlite reformers simply gave them coherent expression as they deployed simple concepts in simple language. The Chuhras absorbed, accepted, and reconstructed these concepts and this language into their own political and everyday lives. Hindu organizations, therefore, gave their ideological discourse coherence by presenting their 'class objectives as the consummation of popular objectives'.[52] Hindu reformers understood the 'truth and cleanliness' slogan from the standpoint of the production of more effective workers as well as more acceptable and pliable citizens. Talk of cleanliness

---

[51]*Panjab Achut Udhar Mandal Report, 1926–31*, pp. 16–17.

[52]Ernesto Laclau, *Politics and Ideology in Marxist Theory: Capitalism, Fascism, Populism* (London: Verso, 1977), p. 107.

encompassed the dalits' earlier criticism of the municipality's aban-
donment of dalit neighbourhoods and talk of diets encompassed the
dalits' earlier critique of the wage structure that made them scavengers
for their sustenance. The Left (socialists, communists and Ad-Dharmis)
simultaneously attempted to elaborate the structural components of
Chuhra thought, but these formations were not strong enough to
overcome the tidal pressure of the Hinduization movement of the 1920s
and the 1930s.

The domain of the people and of democratic and popular struggle
was colonized at this crucial moment by bourgeois Hindu ideologies.
Hindu organizations during the 1920s inserted themselves into the
domain of the social as the very voice of the Hindu, the consummation
of the popular objectives of the Hindu masses. When dalit organizations joined the struggle a decade later, they confronted the Hindu
reformers on this terrain. A disturbing element in the character of the
initiatives from above was the paternalism of Hindus as well as their
inability to analyse the causes of untouchability beyond an inversion of
culpability (by attributing to dalit habits and customs the cause of their
oppression). At the core of the Hindu reformers' reconfiguration of
dalit notions lay a markedly anti-Muslim argument.

AD-DHARM VISIONS AND DALIT DIVISIONS

In the mid-1920s, radical dalits sensed the inadequacy of the programme offered by the Hindu reformers and they responded by starting
their own political movements. Across the subcontinent, movements
emerged which represented people who claimed to be the aboriginal
inhabitants of the land with links beyond antiquity, the Adi-Dravidas,
the Adi-Andhras, the Adi-Karnatakas, the Adi-Hindus and the Ad-
Dharmis. Trilok Nath argues that 'the whole "Adi" myth was inspired
by the scholarly theories about the Harappan civilization based on the
excavation discovery of Harappa by Sir John Marshall, Director of
Archeology in India in 1921'.[53] Marshall's discoveries provided
sustenance for the Adi-Hindus' histories which argued that the dalits
were the original inhabitants who were disenfranchised by the invading
Aryans; the dalits, therefore, were the inhabitants of Harappa and the
other recently excavated cities. The All India Jati Sudhar Mahasabha,

---

[53]Trilok Nath, *Politics of the Depressed Classes* (Delhi: Deputy Publica-
tions, 1987), p. 6.

founded in March 1922 in a dalit neighborhood in Delhi, declared that 'before the advent of the Aryans, we were a flourishing nation. But when the foreign Aryans conquered us they wanted to reduce us to slavery and so they branded us as "untouchables" so much so that it received sanction in their religious books, e.g. the Rigveda'.[54] The myths of the dalits began to be revised in line with this new historiography. Older Chuhra stories told of a time when there was only one caste, when Brahman brothers roamed the land. A betrayal brought forth a fall and other castes were born. In the new myths, the Chuhras claimed a golden age, the age when they ruled the land before the Aryan invasion. The Brahmans or Aryans were not of the land, but conquerors. The consequences of this new myth of origin was that the dalits were encouraged not to trust their *suvarna* (of non-dalit status) benefactors, not to assume any primordial racial bonds and therefore, not to work with them. The feeling of being aboriginal began to hold sway, to be the dominant norm in the political lives of the dalits.

Hindu reformers in the 1920s simply posited a community of Hindus without much interrogation of the material reasons for the antagonism between Hindus and dalits. The Adi movements, on the contrary, emphasized the differences to do three things: (1) to highlight and transform the miserable conditions in which the dalits lived and worked; (2) to elaborate their own institutions and ideologies, and (3) to ensure that the dalits do not get absorbed into the Hindu movement in a subordinate position. The Jati Sudhar Mahasabha declared in 1931 that it had 'no confidence' in such Hindu groups as the SDS, the Achutudhar Committee (Allahabad) and the Dayananda Dalitudhar Mandal (Hoshiarpur). These organizations, the Mahasabha declared, 'are run by high caste Hindus for their own benefit; their efforts are directed to retard any improvement or progress that the depressed classes may try to achieve'.[55] The past without Aryans allowed the dalits to argue for the possibility of forming independent dalit organizations. The Adi movements, based on antipathy to Brahmans and to the common assertion of a glorious aboriginal past, provided the political ground for a *national* dalit community. Jurgensmeyer, in this regard, argues that Ad-Dharm was not 'the religion of a caste group, it was the religion of a people'.[56] The ground for the claim to nationhood

---

[54]NAI, Home (Public), File no. 490/31-Public.

[55]Ibid.

[56]Mark Jurgensmeyer, *Religious Rebels in the Punjab: The Social Vision of*

was made through history, and here a history of independent creation provided the elements for a *dalit nationalism.*

The Adi groups decided to take their claim of racial and religious difference to the 1931 census in order to thwart the Hindu militants' attempt to claim them for political reasons and to prove their numerical strength as a viable political force.[57] At the first Ad-Dharm conference, the dalits requested the government not to list them as Hindus in the census since their faith was Ad-Dharm. 'We are not a part of Hinduism', they argued, 'and Hindus are not a part of us'.[58] The Ad-Dharmis began to travel the countryside distributing posters and tracts as well as telling dalits to return themselves as Ad-Dharmis. One government report tells us that Mangoo Ram claimed that the 'Sirkar will *grant land, give jobs and grant equality of status* if they show themselves as "Ad-Dharmis". This has had a magic effect on those classes'. In the tracts, the Ad-Dharmis used the Sarkar 'in a very mischievous manner'. They encouraged the dalits and other members of the working-class 'to stand on their hind legs, and defy the threats of the zamindars', since the Sarkar was on the side of Ad-Dharm. This 'frightened the ignorant zamindars that they should not go against the Sirkar'.[59] In the initial days of the campaign, the diverse tactics of the Ad-Dharmis seemed to help them spread their message. The feeling of independence produced a feeling of solidarity amongst the dalits which allowed the Ad-Dharm groups to actively combat the Aryas. Prodigal dalits were welcomed back to the fold after being chastized for their relations with the Hindus. When the Chuhra leader Chunni Lal Thapar attended a rally in Ali Mohalla in Jalandhar, Dogarmal Pradhan, an Ad-Dharm activist, asked him to apologize for his extended relationship with the Arya Samaj. From the podium, Thapar asked for forgiveness. 'The rights of the untouchables have been robbed by the Hindu, and you sit there looking very sad', he said. 'Chunni Lal is also an untouchable (*'Chunni lal bhi hai achut'*), he has committed a mistake, yet he returns in penance and supplication (*'voh bhi minnata kar kar'*).[60] Bansi Lal, a

---

Untouchables (Delhi: Ajanta, 1988), p. 50.

[57]*Times of India*, 14 October 1928; J. E. Sanjana, *Caste and Outcaste* (Bombay: Thacker and Co., 1946), pp. 234–5.

[58]Jurgensmeyer, *Religious Rebels*, p. 74.

[59]NAI, Home (Political), File no. 222/1932-Poll.

[60]Rolu Ram, Jalandhar, 3 April 1993; Bakshi Ram, *Balmiki Sabha da Itihas, 1901 to 1991 tak* (Ludhiana: Panjab Pradesh Balmik Sabha, 1991); 'Baba

Chuhra who was a representative in the Legislature, told a meeting of dalits at Lahore in 1931 that he called himself a Hindu to get the active support of the Congress. The dalits enjoyed his renunciation of the Hindu movement; Hindus, on the other hand, began to bitterly refer to Lal as 'Bhangi of Lahore'.[61] Unity was in the air for the dalits.

British officials deliberated for as long as they could before pronouncing judgment on the delicate matter of allowing the dalits to be returned in the census as Ad-Dharmis. At first, they decided that it would not matter if the Ad-Dharmis were allowed to return as such for they estimated that those numbers would not be much. With the Chuhras, however, they came upon a familiar problem, whether to return them as Lalbegis, Bala Shahis or as Hindus. 'The question in my opinion', wrote the Census Commissioner J. H. Hutton, 'turns on whether or not the Chuhras are a definite tribe with a tribal religion distinct from Hinduism. Knowing little or nothing of the Punjab, that is a point on which I am not prepared to offer an opinion, but my own impression was that the term included almost everyone of the scavenging class and had no reference to any specific tribe with uniform customs'. Chuhras are not a tribe or a community, he argued, but an occupational group, scavengers. In this case, and in the 'absence of general proof', Hutton concluded, 'Lalbegis cannot be considered as having a tribal religion', or be part of the Ad-Dharmis. ' "Balmiki" was I think the name of a Hindu Bhil ascetic and a return of Balmiki unqualified would probably be taken as Hindu, failing some indication to the contrary', he argued. 'Chuhras who fail to return any religion are to be classified as "Hindu" unless they state explicitly that they are not'.[62] In the case of the Chuhras, the Census Commissioner decided in favour of the Hindus. Even though the issue was left to the enumerators, evidence suggests that they counted most Chuhras as Hindus without much ado.

The Hindu organizations protested the vague decision of the Census Commissioner, which they argued was a 'result of a deep laid conspiracy to divide and weaken the Hindus of the [Punjab]'.[63] In response,

---

Chunni Lal Thapar ke Ludhiana mein Shraddhanjali', *Jago, Jagte Raho*, April 1978.

[61] *Times of India*, 25 February 1931; Sanjana, *Caste and Outcaste*, pp. 235–6.

[62] NAI, Home (Public), File no. 45/56/30-Public.

[63] NAI, Home (Public), File no. 444/31-Public; NAI, Home (Public), File no. 45/67/31-Public.

the Hindu and Sikh èlite began their own campaign to malign the Ad-Dharmis and to put pressure on their tenants and their field labour to return themselves as Hindus and Sikhs.[64] The protests of the Hindu organizations demonstrated their distaste for autonomous mobilization among the dalits, something which the Chuhras took to heart. The motives of the èlites became clear, and it allowed for a moment of solidarity among dalits just as it revealed a deep-seated fear among the Hindus. This momentary solidarity provided the dalits with the grounds for asking for separate electorates.

Independence was central to dalit nationalism and its embodiment was B. R. Ambedkar. His fight against Gandhi and the Congress for separate elections was a rallying cry for radical dalits and his own dalit heritage allowed for a sense of pride (that Ambedkar was a Mahar from Bombay Presidency shows how widely the community was defined). From Jalandhar, thousands of Chuhras sent their signatures in blood to London in support of Ambedkar. The Ad-Dharm Mandal and Balmiki Sabha of Jalandhar wanted to send firm proof that Ambedkar spoke the truth when he declared that dalits had been cast out by Hindu society. In order to test the will of the local Hindus, some dalits took a bucket and a rope and went to the Laal Bazar well. They tried to fill water, but were stopped by orthodox Hindus. The Hindus offered to give the dalits water, but the dalits wanted to take it themselves. A fight broke out and the bucket fell into the well. The incident was reported in local newspapers, cuttings of which were sent to Ambedkar as proof of the recalcitrance of Hindus to allow dalits dignity.[65]

On 20 September 1932, six days before the Poona Pact which resolved the issue to the satisfaction of Gandhi, the Balmiki Ad-Dharm Mandal met at Shimla to discuss its fate.[66] The major dalit leaders of the Punjab attended, as well as some prominent Arya Samajis. Mangoo Ram presided, while Chunni Lal Thapar marshalled his forces against the Hindu, L. Devi Chand. Issues of commensality, intermarriage and temple-entry came up for discussion, with predictable positions taken by the Hindus and the dalits. The Hindus claimed that Aryas regularly ate with dalits and allowed them to enter temples. Shanno Devi, an Arya Samaj *updeshak* (missionary), told the dalits that 'no one can stop

---

[64]NAI, Home (Public), File no. 1/58/32-Public.

[65]Rolu Ram, Jalandhar, 3 April 1993.

[66]NAI, Home (Political), File no. 31/113/32-Poll. and unprinted K.W; Bakshi Ram, *Balmiki Sabha*.

you from going to temples ... Though the Hindus have given you trouble you should combine with them now'. If the Hindus behaved badly, they are sorry; they now want to be your friends, to welcome you into their family. This was the totality of the Hindu position expressed by Arya Samaj representatives at the conference. The dalits declared that they would not be taken in by these hollow promises and occasional dramatics. When Dr N.L. Varma, an Arya, said that he carried refuse from the latrines before the conference, Chunni Lal cut him off by saying that 'he cannot accomplish the work fully well' unless he does it for at least ten or fifteen days. The dalits were forthright in their revolt against political theatre, yet, at times some dalits succumbed to the Arya's drama. After the conference, Shanno Devi took a few dalit women to the Sanathan Dharm temple in Shimla and 'no one objected'. We do not know what happened during their attempt, but in another incident in 1932 at the Sanathan Dharm temple in Shimla, seven Balmikis along with some Arya Samaj Congressmen were asked to leave by the temple priest.[67]

At the conference, Chunni Lal's temper flared at one crucial moment when Varma charged the dalits with being induced by the government and the Muslims to disrupt Hindu unity. 'We are not such fools to act in the hands of the Muhammedans or the government', Thapar said. 'We shall abolish this untouchability ourselves. We will forcibly enter your house and then we will dare you to drive us out. We want to remain untouchables. We want to preserve this community which history has bequeathed us. We want to change our status through political negotiation across the divide which separates us. We want to fight for our rights. We do not want you to help us, for we want to fight against you. This is not a place for mutual understanding, because the balance of power is on the side of the Hindus; therefore, any mutual understanding itself is not possible.' These lines are memorable. A pitfall of nationalist consciousness is the desire to idealistically will away the divides without struggling to undo their structural realities. 'You call yourselves untouchables', Shanno Devi said, 'but in reality you are Hindus'. In the seemingly innocuous act of naming, so many political issues were in danger of erasure.

The conference also demonstrates the limits of the independent political theory put forth by the dalits. 'We are the original inhabitants

[67]Pamela Kanwar, *Imperial Simla: The Political Culture of the Raj* (Delhi: Oxford University Press, 1990), p. 185.

of the country', said Chunni Lal Thapar, 'and we therefore fight for our rights. We strongly urge foreign communities to leave this country. We have not claimed that we solely should rule over it, but the idea is that all communities should share in the administration. We are not ready to compromise with the Hindus, unless we are given an assurance of a fair agreement'. The desire for independent initiative was strong, so strong that Chunni Lal was able to set the dalits in opposition to the entirety of the non-dalit population (Muslims, Hindus, British—all foreign). The power of Chunni Lal's statement relies upon the assertion of dalit power regardless of its implications for quotidian politics. The élan of the statement replicates the boldness of the entire movement which was designed to win concrete victories but which also produced the idea that dalits could lead the struggle for their freedom. The latter sensibility was historically more significant than the limited gains which the Ad-Dharm movement was able to secure. Nevertheless, Chunni Lal moves from the strong statement into a language of parliamentary politics, a language ruled by compromise and pragmatic governance. The tension between autonomy and negotiation was not clarified in the Ad-Dharm movement which was often content to use the strong statement as a bargain for the moderate victory.

Mangoo Ram's three part resolution (that the Ad-Dharm movement will continue, that Gandhi should continue his work among Hindus and that Dr Ambedkar be authorized to make any agreement with Gandhi) was passed with much noise. The inspiration for a struggle governed by the dalits was sought through Dr Ambedkar; in 1930, he told the dalits that 'nobody can remove your grievances as well as you can and you cannot remove them unless you get political power in your own hands'.[68] Two years later the position taken by dalit organizations showed that they wanted to assume political power and responsibility. This was Ambedkar's greatest moment, the embodiment of all the men and women who fought so hard to put their telegrams on the table and make them work. When history such as this is made, it is tragic to report its outcome as failure. To honour the third part of their resolution, the Balmik Ad-Dharm Mandal accepted the Poona Pact on 28 September 1932, two days after Ambedkar had signed it. It was commonly known among the dalits as Dr Ambedkar's agreement, and

[68]Trilok Nath, *Politics*, p. 245.

it was signed 'in the interests of India'.[69] Whether these interests were the same as the interests of the dalits is not mentioned.

The Ad-Dharm alliance, in all fairness, did not fail only because of the government and the militant Hindus. It also failed because the hope for a dalit communality could not overcome the genuine fissures between the Chuhras and the Chamars. In 1927, the Chuhras formed their own Balmiki Ad-Dharm Mandal, but that was largely to develop leadership among the Chuhra community to work alongside the Ad-Dharm Mandal itself. In the 1930s, the alliance began to dissolve as a result of the clash between respective caste heritages, for the Chamars of Raidas/Ravidas and for the Chuhras of Valmiki. Raidas, whose songs are found in the *Granth Sahib*, was (along with Kabirdas) a strong critic of caste and social inequalities. Punjabi Chamars began to build temples to him in the 1920s (in Delhi a Ravidas temple was set up in Jangpura in 1922). The Chuhras, by the 1930s, called themselves Balmikis and they claimed Valmiki as their preceptor. The Balmikis clashed with the Chamars over which guru should take precedence. In the early days of the Mandal, statues of both preceptors adorned the Mandal office in Jalandhar. One of the early disputes occurred when the Chamars, allegedly, removed the statue of Valmiki from the office.[70] It is not for nothing that Mangoo Ram told Mark Jurgensmeyer that the Balmikis had no part of his movement; in the same coin, I was told by Balmiki leaders that they had the entire show running before Mangoo Ram returned from his sojourn overseas. Antipathy runs deep between these two communities, moulded by the limited stakes at hand.

In order to continue the potentialities of Ad-Dharm radicalism, even if only through the limited community of Balmikis, Gauri Shankar Acharya launched an unusual movement, the Nishkalank (Immaculate) Panth in Jalandhar in the early 1930s.[71] Acharya drew upon the resource of Valmiki to become the preceptor of his people, a people, he argued in his 1933 tract, *Sanskar Vidhi*, who have their own socio-religious practices. Rather than serve as a bridge to Brahmanism, Valmiki was to be an admonition to his people to be wary of the political and economic traps set by militant Hindus through the Arya Samaj. Instead of Brahman mantras, Acharya made up his own

---

[69]NAI, Home (Political), File no. 41/5-Poll. and K.W., 1932.

[70]Bhagmal 'Pagal', Banarasi Das Nahar and Roop Lal Shant, Jalandhar, 2 and 3 April 1993; Bakshi Ram, *Balmiki Sabha*.

[71]Bhagmal 'Pagal', Jalandhar, 2 April and 4 April 1993.

incantations that would promote the dignity and self-respect of the Chuhras, as he argued in his tract *Haloona*. His use of Valmiki enabled him to do two things: to stay away from Brahmanism while keeping ties with the Hindu reformers and to carve out an alternative path from the Chamars who, he felt, had taken over the Ad-Dharm movement. R. C. Sangar characterizes the Nishkalank Panth as both progressive and reactionary, the former because there was a need for a separate entity for the political development of the community and the latter because 'we could not be saved from Hinduism since we took our name from Brahmanical Hinduism'.[72] Acharya's radicalism was compromised at crucial moments, such as in his argument that Ambedkar's position at the Round Table Conference stalled independence. He wanted the Balmikis to forsake Ambedkar and to follow Gandhi.[73] In 1936, Acharya founded a Balmiki Ashram on Mandi Road in Jalandhar to house his Nishkalank Panth. Today, amidst the offices of distributors of Punjabi cinema stands the Ashram where Acharya's son continues his father's legacy. Few turn to it with any seriousness.

THE EMERGENCE OF BALMIKI

The aboriginal radicalism of some dalits and the popularity of Dr Ambedkar drew a strong response both from Gandhi (who started the Harijan Sevak Sangh and drew in many of the militant Hindu organizers) and the militant Hindu organizations (like the Arya Samaj and SDS) who now orchestrated shuddhi amongst the dalits. In Lahore, in 1930, the Arya Samaj conducted a shuddhi of 6000 Balmikis; in 1933, about 1500 more Balmikis joined their brethren in the realm of purity promised by their Hindu friends.[74] In 1933, some concerned Aryas called a meeting of their active workers in Lahore to discuss the issue of *dalitudhar* (uplift of the dalits). They felt that Muslims and Christians had made notable inroads into the Chuhra community, and now the Ad-Dharmis had secured some measure of influence among the dalit-Bahujans. A prominent Brahman pleaded with the workers that this must be stopped. In order to do so, he urged someone to volunteer to work full-time among the Chuhras. A young man who hailed from the United Provinces, Ami Chand, volunteered. He took up residence in

---

[72]R.C. Sangar, Jalandhar, 3 April 1993.
[73]Gauri Shankar Acharya, *Bharat Sarguzasht* (Jalandhar, 1932).
[74]Vidyalankar, *Arya Prathinidhi Sabha Punjab ka Itihas*, pp. 372–7.

Neela Gumbad in Lahore, from where he preached under the banner of the Dalitudhar Mandal in 1934–5. Charged with the power of Ad-Dharm and the songs of Bala Shah, the Chuhras initially cursed him and showered him with stones. In the sweepers' strike of 1935, Ami Chand joined the marches and was imprisoned for six-and-a-half months for his pains, an experience that earned him the sweepers' trust. Within the year he was joined by Chennu Devi of the Kanya Maha-vidyalaya, Hans Raj and Sadhu Yodhnath, and together they worked to win over the Chuhras to Hinduism. Sadhu Yodhnath composed hymns and songs which were sung as the Balmikis introduced the worship of Maharishi Valmiki into their lives, and Ami Chand wrote *Valmiki Prakash* in 1936 which became the staple tract of the Balmiki commu-nity.[75] *Bhajans* (devotional songs) were crucial to the activism of these Arya Samajis, for much of their politics revolved around promoting the worship of the Rishi. G. D. Birla urged Thakkar and the Harijan Sevak Sangh in 1936 to initiate such a politics. 'Millions of Harijans may be lost to the Hindus', he wrote, and 'the only thing we can do to prevent such a thing is to serve the Harijans in those areas [of religion] and to some extent, I feel that we should also increase our expenditure on Bhajans and Kathas . . . this is the only way to prevent the mischief [of conversion]'.[76] While Ami Chand and Sadhu Yodhnath appreciated the importance of bhajans, they also stressed the pedagogical value of Ami Chand's tract. The first part of the *Valmiki Prakash*, after all, is written as a conversation between a Ram Sevak and a Balmiki man. It is just after dawn. The Ram Sevak is at his temple, reading from the *Ramay-ana*. As he takes the name of Valmiki in a stray *shlok* (hymn), a Balmiki man who has been sweeping the street comes up to the temple filled with curiosity. He asks the Ram Sevak a series of questions about Valmiki and the Balmikis. In the conversation which follows, the Ram Sevak makes a number of interesting observations which we will follow through a close reading of this programmatic tract.[77]

[75]*Who's Who, Delhi Freedom Fighters.* Ed. Prabha Chopra (Delhi, 1974), vol. 1, p. 24; Bhagmal 'Pagal', Jalandhar, 2 April 1993 and Guruji, Balmiki Colony, Delhi, 1 March 1993.

[76]Delhi CID, SB (Non-Current) Records, 3rd installment, no. 27, NMML and G. D. Birla, 'Hinduaun ko naitik chunauti', *Saraswati* (January 1936).

[77]Ami Chand Sharma and Sadhu Yodhnath, *Shri Valmiki Prakash* (Dilli: Dehati Pustak Bhandar, 1936).

Ami Chand situates his tract himself. It begins as a sustained attack on the Ad-Dharm movement, particularly on the characters of Achutananda (of Kanpur) and Shudrananda (of Jalandhar). He accuses them of being either Christians or Muslims, since they wish to separate dalits from Hindus. He declares unequivocally that 'Adi-Hindu is not a jati', a community. 'We ask Achutananda that if you are Adi-Hindu, then what is your esteemed holy book? Who is your main deity? What are your flags and symbols? To these questions of ours Achutananda has no answer; yes, sometimes they say that our guru is Kabir and Raidasji. Then we say that if Kabirdas and Raidas are your gurus, then we ask is it not true that Kabir was the disciple of the famous Bairagi, Ramananda, and worshipper of Ram?'[78] In the same spirit, Ami Chand argues, Raidas was a worshipper of Krishna. If this is the case, then the Adi-Hindus cannot be a religious community. To one who tries to deny the rigidity of his definition, he has this to say: 'If you say that you do not have a religious book, no guru, then you are an irreligious atheist [*dharamhin nastik*]'.[79] 'Keep it in mind', he concludes, 'these people [the preachers of Ad-Dharm] are bent on destroying our house and destroying us. For this reason, do not listen to them. The eternal Hindu religion and Hindu jati should receive devotional acclaim'.[80] The Balmiki man brings the discussion to that very Hindu religion by asking the Ram Sevak about Valmiki. The Ram Sevak narrates a number of stories, mostly from religious scripture, but also from popular legend and folklore, although he gives them a pedagogical value which is unmistakable. In one story, Valmiki was kidnapped by a Bhil woman when he was a child. It was god's will that Valmiki go to the Bhils because 'if Valmiki did not go to the houses of the Bhils, there would not have been reform for the Bhils'.[81] The word used is *udhar* (reform), the word which the Arya groups used for their own activities among dalits. Just as it was god's will for Valmiki to go to the Bhils, so too it is divinely ordained that the Aryas go to the Balmikis.

The Balmiki man interrupts again, and asks a question which logically follows from the imputed link between the Balmikis and Valmiki—was Valmiki of the dalits as well? 'Maharaj', asks the Balmiki, 'tell us if Valmiki was our ancestor [*pita guru*] or our teacher [*shiksha*

[78]Sharma and Yodhnath, *Valmiki Prakash*, p. 7.

[79]Ibid., p. 7.

[80]Ibid., p. 8.

[81]Ibid., p. 10.

guru]?' The Ram Sevak replies, 'Shri Valmikiji is your teacher not your ancestor'.[82] If Valmiki was the ancestor of the Balmikis, that would mean one of two things: that the Hindus revered a book written by a dalit or that the Balmikis are not dalits at all and therefore, they should be exalted in status. Neither was acceptable. In one of the stories which the Ram Sevak had recited earlier, he mentioned that Valmiki was considered a Bhangi because at a Pandav sacrifice he said that he was a Chandal; this is a statement of alliance with the low castes rather than a statement about bloodlines.[83] The Balmiki perseveres, 'then what is our ancestry?' The Ram Sevak recites a shlok—'*Brahman Shudra Sansargat jat: Chandalmuchyate*'. In the contact between a Brahman and a Shudra, the Ram Sevak translates, the Mehtars were created 'and in memory of this comes the Mehtars work of sweeping and removing nightsoil. For this reason you are a Hindu'.[84] Of course, the shlok neither mentions sweeping nor nightsoil, nor does it say anything of Mehtars or Hindus. What it says is that the Chandals emerged through the union of a Brahman and a Shudra. The rest is a loose interpretation of the various strands of logic which emerge out of the Arya rewriting of history. It is remarkable how the very act of reciting from Sanskrit and then translating so loosely can be used as the centrepiece in a very contentious argument; but, who among the Balmikis had access to Sanskrit to challenge these words which the Brahmans charge with the divine itself (this although they may have understood the terms Brahman, Shudra and Chandal)?[85]

If Valmiki is not the ancestor of the Balmikis, then why should they revere him? 'When and why did we make Valmiki our guru?', asks the fictional Balmiki. The Brahmans, the Ram Sevak answers, did not allow others to read the vedas. Valmiki said that all people, from Brahmans to Chandals, can read the *Ramayana*. 'Seeing the kindness of this man, your elders thought it fit to revere him since he allowed you to read the *Ramayana*'. He was chosen as a guru, for gurus are necessary. '*Guru bin gati nahin, Shah bin pat nahi*', says the Ram

[82]Ibid., p. 22.

[83]Ibid., p. 11.

[84]Ibid., p. 22.

[85]*Adi Danka*, an Ad-Dharm paper, reported in the late 1920s that 'Smritis were in force which ordained that molten lead should be poured into our ears if we heard the Vedas recited and that our tongues should be cut out if we recited them'. *Times of India*, 7 November 1928.

Sevak, without a Guru there is no way (to God), without a ruler there is no honour. Hindus do not like to see the face of a man who has no guru, the Ram Sevak pointed out, hence it was fitting to take a guru.[86] What proof is there, the Balmiki asks, that Valmiki is the guru of Balmikis? Balmikis keep the *Ramayana*, the Ram Sevak replies, they sing songs which mention the Maharishi and they keep his statue in their homes. For example, writes Ami Chand, in Lahore's Dilli Darwaza area there is a Balmiki called Kajjaram who has a picture of Valmiki. 'I have seen it with my own eyes', says the Ram Sevak.[87]

If a guru is necessary, the Balmiki asks, why do we not simply revere Lal Beg? On this point the Ram Sevak is categorical, 'Bhai, Lal Beg is a disciple of Valmiki'. He then begins a ferocious attack on the 'Qadiani Maulana Ahmediya', i.e. Mirza Ghulam Ahmad of Qadian. 'Those people who call themselves Lalbegis are mistaken. You people should call yourselves Balmikis forever'.[88] The tone is angry, almost intolerant. The very mention of Lalbegi, even in a staged discussion, raises his ire. The anti-Muslim tenor of Ami Chand's book falls in line with a long-standing attempt by militant Hindus to attribute to Muslim practices in the lives and faith of the Chuhras the reason for their backwardness. For instance, the manner of burial. Delhi Mehtars buried their dead and chanted '*Allah ki sipurd*' on their return from the graveyard. The Aryas wanted the Mehtars to adopt their neo-vedic rituals. When SDS took up the issue of disposal of the dead, one of their dalit preachers of Delhi, Nanak Chand, fought with his caste fellows to cease burial in favour of cremation. He, along with his friend Karam Chand, was able to make the elders accept cremation at the edge of the cremation grounds at Nigambodh Ghat, a slur which the elders accepted grudgingly.[89] From ritualized eating practices to myths, the dismissal of anything Muslim was carried out efficiently and ruthlessly. In February 1993, Madan Lal Parcha told me that it was the Khaksars who printed a book about Bala Shah and Lal Beg and invented the entire story. '*Zabardasti ka mazhab banaya gaya*' (the religion was built by force), he said, and that too by Muslims. Hindu militants also promoted stories which calumniated Lal Beg and Bala Shah. The most

---

[86]Ibid., p. 24.

[87]Ibid.

[88]Ibid., p. 25.

[89]Faqir Chand, Ghi Mandi, 25 March 1993 and Jagdish Pujari, Delhi, 15 June 1992.

common story, still in circulation, is that Lal Beg was a nawab who raped a number of dalit women on their wedding-night. It was said that he was called Mansur Badshah. One night he entered the home of a Mehtar and raped a woman. He was killed by the *pahalwans* (wrestlers, body-builders) of the community. Interestingly, the story goes on to say that the police arrived in search of him; in haste, the Chuhras put two bricks over his body and began to pray to the bricks. The police entered the house and called Lal Beg's name. Hence the tradition of calling the name of the pir as the Chuhras face the shrine. I was told that *'Lal Beg ka lalmurga kat'*, was a slogan forced on the Chuhras by the Muslims. Nanak Chand insisted that his caste fellows remove other traces of Muslim custom such as the offering of a red cock to the shrine of Bala Shah and then eating the chicken off one large communal plate (called *tabak*, or literally, a superstitious practice to ward off evil spirits).[90] These stories are but the tip of an unpleasant iceberg of myths and half-truths.

If the dalits exorcized Muslims from their everyday lives, would that ensure their freedom? 'If we are Hindus', the Balmiki man in Ami Chand's *Valmiki Prakash* asks, 'then why are we considered to be untouchable and will untouchability ever be abolished?' This question calls for a long answer, which turns on the notion of *karma*. Those who do bad things, Ami Chand argues, are dalits. Look at the Bhil woman, the Ram Sevak says, from whose hand Ram ate her *jootha*, her leavings. After Valmiki said that he was a Mehtar, even Krishna ate with him. Brahmins ate with Kabir. If you are clean, then there should be no objection to eating with you. Yet, the Ram Sevak rehearses the story of Guru Jhaumpra and the betrayal and fall of the Chuhras. The dalits were punished for moving the cow, but they will be allowed re-entry into the fold in the fourth age, in the Kalyug. Of course, the story is told differently, for in the Chuhra version the brothers say that they will allow Jhaumpra back in the fourth age, but god says that in the fourth age only the Chuhras will gain resurrection while the Muslims and Hindus will tremble with fear. Ami Chand used the traditions in a creative way, transforming the dalits' overall argument of betrayal in order to make Hinduization more amenable. The fourth age is here, he announces, so dalits should join their Hindu family. In an inspired move, Ami Chand criticizes the decline in Hinduism (such as Brah-

[90]Sadan Lal and Madan Lal Saugwan, Kalan Masjid, 21 March 1993 and Bannu Devi, Ajmere Gate, 5 May 1992.

mans eating meat, drinking liquor and marrying Shudras), whose reform includes the end to untouchability; the reform, however, comes with an end to intermarriage, which remained a point of contention.

The Ram Sevak makes a series of familiar pronouncements which carry the message that the dalits will not be treated as untouchables if they lead clean lives. Give up meat (especially beef), stop drinking liquor and do not gamble. Clean your homes and your clothes. Be constant in your devotion to Valmiki: 'It is the duty (*dharm*) of every Balmiki brother to propagate the *Valmiki Prakash*.'[91] Above all, the book argues, leave all Muslim customs and adopt Hindu manners. Do not bury your dead, only cremate them. Muslims should not be allowed in your ceremonies; if they come, god will not accept the ceremony.[92] If this prescription is followed, writes Ami Chand, the Hindus will not be distant from the dalits, particularly the Balmikis. 'Your untouchability will go if you stop doing bad karm things': *your* untouchability, the untouchability of the low castes which they bring on themselves by their conduct.[93] 'Keep it in mind', Ami Chand wrote in the preface, 'I am offering in all simplicity a sermon on righteousness (*dharm*). My view is that when you attain strength with your religion, then you people will be able to develop in all sorts of ways'.[94] Religious community and loyalty provide the firmest basis for the removal of untouchability. This, in sum, was the message of the Aryas to the Balmikis: 'You are Hindu, your religion is Hindu, Vedas are your holy books, Valmiki is your guru. Those who do circumcision, get married in the Muslim style, do their funerals in the Muslim style, they do a great sin . . . Your guru is Valmiki, your God is Ram. This is because you are Ram Bhakts, for this reason you must be devoted to Ram in order to gain deliverance'.[95] The Balmiki then says, 'the Hindu jati is what binds us with blood. For this reason, whatever the Hindu community does is for our good. No one else will do things for our good'.[96] Community loyalty is a populist element which can be articulated for any form of politics; when community is constructed around blood-lines, the racial boundaries circumscribes the dalits' choices. Forging

[91]Sharma and Yodhnath, *Valmiki Prakash*, p. 8.

[92]Ibid, p. 31.

[93]Ibid., pp. 26–8.

[94]Ibid, p. 6.

[95]Ibid, p. 28.

[96]Sharma and Yodhnath, *Valmiki Prakash*, p. 40.

ties with those who do not share blood becomes improbable, an idea that worked against the grain of those who attempted to craft wide solidarities for political struggle.

The tract was distributed extensively, having been given the stamp of approval from major Arya Samaj and Gandhian leaders. Most Balmikis appreciated the bhajans which made up the second half of the book, for these allowed them to conduct religious services in line with the argument in the first half of the book.[97] The Mehtars of Delhi began to refer to Ami Chand as Maharaj, to indicate their respect for him, but also ironically to mock his pretentious rendition of their history. He was, to be sure, a very young man in the eyes of the elders, and he did make some very bold and audacious statements.[98] To some, Ami Chand made a persuasive argument. While it revealed the limitations of Hindu reform, it put forward its point as the only way for the Balmikis to gain some measure of status in their larger social networks. If the Balmikis conducted themselves in the appropriate manner (which includes distancing themselves from Muslims), then they will gain respect from Hindus. In an attempt to flatter the Balmikis, the Maharishi is given to them as someone to revere. He, however, is not offered as an ancestor. It is on this point that the Balmikis clashed with Hindu militants, but to begin the argument is already to enter the terms of Ami Chand Pandit. The debate is not about whether the Balmikis are Hindus or not, but whether they can claim the Rishi as their own as Hindus. To hold Valmiki back, in fact, is a way for Ami Chand to deny the dalits parity in a distant past at the same time as other Hindus offer it by saying that the dalits are fallen Rajputs. Both arguments reinforce the claim that the dalits have an intimate relationship with Hinduism. The debates which follow are academic, for the Balmiki now debated from within a Hindu community.

Two examples from the 1950s offer us insight into how the traditions of Bala Shah became submerged within the collective consciousness of the dalits. Santram, the founder of the Jat-Pat Torak Mandal,

---

[97]Sant Chandrabhan, 21 February 1993, Ratan Lal Balmiki, April 1992 and 20 March 1993, Balmiki Colony, New Delhi; Lahori Ram Balley, 2 April 1993, Jalandhar; Radha Shyam Pareek, *Contributions of the Arya Samaj in the Making of Modern India, 1875–1947* (New Delhi: Sarvadeshik Arya Pratinidhi Sabha, 1973), p. 159; Bharatiya Shraddhanda Dalitudhar Sabha, *Annual Report, 1927*, pp. 18–20

[98]Mangal Ram, Ghi Mandi, 25 March 1993.

argued that the Chuhras had two different religious traditions, one, under Muslim influence, took Lal Beg as its icon of worship and, the other, recognized Maharishi Valmiki as the teacher of the Balmikis. The former had to be actively forgotten, he argued, while the latter had to be championed.[99] Gyaneshwar, a dalit activist in Delhi, put these two traditions into one by writing a version of the *Ramayana* in which Valmiki appears as a radical Chandal.[100] Unwilling to let go of the idea of a radical and antagonistic tradition, Gyaneshwar wrote against a sterile adoption of the will of the Hindus (the second tradition of Santram). Madan Lal Saugwan who told me of Gyaneshwar in 1993 also said, with a glint in his eye, that he lost the last copy of the text during the 1960s. I am tempted to read that loss as a metaphor for the disappearance of the tradition of the radical Bala Shah who boldly castigated the powerful.

TESTING HINDUISM

In order to actualize their claim to Hinduism, Balmikis and other dalits put forward three basic demands for reform, temple-entry, intermar- riage, and inter-dining as means towards the abolition of untouchability rather than as their goals. As means, the demands aimed to accentuate the caste contradictions and to challenge the liberalism of Hindus. The demand for reform was not only initiated to palliate the contradictions, to make them adapt and ameliorate the lives of the dalits. The dalits called for reforms to help their daily lives, no doubt, but also to stress their demand for the removal of the conditions which required reform. Dalit groups, therefore, demanded access to temples only so that they might enjoy the fruits of Hinduism 'as long as we are counted as Hindus and undue advantage is taken of our numbers by the Hindus'.[101] The bitter tone came from the anger that dalits are needed as labourers and voters, but not as friends and family. But the demand for reform was also an ironic challenge, for the dalits knew that Hindus would not pursue the reforms. In that sense, the demand for reform was a political instrument, devised to demonstrate the illiberalism of the liberal reformers. The cry for reform, therefore, must be heard as a demand (however inchoately formulated) for recognition of the political

---

[99]Santram, *Hamara Samaj*, p. 124.
[100]Madan Lal Saugwan, Kalan Masjid, Delhi, 28 March 1993.
[101]NAI, Home (Public), File no. 490/31-Public.

initiative of the dalits, since that cry is a weapon to illuminate the social contradictions of lived Hinduism. The demand for reform also shows the gradual incorporation of the politics of the Balmikis, as they turned to the very framework of reform set by militant Hindus.

The Vaikom Satyagraha in Travancore in 1924 brought the issue of temple-entry to the fore as well as demonstrated the various uses of reform. In 1925, at a Depressed Classes Conference at Nipani, Ambedkar extended a challenge to Hinduism. The issue before the dalits was not temple-entry as such, but the value of the Brahmanical scriptures as Vaikom priests coaxed Gandhi with quotations from the Shastras to justify their rules. To Ambedkar, this clearly indicated that 'either we should burn all these scriptures to ashes or verify and examine the validity of their rules regarding untouchability'. If the priests' claim for untouchability was proved, what should the dalits do? Should they submit to the Shastras, or should they argue that 'these scriptures are an insult to people'.[102] The scriptures set the limits of liberalism, and to demonstrate that, temple-entry was a viable political tactic and a challenge to militant Hindus. In 1930, at Parvati, Ambedkar clarified his challenge and threat to Hinduism. 'Your problems', he said to the dalit Satyagrahis, 'will not be solved by temple-entry. Politics, economics, education, religion—all are part of the problem. Today's satyagraha is a challenge to the Hindu mind. Are the Hindus ready to consider us men or not; we will discover this today'.[103] In this context, in the late 1930s, Ambedkar challenged some Lahori Hindus to show him a Sanathan Dharm temple which would open its door to dalits. Mahatma Hans Raj asked Santram to find a priest who might allow dalits to enter his temple; after that transgression, the priest was to be paid Rs 50 to purify the temple with holy water from the river Ganga.[104] The deception did not take place, but it demonstrates the risk of symbolic reform: if reform is a tactic, it can be so for both sides. Temple-entry functioned as a challenge, as a way to provoke Hindus to deliver on their promises, but it also provided Hindus with an easy way to side-step structural change, by allowing symbolic tours of temples by dalits.

[102]Eleanor Zelliot, 'Dr Ambedkar and the Mahar Movement' (Philadelphia: University of Pennslyvania PhD, 1969), pp. 99–100.

[103]Zelliot, 'Dr Ambedkar', p. 114.

[104]Santram, Oral History Transcripts no. 238, NMML.

Intermarriage and commensality provided Hindus and dalits with further issues for challenge and symbolic ripostes. Ritual inter-dining was a major part of most Congress campaigns for dalitudhar as a few Congressmen or other reformers entered a dalit hamlet, gave a speech, took a tour of the hovels, and then, shared a meal with some dalits. The dalits and Hindus did not even eat from the same plate, but they sat side by side, a symbolic act that was seen as sufficient for the dalitudhar of the militant Hindus. In 1937, Gandhi announced that 'given the proper confirmation with the rules of cleanliness, there should be no scruple about dining with anybody'.[105] Yet, Gandhi's concern for the orthodox led him to be cautious and he feared that the 'time has not come for that call [for inter-dining]. The people won't respond to all my calls and rightly'. Besides, he felt that inter-dining was not essential for the removal of untouchability.[106] Shraddhananda offered a version of inter-dining that did not worry the orthodox, since he was opposed to 'promiscuous eating out of the same cup and dish like Muhammadans, but partaking food in separate cups and dishes, cooked and served by decent Shudras'.[107] We will allow them to serve us, he says, only if they are decent and clean. In 1923, Malaviya 'appealed for the removal of untouchability', but he did not 'of course . . . force high class Hindus to eat with them or intermarry'.[108] To force these issues on the orthodox Hindus was seen as counter-productive by the Hindu reformers, a fear which provoked the reformers to avoid the issue entirely.

'The real remedy for breaking Caste is intermarriage', Ambedkar wrote in a lecture he was to deliver to the Jat-Pat Torak Mandal in Lahore in 1936 (but which was cancelled because it questioned the scriptures). 'Nothing else will serve as the solvent of Caste'. Ambedkar held that marriage norms are the 'source of the disease' and since many Hindus hold such beliefs as sacred, 'the real remedy is to destroy the belief in the sanctity of the Shastras'.[109] Gandhi adamantly argued that

[105] *Harijan*, 13 February 1937.

[106] N. R. Malkani, *Ramblings and Reminiscences of Gandhiji* (Ahmedabad: Navajivan, 1972), p. 103. The Harijan Sevak Sangh's Constitution did not require inter-dining, but encouraged the setting up of 'good restaurants for Harijan Hindus', *Constitution of the Harijan Sevak Sangh* (Delhi: Harijan Sevak Sangh, 1935), pp. 18–23.

[107] Shraddhananda, *Hindu Sangathan*, p. 136.

[108] *Oudh Akhbaar*, 6 January 1923.

[109] B.R. Ambedkar, *Annihilation of Caste* (Delhi: Arnold reprint, 1990), pp. 82–3.

'the giving or taking of son and daughter in marriage, to or from any person one likes [is] mere license'.[110] License meant that it was freedom without restriction, without any form of social mediation, but that sort of freedom is impossible, since social interaction calls for some form of mediation. The dalits protested against one form of mediation, the practice of untouchability, and called for its abolition. If untouchability was secured through blood lines, through the mechanism of heredity, then marriage relations were a necessary place for change. Ambedkar and other radical dalits argued for social mediation founded on an alternative ground than blood, but their claim put at risk the very mechanisms of power which participated in the reproduction of the status world. To stabilize that status world, the only resolution which was offered to the social contradictions was symbolic acts which worked as metaphors and not as examples for social practice. Symbolic intermarriage was a difficult thing to accomplish, but the cinema was a good place for it. *Achut Kanya*, made by Himanshu Rai in 1936 (Bombay Talkies), is a story of unrequited love between a dalit girl, Kasturi (played by Devika Rani) and a Brahman boy, Mohanlal (played by Ashok Kumar). The lovers cannot consummate their attachment, so each marries within his or her caste. Towards the end of the movie, Kasturi's dalit husband starts a fight with Mohanlal, with whom he thinks Kasturi might flee. To stop the fight, Kasturi jumps in front of a moving train. Two points need to be made about this film. One, it is the dalit woman in the end who sacrifices herself in order to stop the battle between the dalit man and the Hindu man. It is her tragic end which is to bring the men together. Second, the movie was made possible in large part because of Devika Rani's own privileged position, one which allowed no real transgression to take place. Even here symbolic action is inserted as a way of easing social conflicts and tempering the realization that popular objectives (such as equality) are posed with severe limitations. A visible and symbolic action of this period was the construction of temples for the Balmikis, and it is to that which we shall now turn.

BALMIKI ENSHRINED

One of the most striking things about the temples dedicated to Maharishi Valmiki is the universal claim of their antiquity. Whether in

---

[110]Sanjana, *Caste and Outcaste*, p. 25.

Jalandhar, Karnal, Delhi or Shimla, the local Balmiki population proudly proclaim the pre-historic roots of their shrines as well as their ancestral connection with the Maharishi. Age and community play central roles in the imaginations of north Indians, as the rishis in folklore live for hundreds of thousands of years to indicate for us their immense wisdom. Each community and caste provides us with elaborate stories of the formation of their people into a community, often being premised upon the divine origin of the founder of the community. For these reasons, the location of Maharishi Valmiki at the centre of the Balmiki community's self-definition is perhaps under-standable. It was with a sense of unease, therefore, that I probed the divine origin of the founder of the community. Elders told me the stories of the founding of their temples, who built them, what structures existed on the sites before, who funded the temples, etc. The temple in Ali Mohalla in Jalandhar was the most difficult, since it had been recently rebuilt. It seemed that I would never know when the older shrine had been built. Despite the desire to claim antiquity for our shrines, it is only rarely that we put up commemorative stones which indicate foundation details. There was a stone at Ali Mohalla, but it only recounted details of the recent rebuilding. The important history here was the recent one, the one which was most meaningful. After all, whenever I broached the question of the older shrines, the Balmikis asked me to comment on the beauty of the new one. It was a dramatic structure, towering in the main bazaars of Jalandhar city. By all indications, it provided the community with meaning and sustenance.

Om Prakash Gill, an aging leader from the Balmiki community, who was interviewed by Mark Jurgensmeyer a decade ago, was familiar with the questions of historians. He was startled by my knowledge of the old traditions, the stories of Lal Beg, which I recounted to him from my readings of colonial ethnography. It was a curious moment, to be telling the native what the colonial official had stolen and what the Hindu nationalist had told him to forget. I had come to him through people whom he trusted, Bhagwan Das and Lahori Ram Balley, both fiery Ambedkarites whose service to the dalits of Punjab is unparal-leled, and I came along with R.C. Sangar, an intellectual of the Bahujan Samaj Party (Ambedkar faction). Gill smiled as I recounted the stories, stories which the younger militants took as a charter for their recent disenchantment with the Hindu nationalists. After a short time, he took my hand and told me what stood on the ground before the temple was constructed. The shrine was known as Darbar Saheb, he said, and it was a shrine to Bala Shah Nuri and Lal Beg. As the faithful entered that shrine, he said, they saw a series of niches on the far wall. In each niche, the faithful lit a small lamp.[111]

Scattered across the verdant landscape of the Punjabi plains, in the midst of the dalit hamlets, stood many such shrines which resembled the upright tail of a cow ('*gai ki dum ki shakal*') from afar. They faced the east, and on one wall facing the door there were niches for the faithful to place lamps in honour of Bala Shah. On Thursdays, the faithful gathered at these shrines and offered sacrifices which included *churman*, an offering made from bread crumbs, butter and sugar. Chuhras offered animal heads at the consecration of the shrines during which time they buried it along with the sacrificial knife.[112] The Chuhras worship Bala Shah, we are told, 'by erecting mud mounds, generally of very simply structure, but sometimes terraced, on which is planted a bamboo with a coloured rag attached by way of flag'. On the mound, the Chuhras burnt *chirags*, little oil lamps, and bowed down 'to ask for temporal favours at the hand of their guru'. Our informant tells us that the 'bamboo and rag are almost always very short, unlike that which *faqirs* put up: the reason being, I presume, that the higher castes would not allow the Chuhras to manifest too prominent a symbol of their faith'.[113] The *gyani* (wise person, mediator) encouraged the faithful to light lamps and to honour the various pirs who revealed the glory which is due to the Chuhras at resurrection. In the 1920s, all this changed. A cardboard cutout of Valmiki was installed in the Ali Mohalla shrine which was renamed Valmiki Darbar. A shrine in Mohalla Sangra, known as Bala Shah ka Mandir, was also offered to Valmiki. The people who effected the conversion were surprisingly those who were most suspicious of Hinduism, Balmiki Ad-Dharm activists.[114]

Just as Balmikis claim that the Ali Mohalla temple is the first temple to Valmiki, so too do they claim that the most famous Valmiki temple stands in New Delhi on Mandir Marg. Mandir Marg is a celebrated place in itself, being on both tourist and pilgrimage maps. Buses filled with believers in god and culture come to marvel at an entire road

---

[111]O.P. Gill, Jalandhar, 4–5 April 1993 and Bhagmal 'Pagal', Jalandhar, 2 April 1993.

[112]Youngson, 'The Chuhras' (December 1906), p. 355.

[113]H.U. Westbrecht, *Indian Notes and Queries*, vol. 4, no. 47 (August 1887).

[114]Dravid Desraj, Vishnu Dev and Rolu Ram, Jalandhar, 3 April 1993.

blessed with shrines, including the Laxmi Narayan (Birla) Temple (after whom many believe the street was named). This is indeed a confluence within the capital, Delhi's Prayag. The oldest building is a different sort of temple, the Harcourt Butler school (1917), built to facilitate the newly arrived children of the senior government services. The major building activity began in the 1930s. First, the Saint Thomas Church, whose foundation stone was laid by the Viceroy's wife, Lady Willingdon on 30 January 1932. That same year, a few hundred yards down the street, the NDMC set up its solitary sanitary store to hold supplies as well as to house bullock carts and bullocks.

Save one temple, the New Delhi Kalibari built by Bengali bureaucrats in the 1930s, the other temples have one family in common: the Birlas. In 1937, the Birla family paid for the Mahabodhi Society Buddhist Temple, which was opened in 1938 by Gandhi. In 1938, the Sanathan Dharma Laxmi Narayan Temple was opened, funded by Seth Raja Baldev Dass Birla. In 1939, the Hindu Mahasabha building was opened, thanks to the generosity of the sons of B.D. Birla. Further down, at the end of the road, the Birlas funded another temple, one which they graced only on special occasions, the Maharishi Valmiki Temple (1937). Why did the Birlas spend a fair sum of money on a temple not a mile away from one of the biggest temples in north India, the Laxmi Narayan Temple? This was odd because outside the Laxmi Narayan Temple, a large sign proclaims that 'this temple is open to all Hindus (including Harijans subject to the prescribed conditions of cleanliness, full faith and sincere devotion)'. In all likelihood, to give the Balmikis their own temple, dedicated to their own guru, was one way of preventing their frequent presence at the Birla Temple.

The 1937 Valmiki temple came after almost two decades of struggle by the Balmikis to build a religious shrine at the site. Around 1918, Master Prabhu Dayal, Devli Kheema and Nihal Chand decided to build a shrine in the area beside the ridge. Some have suggested that a few Chuhras might have been living here, but this is not proven. Prabhu Dayal had just migrated to Delhi from Meerut district where he worked along with the Arya Samajis. Initially, these three pioneers erected a crude shrine, perhaps to Baba Shiv, the guru of many Bhangis of Meerut district. When I spoke of Lal Beg, the Sant indicated that both Baba Shiv and Lal Beg are gurus, although in Meerut Baba Shiv was more popular.[115] The shrine, however, was *kaccha* (temporary) and a

[115]Sant Chandrabhan, Guruji, Krishna Kumar Vidyarthi, Rattan Lal Balmiki

decade later it needed to be renovated. A decade later, however, the activists of SDS urged the Chuhras to kill Bala Shah and to worship Valmiki. When Lila Ram and Dhannath approached Ganpat Rai, who was then the secretary of the Hindu Mahasabha, they did so in the context of the delegitimization of their worship practices. Lila Ram and Dhannath were both workers in the NDMC, and they were involved with Ganpat Rai in the Mehtar Union. Further, the Mahasabha building was being built next door and they felt that he might help them with their construction of a permanent structure. They wanted to build a temple, a room for a *pujari* (priest), a hall for the education of the children and an attached bath and toilet. They told Ganpat Rai that they had no money to construct the building, and that the DMC threatened to confiscate their land if they did not build on it. Ganpat Rai and Murli Dhar Taneja (of the Hindu Mahasabha) approached some philanthropists, such as the Birlas. In order to institutionalize their relationship with the Balmikis, they formed the Balmiki Hindu Mahasabha and the New Delhi Balmiki Hindu Sabha, involving Lala Banwari Lal, a prominent Arya and a wealthy contractor, as a major financier. The Sabha approached Major Dean of the Delhi Improvement Trust and assured him that they had begun to collect funds for a temple. Jugal Kishore Birla, Thakkar Baba of the Harijan Sevak Sangh, leading contractors of Delhi and donations from the Balmiki locality made up the shortfall. In 1937 the temple was inaugurated by the senior vice-president of the Delhi Municipal Corporation, Rai Bahadur Harish Chand.[116] Valmiki had a place in Delhi.

The second major Valmiki temple was built at Ajmeri Gate, and its history is similar. In front of Ajmeri Gate in the old city of Delhi, there was a large tank and a field which made the Gate cool and peaceful. Around an arch in the city wall, dalit men and women sat and enjoyed the air. Khwaju and Chandu spent most of their time there at the turn of the century, smoking *charas* (*Cannabis sativum*, a psychotropic substance) and occasionally plying their trade of cutting hair and shaving beards. The alcove was known as Khwaju ki thek. Sharing their alcove, was a statue of a goddess, the immortal Devi, goddess of the dalit-Bahujans. In the next alcove, there was a *sikr* to Baba Shiv,

---

and others, Balmiki Colony, New Delhi, 1992–3.

[116]*Hindustan Times*, 12 June 1937 and *Harijan*, 15 April 1939; the following Oral History Transcripts, NMML, no. 211 (Murli Dhar Taneja), no. 330 (Ganpat Rai) and no. 177 (Jugal Kishore Khanna).

that deity of the dalits of western UP, beside which the famous Safel wala Baba held court. Today there is a *mazhar* to this Syed or Safel wala Baba and dalits such as Chamars, Khatiks, Dulaks, and Balmikis come to pay homage to him. Mangal Singh, Jauri Chaudhuri, Nanak Chand and Ginna Pandit, all of them working with the Arya Samaj, came to Khwaju in the late 1920s and told him to place a *murti* (idol) of Valmiki next to his spot, since he used to sit there anyway. Khwaju agreed, and when the wall was broken (after 1947), a permanent temple was erected there.[117] Soon Valmiki temples began to be constructed everywhere, in Shimla in 1931, in Hoshiarpur, in Patiala, in Allahabad, in Meerut, in Dehradun, in Lahore. Bala Shah Nuri was on the way to his death, and Valmiki was on the way to his birth.

ON THE BACKS OF MUSLIMS

'Keep faith in yourself', Ami Chand Pandit wrote, 'look after yourself and try to achieve things with valour'.[118] Ami Chand, in a shrewd appropriation of the popular desire for autonomy, physical strength and self-determination, suggested that valour is the means to worthy ends. The word is *purusharth*, which carries suggestions of manhood and virility as well as valour. Be manly, be virile, be valourous. As an example of valour, the Ram Sevak of Ami Chand's imagination told the Balmiki the story of two brave Balmikis. When Teg Bahadur was beheaded in Delhi by Aurangzeb's army, his son Guru Gobind Singh wanted his body back in the Punjab. Two Balmikis, Ghasita and Jena, took the body and brought it to the guru.[119] In this tale, valour was duty and fealty, as well as honour. To achieve things with valour, however, had a more militaristic invocation; to achieve things with valour is a call to arms. Militarism found expression in the akharas at which Hindus offered their martial tradition which included historical and legendary figures such as Bhima, Shivaji and Hanuman. The militant Hindus organized wrestling tournaments 'at which sweeper young men took a prominent part'.[120] The militant Hindu groups also trained their dalit supporters to wield sticks and swords as a mark of their liberation. This martial capacity was not to be turned against the British, however,

---

[117]Dharam Singh Pujari, Ajmere Gate, Delhi, 28 March 1993 and Ram Krishen Saugwan, Himmat Garh, Ajmere Gate, 21 March 1993.

[118]Sharma and Yodhnath, *Valmiki Prakash*, p. 22.

[119]Ibid., p. 23.

[120]*Hindustan Times*, 27 October 1928.

but against their own neighbours, the *razil* Muslims.

From the very inception of the dalitudhar movement in Delhi, the question of the liberation of the dalits was brought to a crisis by transfering the problem to the Muslims. Each symbolic action was designed in such a way as to put the blame for untouchability and the difficulty of its abolition on the Muslims. In 1921, in a letter to Gandhi, Shraddhananda described an incident which occurred as he took some dalits to draw water from a well in Delhi City. The 'Muslim Congressmen stood in the way', he complained, 'and it seemed that even the Arya Samajists would not be able to keep the depressed classes free from the machinations of the bureaucracy'. Since a fair number of rais Muslims worked for the DMC, their actions were taken as representative of Muslim actions. That they acted according to the dictates of the colonial municipality or that their fears (shared with most Hindus) of the transmission of impurities from the dalits, was not to enter into the context; only that they were Muslims. 'A musalman trader of Sadr', Shraddhananda wrote, 'went to the length of saying that even if Hindus allowed these men to draw water from common wells, the Musalmans would forcibly restrain them from drawing water because they (the Chamars) ate carrion'.[121] This does not inspire a discussion on the hold of these notions of purity on segments of the population, but it simply allowed Shraddhananda to reflect on the barrier which the mythical Muslims posed against dalitudhar.

Another indication of the sustained attempt at inserting the Muslim between the dalits and liberty is from 14 February 1924. Shraddhananda and Deshbandhu Gupta took some dalits to draw water from a well in Hauz Qazi, a predominantly Muslim locality. The previous day, Malaviya called for the admission of the dalits into the 'inner circle of Hindu society', a statement which inspired this adventure. But the reformers did not go anywhere near Hindu society, as they stumbled into the inner circle of Muslim society. Some local Muslim leaders took offence at this action and a dispute arose. Why did the reformers bring the dalits into their locality, they asked, especially when they had wells in the Hindu localities which were not open to dalits and needed to be challenged? Why did the reformers wish to prolong their hypocritical politics of opening wells which did not matter to them and to their orthodoxy? It was SDS's gall which piqued

[121]Swami Shraddhananda, *Inside Congress* (Bombay: Phoenix, 1946), pp. 134–48.

some Muslim leaders, as they questioned the motives behind the march. A fracas ensued, as the SDS activists felt that violence was the answer to these questions.[122]

Temple-building as well had a strong anti-Muslim tendency. In the late 1920s, SDS encouraged the building of a temple in Nabi Karim, a locality in which Balmikis and Muslim artisans lived. The land upon which the temple was built was apparently an old graveyard of the neighbouring Muslim community.[123] The graveyard was not the only problem, since the temple was to be built not fifteen feet away from an active local mosque. When the local Muslims asked the Balmikis to move the temple, Seva Das (alias Chajju Maharaj) refused to move from the spot and so, a temporary temple remained on the contentious ground. For almost fifteen years, the issue remained unresolved, with relations between the Balmikis and Muslims getting strained. Flushed with passage of temple-entry legislation in his state in 1936, Travancore's constitutional advisor, Sir C.P. Ramaswami Aiyar laid a foundation stone for a permanent structure on 1 December 1940. The money for the temple came from none other than Jugal Kishore Birla (who offered to donate a silver statue of Valmiki). In a letter to the local authorities, Ganpat Rai declared that 'the Muslims of the locality have been threatening breach of peace'. On the basis of this piece of information, the government posted police in *mufti* (civilian attire) at the spot as a result of which the construction of the temple had to be postponed. In February 1941, the Balmiki Sabha resubmitted its plans for the temple to the DMC, which passed the plans in May 1941. The Sabha had a legal right to start construction of the temple at their will. The government was worried about the outcome of such a policy, and advised the leaders of the Sabha to suspend plans to build the temple. Negotiations carried on for two months, at which time 'through the genuine cooperation of Mr Ganpat Rai', the Sabha agreed 'to give up their claim to build a temple at the present site, if they were given some other suitable site for building a temple'. Through negotiations and parley, the deadlock appeared to be over and a plot of land was selected in Basti Ara Kashan. Another minor administrative detail—the need for permission to have a shop in the temple in order to allow it to be self-

[122]*Eastern Mail* (Delhi), 15 February 1925.

[123]D.S.P. City's *Report*, 8 December 1940 and 14 January 1941; *Report of the Station House Officer*, Sadr Bazar Police Station, 21 December 1940; City Magistrate's *Report*, 31 January 1940.

supporting—held up the temple. The District Commissioner, with imperial magnanimity declared that 'I see no objection particularly in the case of a temple serving needs of a poor community such as the sweepers. Indeed, it would appear preferable if such permission should be accorded, since, were the temple to be denied this source of income it might endeavour to derive income from less desirable sources, such as gambling, prostitution, etc'.[124] Despite permission, nothing happened and the Balmikis returned to their original graveyard land and built their temple. When Muslims from the area left in 1947 for their long and bloody trek to Pakistan, their land was taken by the local Balmikis who rebuilt and enlarged their temple. The local Balmiki leaders placed the foundation stone laid by Ramaswami Aiyar face down in front of the deity, a futile declaration of sovereignty in their own domain.

The temple was, however, only partly the domain of the Balmikis who now joined, however tentatively, the community of the Hindus. A striking feature of this alliance was that the nodal point of organization for the Balmikis continued to be their jati, so that their entry into the Hindu fold was mediated by their caste. The Chuhras now worshipped in temples, but not in the temples of other Hindus, since they had their own Valmiki temples (at which other Hindus almost never worshipped). For a brief moment in the 1930s, radical Chuhras and other dalits attempted to create a dalit identity to unite all oppressed castes, but this attempt failed as a result of the insufficient preparation for unity amongst the castes whose everyday lives remained in mutual conflict. The importance of the jati for the urban Balmikis may be explained by their intensified segregation into the sanitation trade and into the pockets of sweeper mohallas where they developed segregated solidarities, cultures and interests. Even though the various castes confronted each other as workers and Jamadars, as employees and employers, as consumers and merchants, as servants and masters, the Hindu and Muslim bourgeoisie lived in social isolation from the dalits. The silent decree of society left the dalits outside the mechanisms for cultural and social fusion with the emergent nation at the same time as the militant Hindus demanded that the Balmikis conjoin themselves politically into the Hindu community (and ideologically, from a distance). For these reasons, the level of corporate caste remained

[124]DSA, CC (Local Self-Government), 1941, File no. 1 (100) and DSA, CC (L.S.G.), B Progs., 1944, no. 1 (95); Madan Lal Parcha and Prem Prakash Ujjainwal, Nabi Karim, 24 February 1993.

important and it was the main avenue through which the Chuhras acted in the militant Hindu movement (now as Balmikis). The resilience of the corporate jati kept alive certain oppositional traditions, such as union militancy and the anti-Hindu customs, even if these only appear fleetingly. Since caste oppression is a real phenomenon, the struggle against it cannot deny its existence at the point of organization. The Balmikis, whatever their tactical sacrifices (in light of the militant Hindu intervention), continue to be sustained by the vitality of the social contradictions which oppress them.

5

Harijans

In 1930, M.K. Gandhi began to refer to the dalits as 'Harijans', meaning children of god. Many dalits remained puzzled by the name, since it singled them out for a divine lineage, whilst the rest of the population were not invested with the priviledge of such Gandhian nomenclature. When the dalits came in for special mention 'did it not merely mean that attempts were being made to make their conditions tolerable rather than destroy the system which bred inequality?'[1] In 1946, when Gandhi lived amongst the sweepers of Delhi for a few months, he referred to them as 'Bhangis', using a word that the dalits generally disliked and for which he was criticized. At this juncture, Gandhi noted that 'it mattered little as to which of the current words was used for the same occupation. In spite of being considered the lowest occupation, it was in fact the highest inasmuch as it protected health and [the dalits] should be indifferent to the name'.[2] The question of the name, itself the start of the self-conscious Gandhian intervention into the lives of the dalits, was superceded by a drive to transform the perceptions of the dalits amongst other castes and to conduct minor reforms in the lives of the dalits. Gandhi's intervention in dalit politics began almost from the start of his leadership of the Indian National Congress in 1917, for he was a central character in the pact by which the Hindu militants claimed dalits as their domain. By the early 1930s, however, Gandhi took charge of dalitudhar himself and he controlled the dynamic that disallowed the sweepers' struggles to take a radical direction. Reform was central to the idiosyncratic Gandhian view of sweeper emancipation, so that freedom instead of being emancipation from the bondage of sweeping became a re-valuation of sweeping itself. That is, rather than remove the prejudice against sanitation and urge others to join the sanitary corps, the Gandhian solution, for the

---

[1]B.K. Roy Burman, 'The Problem', *Seminar*, no. 177 (May 1974), p. 10.
[2]*Harijan,* 12 May 1946.

most part, entailed a valorization of the dalits as sweepers, not now to be seen as the 'lowest occupation', but indeed as the 'highest'.[3]

THE CONUNDRUMS OF GANDHIANISM

Gandhi was very particular about the Order of Varnas (*Varnashrama-dharma* or *Chaturvarna*), for, he wrote, 'caste has a close connection with the profession of one's livelihood. Everyone's profession is his own "dharma". Whoever gives it up, falls from his caste, and is himself destroyed, that is, his soul is destroyed'.[4] This did not mean that he was wedded to the chauvinism and arrogance of the upholders of a dying order, such as the Sanathan Dharma Sabha, Sri Bharat Dharma Mahamandal and the All-India Varnashrama Swarajaya, all of which believed in the unbridled power of the Brahman over the rest of society and the creation of a society based on the vehemence of the *Manusmriti*.[5] For Gandhi, custom is historical because human history had not yet entered the realm of Truth (God/Humanity). Religious traditions and philosophies worked as guidebooks towards a free society. The struggle to produce or discover Truth meant that previous attempts must be studied and explored, but not worshipped as a fetish. The future, in his philosophy of history, was far more important than the past. For that reason Gandhi categorically denounced all those attempts to find the origin of untouchability and especially to pin the blame for it on the Muslims.[6] Gandhian intervention in the lives of the dalits, did not correspond with the claims of Hindutva.

Gandhi's denunciations, however, came, in the main, after the militant Hindus had already made their forays into the dalit neighbourhoods and established a language of reform similar to that of the Gandhians who would follow them there. Until 1932, the militant Hindus worked in dalit neighbourhoods by agreement with Gandhi and outside his control. They did so under the aegis of their organizations (Dayananda

[3]B.R. Ambedkar, 'What Congress and Gandhi have done to the Untouchables [1946]', *Writings and Speeches* (Bombay: Government of Maharashtra, 1991), vol. 9, pp. 292–3.

[4]Sanjana, *Caste and Outcaste*, p. 26.

[5]Swami Chidananda Sannyasi, *Shuddhi Vyavasta* (Delhi: Bharatiya Hindu Shuddhi Sabha, 1928).

[6]*Navajivan*, 18 May 1924 (*CWMG*, vol. 24, p. 40), *Navajivan*, 29 June 1924 (*CWMG*, vol. 24, p. 321), *Young India*, 5 February 1925 (*CWMG*, vol. 24, p. 73) and *Yervada Mandir* (Ahmedabad: Navajivan, 1945), ch. 9.

Dalitudhar Sabha, the Shraddhananda Dalitudhar Sabha and the Punjab Achutuddhar Mandal). Between the 1910s and 1932, Gandhi was engaged in guiding the nationalist movement through its valiant years.

Gandhi in Harijan Colony, 1946 (Courtesy: Nehru Memorial Museum and Library)

The Salt March and the First Civil Disobedience struggle (1930–1) culminated in the staged legalism of the Round Table Conferences and the Gandhi–Irwin Pact. These agreements were far short of the peasantry's radical no-rent, no-tax demands which tried to push the Congress during the campaign. In 1932, Gandhi initiated the formation of the Harijan Sevak Sangh to work intensively among the dalits, to bring them to Hinduism under the rule of the Congress. Gandhi, in 1933, sounded the call to Thakkar, a call which demanded the continuation of older policies, but now under the control of Gandhians. 'Propaganda we must have, and plenty of it, both among Harijans and caste men. But we have to make the propaganda practically self-supporting, especially among caste men. In my opinion, the best propaganda is constructive work among Harijans'.[7] In a meeting with Hindu youth, Gandhi told them that 'the best propaganda is that of personal example. Let every Harijan sevak lead a model life of purity and simplicity, clothe the Harijan with love, and I am quite sure no counter-propaganda will be necessary'.[8] Gandhi's fast in 1932, the founding of the Harijan Sevak Sangh, the publication of *Harijan* and his Harijan tour of 1933–4 drew the issue of untouchability into the nationalist mainstream. Previously local movements, whether dalit or Arya Samaji, now gained a wider audience even though this audience never really came to terms with the earlier history of dalitudhar conducted by militant Hindus (many of whom now worked under Gandhi's flag). Even G.D. Birla, in 1934, told the press that the problem of untouchability 'is no more one of platform resolutions', a denial of the decade long work by militant Hindus who set the terrain for the Gandhians.[9] D.D. Kosambi, in 1939, accused Gandhi of launching the Harijan movement 'for the dissipation of the excess of energy available' in the latter half of the First and in the Second Civil Disobedience Movements (1932–4).[10] If this judgment is a bit harsh, without a doubt Gandhi was in no position to launch a radical movement against untouchability given his need to reassert control over the national movement in the early 1930s as well as to prevent the revolutionary drive from turning on the wealthy. With these political limitations, the Gandhians of the 1930s followed the conservative reformation of the 1920s which stressed the transformation of the attitude and behaviour of the Hindus towards the dalits. Since it was sought to transform the attitudes of the Hindus, the Harijan Sevak Sangh only took them as members and

---

[7]Gandhi to Thakkar, 19 March 1933, Gandhi–Thakkar Correspondence, Gandhi Memorial Museum, Delhi.

[8]*Harijan*, 4 April 1936.

[9]*Hindustan Times*, 28 June 1934.

[10]D.D. Kosambi, 'The Function of Leadership in a Mass Movement (1939)', *Exasperating Essays* (New Delhi: People's Publishing House, 1992), pp. 7–8.

asked them to go amongst their dalit'brethren' and help them with their trials. Many of the dilemmas of Hindu militancy came into the practical work of the Harijan Sevak Sangh. One such element is the problem of *Bhangi Mukti* (Emancipate Sweepers).

Modern Indian society, Hindu militancy argued, needed to be refurbished by the ancient system Varnashramadharma, with Brahmins, Kshatriyas, Vaishyas and Sudras adopting their inherited roles without the taint of hierarchy and untouchability. 'Neither birth nor right was the ground for anyone to be called a Brahmin or a Kshatriya or a Vaishya or a Sudra', Swami Sundarananda wrote in 1922, 'but conduct was the only criterion' for people to find their positions in the realm of social production.[11] The caste-collectivist position argues that people develop their skills within family and kin networks and they are able to pursue these skills (whether learned or inherited) through their monopoly or, at least, their right to exercise those skills. While the individualist position appears to be radically different, it too is forced to argue that while individuals may develop their skills through their individual inclinations, the individuals are only able to learn or develop these skills in family and educational networks. The real difference between these positions lies in their explanation of how a society is able to organize itself so that all occupations are staffed. The individualists hold that the market (like god) produces an optimum society (but if this is so, then individual inclinations are not the basis for one's task, but the market is that basis) and the caste-collectivists hold that a divine hand produces optimality. There is an unresolved contradiction in both approaches, between the principle of an individual's choice of occupation and society's ability to achieve an optimum workforce. The approach that privileges equality is often caricatured as the civil libertarian idea that all people must be the same (and not struggle to build a complex, yet equal society). Without an interrogation of the problem of equality and labour and the question of structural change to realize equality, the caste-collectivist thinkers simply call upon those in positions of privilege to treat the oppressed better. 'Fundamental rights have been snatched away from [the dalits] for the accident of their birth and for undertaking professions which, although essential for the maintenance of society, are looked down upon from the social point of

---

[11]Swami Sundarananda, *Hinduism and Untouchability* (Delhi: Harijan Sevak Sangh, 1945), p. 25.

view'.[12] Instead of treating the complex of essential labour and fundamental rights, Swami Sundrananda asks Hindus not to look down upon the dalits. From a radical slogan, Bhangi Mukti, the militant Hindus and Gandhians adopted the reformist slogan, *Bhangi Ksht Mukti* (Improve the Conditions of Sweeping). The militant Hindus and Gandhians condemned untouchability, but they were not prepared to abolish the basis of untouchability, the relationship of dalits to menial labour (the notions of purity and impurity, the DMC's practice of recruitment for menial jobs, the privation of most dalits, as Hocart suggested, due to hereditary vassalage).[13] In general, as we will see in detail below, the Gandhians and the militant Hindus did not argue for emancipation *from* dalithood, but for reform *within* dalithood. Some political figures did call for the abolishment of the ground of untouchability, leaders within the communist movement such as M.N. Roy and others such as Ambedkar, but the organizational weakness of the Left movement at this time meant that Gandhian reform held the day.[14]

How was the sweeper to be emancipated? The technocrats put their faith in the water-flush latrine, but this was not to be. Vinoba Bhave, Gandhi's closest disciple, argued, after Gandhi's death, that 'the only possible reform in this profession would be to eradicate it altogether', to emancipate the sweeper by the abolition of sweeping. The people who sweep, he noted, echoing Ambedkar and Jagjivan Ram, must be given land for cultivation and the opportunity to lead a prosperous life.[15] Bhave held that everyone should do some sweeping each day as a spiritual endeavour, for, as Vallabswami wrote, 'it is time for the liberation of the Bhangi. In truth, if every person becomes his or her own Bhangi, that will be the ideal'.[16] Each morning, let every person rise and 'worship the filth' by appreciating the work that it takes to cleanse the world in the 'correct manner'.[17] Saints, such as Gandhi, we are told, cleaned toilets to 'weaken [their] ego and to acquire humility'.[18] This

[12]Sundarananda, *Hinduism*, p. 85.

[13]A.M. Hocart, *Caste: A Comparative Study* (London: Methuen, 1950).

[14]Vijay Prashad, 'Between Economism and Emancipation: Untouchables and Indian Nationalism, 1920–1950', *Left History*, vol. 3, no. 1 (Spring/Summer 1995).

[15]*Harijan*, 22 January 1955.

[16]Vallabswami, *Safai*, p. 34.

[17]Ibid., p. 32.

[18]Vinoba Bhave, *Shanti Yatra* (New Delhi: Sastra Sahitya Mandal, 1950), p.

form of emancipation is extremely personal, for it still does not offer a solution for urban sanitary functions, for Bhave too recognized that while he was able to do the work in a village, he 'doubted if he could do it in a city. The gutters and latrines and the filth of cities was unbearable'.[19] The failure to conceptualize liberation in terms of the city was a consequence of Gandhian socialism's accordance of theoretical priority to the rural and its valorization of the peasant. In urban areas, the Gandhians realized that refuse removal on a grand scale was inevitable, so that they provided some strategies towards the amelioration of sanitary services (Bhangi Ksht Mukti) rather than to abolish a professional sanitation workforce. The emancipation of the sweeper (Bhangi Mukti) was compromised.

Two other approaches of the Gandhians merit discussion. Those dalits who have historically been sweepers must not be allowed to continue this occupation and others must be encouraged to do the work and second, that the conditions for sweeping be improved so that Hindu prejudices against refuse removal may be eliminated.[20] Both of these approaches turn to theories of untouchability amongst Hindu reformers of the fin-de-siecle. These reformers, including Gandhi, utilized the findings of modern science to validate the argument that dirt is bad for health and so, people who encounter dirt should be shunned until they have cleaned themselves. 'If such a Bhangi has been engaged in sanitary work', Gandhi wrote, 'to take a bath (after contact with him) is simple hygiene and is absolutely necessary, but failure to do so does not threaten one with spiritual ruin. There can be no sin in refusing to touch a Bhangi when the occasion requires us to do so. It is sinful not to welcome a Bhangi, who has bathed himself, to take a seat by our side, and it is ignorance to believe that his touch will pollute us'.[21] Dalits are unclean when they do dirty work, but they should not be seen as inherently dirty. The logic being that dirty tasks are dirty because they cause contact with bodily emissions or organic life such as saliva, semen, menstrual blood, faeces, urine, hair, or nail-clipping, so that

---

226. Bhave's social theory is available in his 1940 account, *Swaraj Shastra* (Wardha: Sarva Sewa Sangh, 1955). One must always keep in mind that this is the same man who supported the Emergency and called it an *Anushasan Parva* (an Era of Discipline).

[19]*Harijan*, 5 December 1948.

[20]*Harijan*, 10 May 1942.

[21]*Navajivan*, 17 July 1921.

barbers, sweepers, skinners and others carry the stigmata of occupational pollution. All people are polluted in an episodic fashion, such as when we go to the toilet or else when women are menstruating.[22] While a few Hindu reformers held on to the idea that the dirt removed by the dalits determines their social status (that is, they are infected by occupational pollution), the bulk of the reformers argued that ablutions can erase the mark of the dirt (that is, of episodic pollution).[23] From the 1920s onwards, the dalit's contact with dirt was seen as less of a mark of permanent pollution than a transgression of social norms or a mythical fault or error.[24] Dumont makes the rather functionalist argument that those 'who are most oppressed materially are at the same time seen as supremely impure'.[25] Such an attitude to the question of untouchability neglects the historical shifts in attitudes produced by such movements as Gandhianism. Untouchability is not one thing or another thing, neither merely economic nor merely religious, but it is certainly a political phenomenon that is fought over by various social actors along the axes of the economic and the ritual. Therefore, Gandhi argued, all people can do sanitation work, since the work itself does not determine one's purity. Neither the state nor militant Hindus nor indeed Gandhi, however, counternanced an early withdrawal of dalits from refuse jobs. In December 1932, Appa Pathwardhan conducted a satyagraha in Ratnagiri Jail when he was informed by the prison authorities that prisoners of only certain castes (dalits) can do sanitary work. In a sympathetic pamphlet, *Turungantil Bhagikam* ('Bhangi Work in Jail'), a group of released prisoners recognized that the authorities responded to the prejudices of the Hindu prisoners, but they also noted that 'government, however, cannot avoid the responsibility for the support in the shape of force they have lent for their own convenience'.[26] The state followed what it felt was the bigotry of the people, but it was challeng-

[22]Satish Saberwal, *Mobile Men: Limits to Social Change in Urban Punjab* (Delhi: Manohar, 1990), pp. 201–2.

[23]N.R. Malkani, *Clean People and an Unclean Country* (Ahmedabad: Navajivan, 1965), p. 87.

[24]Shalini Randeria, 'Carrion and Corpses: Conflict in Categorizing Untouchabiliity in Gujarat', *Archives-Europeennes-de-Sociologie*, vol. 30 (1989), p. 172 and Robert Deliége, 'Replication and Consensus: Untouchability, Caste and Ideology in India', *Man*, vol. 27 (1992), p. 170.

[25]Louis Dumont, *Homo Hierarchicus: The Caste System and Its Implications* (Chicago: University of Chicago, 1970), p. 137.

[26]NAI, Home (Political), 1932, no. 31/108/32.

ed only by such visionaries as Patwardhan, certainly not by Gandhi.

While Gandhi did take a remarkable position against the notion of permanent pollution, he did not wish to do so at the expense of the Varnashramadharma which he held as sacrosanct.[27] Each varna, Gandhi felt, comes with certain qualities of social affections and skills and the tasks done by each varna are important, such that no task is given more value than another. 'If the qualities and tasks of each caste are recognized', he wrote in 1930, 'there is no undesirable competition or feeling of hatred among them'.[28] When asked why he supported the Order, Gandhi noted *usmein bara aaram hai* (there is great peace in it), to know, for instance, one's vocation and not to be flustered on this score in one's youth.[29] These inherited tasks ('callings') are to be followed by one with enthusiasm regardless of the task and certainly without any consideration for the tasks of others. 'Do your alloted duty', Gandhi wrote, 'restraining the organs of sense, for that is better than inaction'. Further, do this duty (prescribed by one's varna) with a 'spirit of sacrifice' for 'life is given us for service and not for enjoyment'.[30] 'The law of varna teaches us that we have each one of us to earn our bread by following the ancestral calling', he wrote in 1936, 'it defines not our rights, but our duties'.[31] Gandhi's reconstructed Order of Varnas tried to do away with hierarchy not as a fully-developed sociology (with, for example, a legal principle of equality), but through an appeal to the good faith of all people. Further, Gandhi's reconstruction placed duty at its centre, thereby undermining any possibility of social mobility for the dalits. 'A Bhangi', Gandhi wrote, 'constitutes the foundation of all services'.[32] 'A Bhangi does for society what a mother does for her baby. A mother washes her baby of the dirt and insures his health. Even so the Bhangi protects and safeguards the health of the entire community by maintaining sanitation for it'.[33] The connection between a mother and her baby is not accidental, since it reveals the gendered

[27]M.K. Gandhi, *Discourses on the Gita* (Ahmedabad: Navajivan, 1987), p. 22.

[28]Gandhi, *Discourses*, p. 69.

[29]Santram, Oral History Transcripts no. 238, NMML.

[30]Gandhi, *Discourses*, pp. 15–16 and p. 20.

[31]*Harijan*, 18 July 1936 (*CWMG*, vol. 63, p. 153).

[32]M.K. Gandhi, 'The Ideal Bhangi', *Harijan*, 28 November 1936 (*CWMG*, vol. 64, pp. 86–8).

[33]Ibid.

assumption that some people have duties whilst others have rights. The construction of the New Woman of Indian nationalism, in opposition to the Western Woman and the Common Woman, is along the lines of a helpmate (*sahadharmini*), a pre-political woman who has a duty to perform, but who is not constitutive of the process itself.[34] Such a position pronounces civic death for women and dalits who are relegated to a domain of duties and whose claim to rights is essentially revoked. Damned to eternal quiescence, manual labourers (women and dalits) are asked to trust in the good faith of their overlords, their Hindu male friends who would demand better treatment for them from the colonial state.[35]

Hindus, Gandhi argued, mistake the dalit's diligence for their inherent meniality, an act of bad-faith since it is the bulk of society that relies upon the dalit for the removal of dirt. 'Our woebegone Indian society has branded the Bhangi as a social pariah', he wrote, 'set him down at the bottom of the scale, held him fit only to receive kicks and abuse, a creature who must subsist on the leavings of the caste-people and dwell on the dung-heap'.[36] The Hindu must, in the first place, acknowledge the work being done by the sweeper and offer the sweeper some measure of compassion for the work. Dalits 'should be called artists, who when they look at dirt cannot rest without cleaning it' and Hindus must learn to applaud them, not revile them.[37] To transform the Hindu's view of the sweeper, the very idea of cleanliness needed to be changed from an inherent notion to a spatial notion. 'The meaning of cleanliness is place [*sthan*]', wrote Vallabswami. 'Things must be put in their proper place'.[38] If refuse removal was simply seen as the mundane act of moving things from one place to another then perhaps the social taboo against it might be diminished. But Gandhi was just not interested in a transformation in the culture of the Hindus, for he felt that the dalits themselves engaged in practices that earned them the approbation of the Hindus, such 'bad and filthy habits to which they may be addicted' as 'beef carrion and liquor'. He urged

[34]Suruchi Thapar, 'Women as activists, women as symbols: a study of the Indian Nationalist Movement', *Feminist Review*, vol. 44 (Summer 1993).

[35]*CWMG*, vol. 63, p. 153 and Vallabswami, *Safai*, p. 32.

[36]Gandhi, 'The Ideal Bhangi'.

[37]Vallabswami, *Safai*, p. 6 and Ishwarbhai Patel, *Safai Marg-Darshika* (Delhi: Harijan Sevak Sangh, 1970).

[38]Vallabswami, *Safai*, pp. 3–4.

Hindus to make the dalits lead 'clean lives', an indication that dirt to Gandhi was not just organic, but also cultural.[39] Bhangis, then, are to be the sweepers, but as sweepers, they must be treated better. This improved treatment meant that the Hindus must not be ill-disposed towards the dalits and that the municipalities must provide the dalits with proper work conditions (these in order for the Hindus not to be made to feel repulsed by the dalits).

In general Bhangi Ksht Mukti drove the Harijan Sevak Sangh to fight for an improvement in the working conditions of the sweepers, on the basis of the theory that 'it is possible that the irrational and unscientific attitude towards night-soil may be really overcome by the rational and business-like organization of urban composting'.[40] The 1932 Constitution of the Harijan Sevak Sangh urged municipalities such as the DMC to provide 'special facilities to scavengers calculated to make their conditions of work cleaner and easier', such as running water to wash their bodies, sturdy implements and clean clothes.[41] The 'Bhangi is filthy because he carries our filth', wrote Malkani, so it is the duty of the Hindu to struggle on behalf of the dalits to make the municipality create a clean work environment.[42] 'All scavenging should really be done without soiling the hands or any part of the body', a Congressman wrote in a letter to *Harijan*, and if it is done in this manner, 'the work would assume a dignity which it does not carry at the moment'. Gandhi responded to this by advocating 'bye-laws requiring authorized receptacles, brooms, etc., which would avoid physical handling of dirt and would also prescribe simple working costume'.[43] The DMC was already particular about the dalaos, but this had not changed the way Hindus viewed dalits. On the issue of implements, Gandhi correctly noted the horrid state of affairs for sweepers, since many used mudguards from bicycles, small brooms, broken vessels and leaky head baskets. Faeces pans and wheelbarrows

[39]*Navajivan*, 17 July 1921 (*CWMG*, vol. 21, pp. 1–2); *Harijan*, 11 February 1933 and 6 October 1946; *Annual Report Harijan Sevak Sangh* (1932–3), p. 10; Mahmood Ali Kamlesh, *Suryodya arthat Achutuddhar* (Delhi: Harijan Sevak Sangh, 1935).

[40]Malkani, *Clean People*, p. 72.

[41]*Constitution of the Harijan Sevak Sangh*, pp. 18–23.

[42]N.R. Malkani, 'A Hereditary Proletariat', *Interdiscipline*, vol. 7 (Winter 1970) and Sundarananda, *Hinduism and Untouchability*, pp. 143–4.

[43]*Harijan*, 6 October 1946.

enabled sweepers to cease the carriage of nightsoil in leaky head-baskets.[44] At the Gandhian ashrams, earnest workers developed brooms that did not call for excessive and prolonged bending by the dalits (the real development of the broom awaited Eleanor Roosevelt's visit to India when she recommended the long broom). The issue of the broom reveals the way in which the Gandhians remained at the level of what was already a well-known fetish of mehtardom. In Punjab, for instance, the Mehtars perforce carried their brooms in full-view as they walked down the public street, so that Hindus particular about their prejudices might duck away to avoid the onrush of what they saw as impurity.[45] If the housebroom was considered sacred by Hindus, the sweepers' broom was a reviled instrument except during an illness when others asked Mehtars to cure their child by the sway of the broom.[46] And for the Mehtars of Punjab, the broom entered their *kursinamas* as an instrument of power, 'sweeping with the broom cleans the heart'.[47] The fact that the broom was a sacred and powerful instrument in the lives of the Mehtars meant that the Gandhian activities to produce a better broom must have received some sympathetic treatment from the dalits. On the other hand, as a symbol of the sweeper, the broom was also a reminder of their bondage to this occupation. Instead of surrendering every atom of freedom, the Mehtars took pride in their new occupation and its historic implements to fashion some dignity for themselves (this despite the fact that the stain of the occupation was on such things as their broom).

Apart from the broom, the Gandhians spent much time on the reform of the toilet. The most common toilet in the 1930s was the *sandas* (pit-latrine) toilet which required the sweeper to visit it each morning and physically remove the nightsoil (collected in a basket or else splattered on the floor). The dry earth or ash thrown on the nightsoil was only able to delay the meeting of flies and it did not adequately cut the smell. 'Whosoever devised this type of latrine devised it so as to make it a place of filth and stink—an evil necessity in the house', commented Malkani. 'He also literally made scavenging so filthy that

[44]Patel, *Safai Marg-Darshika*, pp. 103–18.

[45]L.S.S. O'Malley, *Indian Caste Customs* (London: Curzon Press reprint, 1974), p. 145.

[46]Russell and Hira, *Tribes and Castes*, vol. 4, p. 229.

[47]Temple, *The Legends*, vol. 1, p. 533.

the scavenger became identified with filth'.[48] At both the Gandhi Museum and the offices of the Harijan Sevak Sangh in Delhi, there are remarkable exhibits which honour the Gandhian focus on the toilet. Imbedded in a dias about two feet off the ground are a series of toilets designed by prominent Gandhians and others (such as Appa Patwardhan's Gopuri latrine, Dr Kessel's water-closet, the farmer's latrine and the Janata Sandas). In 1963, in Sabarmati Ashram at Ahmedabad, Ishwarbhai Patel and others founded the Safai Vidyalaya to continue research on latrines and sewage systems. These toilets, however, remained useful only in rural areas, unable as they are to deal with the volume of urban refuse and the density of urban habitations.[49] The reconstructed Varnasharamadharma was silent on the city, for the theory of reciprocity could not recast the urban landscape or deal with the prevalence of wage labour.[50] Rather than experiment with sewage systems themselves, the Gandhians tried to produce adequate septic tanks, but these were expensive and required vast amounts of water. On the basis of the Gandhian research, Bindeswar Pathak devised the Sulabh Shauchalaya, the easy toilet that is being used in many Indian cities. Pathak's toilet is set on a layer of soft earth 'so that the water [from the refuse] leaches out and helps easy decomposition and transformation of the excreta into organic manure', a residue that can be removed with only fear of temporary pollution.[51] The Sulabh scheme shows us the importance of public toilets in India, but it does not address the problem of dalit liberation, since Pathak hires only dalits to clean his facilities.[52]

The Gandhians could not but address two other aspects of reform for the dalits, the offer of credit and education. On the former, the dalits recognized the importance of wealth as emancipation from their form of bondage, since some wealth might allow them to buy themselves different histories and power (an example many took from the biogra-

[48]Malkani, *Ramblings*, p. 28.

[49]Vallabswami, *Safai*, p. 66.

[50]The career of Vinoba Bhave is exemplary in this, for in 1950, he began a movement against the money economy (*Kanchan Mukti*), but three years later all he could do was ask people to donate their labour (*Shramdan*) and land (*Bhoodan*) as acts of rural charity rather than socio-economic reconstruction.

[51]Pathak, *Road to Freedom*, p. 54 and *Sulabh Shauchalaya* (Patna: Sulabh, 1981).

[52]Discussions with Sulabh workers, Palam Gaon, Delhi, 1993.

phy of the Chamars). Capital, however, was not available to the dalits in any measure, but the Harijan Sevak Sangh did provide credit for special schemes (such as animal husbandry) that did not wrest the dalits from the imputation of untouchability. Moneylenders and Jamadars offered the sweepers loans, but these could not do more than further entrap the sweepers. Certain well-meaning people, such as Devkinandan Singh, formed schemes to offer loans for the sweepers, but such programmes (Co-operative Credit and Thrift Society of Delhi, 1931) shifted the savings of one sweeper to another who would use the money to cover debts incurred from moneylenders.[53]

Education seemed to be a far more possible means to freedom for dalits and the sweepers fought hard to ensure the schooling of their children. In 1936, the Mehtars' Labour Union of Delhi resolved that 'notwithstanding that several Municipal Committees have passed resolutions for compulsory education, they are not properly acted upon and the education of the children of the depressed classes and particularly of the sweepers' community is not properly looked after'.[54] Gokhale introduced a resolution in the central legislature on education for dalits in 1911, but that was voted down. In quick succession, the government struck down three similiar resolutions—Dadabhoy (1916), Sarma (1918) and Jayakar (1928). In 1916, the Chief Commissioner of Delhi noted that 'I will cause inquiries to be made into the need for the possibility of providing a school within the city itself purely for sweeper children'. The inquiry did not proceed, since the official stated that 'it seems not unreasonable to leave [the sweepers] to work out [their] future by [their] own resources and by such facilities as private enterprise is prepared to extend to [them]'.[55] The only private enterprise at work amongst the dalits were the missionaries whose small schools allowed the DMC to remain disinterested in education for the dalits. Rather than address the problems of dalits who did enter the government schools, the DMC was happy to report that 'it is not an uncommon sight now to see in our schools even sweeper boys rubbing shoulder to shoulder with high caste Hindu boys and the prejudice which was noticeable five years ago against the admittance of boys of depressed classes to our schools has entirely died down'.[56] Dalit elders,

[53]N.R. Malkani, 'A Promising Experiment', *Harijan*, 9 September 1933.
[54]DSA, CC (Education), B Progs., 1936, no. 3 (89).
[55]DSA, CC (Education), B Progs., 1916, no. 169.
[56]DSA, CC (Education), DC Papers, 1931, no. 32.

however, remember these schools as battlefields against Hindu teachers (who beat the dalits students and made them sit outside the classrooms) and bigoted students (who chided the dalits and derided their poverty).[57] Gandhi's notes to teachers of dalits shows some signs of the attitude held by Hindu teachers towards their dalit charges. 'Preliminary training should consist in teaching Harijan children manners, good speech and good conduct. A Harijan child sits anyhow; dresses anyhow; his eyes, ears, teeth, hair, nails, nose are often full of dirt; many never know what it is to have a wash'.[58] With such a vision of dalit children, it should not surprise us to see many teachers make the classroom an inhospitable and derisive space. The oppression of the dalits led to high withdrawal rates, with seventy per cent of boys and ninety-five per cent of the girls leaving school after class 1 and with about fifty per cent of the bulk of the students leaving the next year. By 1939, only six boys and twenty-seven girls reached class 10.[59] Much of the drop-out can be attributed to the parents' need to draw income from the labour power of the children, but there is little doubt from the stories that I heard that the hostility of the classroom did not make the school a space for liberation. That more dalit girls remained in school may have something to do with their ability to negotiate the smaller classrooms, the liberality of the girls in school (for they would have to come from liberal homes to get to school in the first place) and the differential role gender plays in the dalit communities (where success is applauded, despite gender oppression).[60] The Gandhians recognized the importance of education among the dalits, so that they entered the domain, but only to promote vocational study. In 1933, the Harijan Sevak Sangh started a dalit school at its headquarters to teach the dalits crafts so that they might 'refuse to follow the profession of their forefathers'.[61] The children learnt weaving, spinning and other arts

[57]Madan Lal Saugwan, Kalan Masjid, 28 March 1993; O.P. Shukla and O.P. Chauhan, Balmiki Colony, New Delhi, 21 March 1993.

[58]*Harijan*, 18 May 1935.

[59]*Annual Report on the Progress of Education in the Delhi Province* (Delhi, 1936 onwards).

[60]William Houska, 'The Characteristics of Son Preference in an Urban Scheduled Caste Community', *Eastern Anthropologist,* no. 34 (January–March 1981).

[61]Mukt Behari Verma, *History of the Harijan Sevak Sangh,* 1932–68 (Delhi: Harijan Sevak Sangh, 1971), p. x.

whose economic value was minimal in an age of industrial production. 'It is not the intention of the [Harijan Industrial] home to give the Harijan home boarders higher education', G.D. Birla informed Thakkar Bapa in 1934. 'The Sangh has no desire to produce an army of unemployed. Therefore, only such education will be imparted to the students as to make them fit to earn their livelihood as honourable members of Hindu society'.[62] The Harijan home, a characteristic Gandhian intervention into the lives of the dalits, opened in December 1934 with a concentration on leatherwork, carpentry and wickerwork.[63]

'We cannot check the flood or save these people by some of us carrying water away in a bucket', Jawaharlal Nehru wrote as a critique of the Gandhian approach to the dalits.[64] The dalit demand for capital was translated into loans for consumption and their quest for education was reduced to vocational training in anachronistic arts. In 1932, when Gandhi sent some clothes to a dalit locality, the dalits returned the gifts and told Gandhi that 'if you want to give us clothes, then give it for our entire lives. What kind of *tamasha* [circus] is this? With these few pyjamas what will we do? If you want to do economic reform for us, then do it properly'.[65] The mere tokenism of the reforms frustrated many dalits, but for many other dalits the demands of survival drew them to take the crumbs offered. The desperation of the dalits enabled the Gandhians and their merchant partners to offer meagre reforms to their lives. In 1936, G.D. Birla told his fellow businessmen that 'our duty does not end in simply opposing socialism. Businessmen have to do something positive to ameliorate the condition of the masses'.[66] That same year, Jayaprakash Narayan warned the Indian Left that Gandhianism is simply reformism, 'its language is Indian but its substance is international' and 'reformism is interested not in securing social justice,

[62]Delhi CID SB (noncurrent) records, 3rd Installment, no. 25, NMML and *Harijan*, 6 July 1934.

[63]*Hindustan Times*, 15 December 1934.

[64]Jawaharlal Nehru, *An Autobiography* (London: Bodley Head, 1936), pp. 588–90.

[65]Mohan Lal, Oral History Transcripts no. 208, NMML.

[66]Aditya Mukherjee, 'The Indian Capitalist Class: Aspects of the Economic, Political and Ideological Development in the Colonial Period, 1927–47', *Situating Indian History*, p. 262. Birla urged businessmen to do this work 'not as exploiters but as servants of society' to undercut the communists. *Young India*, 19 December 1929.

but in covering up the ugly fissures of society'.[67] One Gandhian, Rameshwari Nehru came to the heart of the matter, when she noted that 'as long as the sweepers live in their present surroundings, no work can be done amongst them by any reformist organization. It is no use trying to teach them to be clean or to keep their children clean when they are forced to live in the filth from which they cannot get away'.[68] The wretchedness of the sweepers has little to do with their will, since Nehru was surprised to see that 'in spite of the nauseating atmosphere, they manage to live such healthy lives. For the interior of their houses are clean and I even noticed an attempt made by certain inmates at beautifying the surroundings by rearing a few flower plants in the pots. How they have the heart to do it and how they manage to keep up their spirits is difficult to understand. They undoubtedly try to make the best of their surroundings'. For Nehru, the social actors who lacked the will to emancipate the dalits included the rais and the DMC, for 'if money can be found for parks and gardens and roads and lighting and a hundred other things, it can easily be found for bettering the living conditions of the sweepers'. The problem, in other words, was not scarce resources, but of resource allocation.

If the Left Gandhians attacked the government for its recalcitrance on the question of dalit liberation, Ambedkar was forthright in his attack on the Gandhians for their inability to allow the dalits any space for independent political initiative. The Gandhians, he noted, have 'collected a swarm of grateful Untouchables who are employed to preach that Mr Gandhi and the Hindus are the saviours of the Untouchables'. The efforts of the Harijan Sevak Sangh, Ambedkar argued, created 'a slave mentality among the Untouchables' and it killed 'the spirit of independence from among the Untouchables'. Under the 'pretense of service' and by its 'petty services', the Harijan Sevak Sangh made many dalits into 'mere recepients of charity'.[69] Congress patronage was widespread, but it came in small doses, so that when G.D. Birla offered some seats to dalits on the Raghumal Charity Trust (Delhi) 'there was such a rush on the part of the members of the depressed classes to get on board' and the businessman was allowed to be magnanimous in his nomination from among the

[67]Jayaprakash Narayan, 'Why Socialism?' *A Revolutionary's Quest.* (Delhi: Oxford University Press, 1980), p. 39.

[68]Rameshwari Nehru, 'Harijan Bastis in Delhi', *Harijan*, 24 April 1937.

[69]Ambedkar, 'What Congress and Gandhi', pp. 266–7 and p. 251.

desperate many.[70] 'The price of the Bhangi is defeat', sang Bhim Pahalwan, 'simple promises are broken'.[71] The dalits, in other words, are easily purchased, an act that itself spells the doom of the community. In 1935, R.R. Bhole, a dalit labour activist who was a Gandhian stalwart, broke with Gandhi because he felt that the Harijan Sevak Sangh did not allow dalits to 'retain independence of action', an immeasurable pedagogical exercise.[72] 'There are no elders here', one young dalit man said to me in 1993, 'only old people'. The elders who should earn one's respect are uneducated and desperate for the crumbs of their municipal patrons; the educated old people are so corrupt that they cannot be respected.[73] Instead of political power, the sweepers thrived on patronage and other flotsam from their Gandhian heritage.

REVOLTING LABOUR

'The sweepers had just struck', E.M. Forester wrote, 'and half the commodes of Chandrapore remained desolate in consequence'.[74] When the sweepers went on strike more than half the commodes felt neglect, for no one would take their place without fear of retribution. The Mehtars enforced their control over localities through informal and formal organizations and evidence from eastern UP shows us that they even had a *panchayat* to protect their rights.[75] In the Punjab region there is no evidence of the panchayat as a central institution in the dalits' lives, but by the 1910s there is some evidence for the formation of caste organizations. At the Dussehra festivities in Jalandhar in 1910, a Chuhra organization known as the Valmiki Samaj opened a sweet shop that announced, 'Let it be known to the *High-Born* that Hindus and Mussalmans are prohibited to buy sweets here. Chuhras and all others are welcome'.[76] Such militancy was to be given full rein in the

---

[70]G.D. Birla, *In the Shadow of the Mahatma* (Bombay: Vakils, Feffer & Simons, 1953), pp. 74–5.

[71]Bhim Pahalwan, Pahargunj, New Delhi, 20 March 1993.

[72]R.R. Bhole, 29 July 1936, R.R. Bhole Papers, NMML.

[73]Rakesh Milind, Balmiki Colony, New Delhi, 5 June 1993.

[74]E.M. Forester, *A Passage to India* (Harmondsworth: Penguin, 1961), p. 209.

[75]Greeven, *The Knights* and E.A. Blunt, *The Caste System of Northern India* (Oxford: Oxford University Press, 1931), pp. 110–4.

[76]J.N. Farquhar, *Modern Religious Movements in India* (New York: YMCA, 1915), pp. 369–70.

labour unions that the sweepers formed (variously called Mehtars Unions, Safai Mazdur Unions and Sweepers Unions). In the late 1920s, the sweepers moved from the guild form of protection to form unions, mostly drawing inspiration from their friends in the working-class who inaugurated the modern labour movement in India.[77] The authorities did not take these unions seriously, for their archives mention them only fleetingly and the officials did not care to make a note of their demands. But the veteran unionists retain the memory for these organizations and they tell us that the unions fought for workplace issues (permanency, wages) and for neighbourhood issues (schools, houses, recreation, familial relationships, such as their segregation, the alcoholism among the men, the poor quality of the teachers).[78] These unions posed an antagonistic challenge to society.

By the 1930s, the language of class emerged on the Indian political landscape and this was to make some difference to the sweeper unions. In 1931, the Congress Socialist Party declared that it would fight for 'the establishment of a new economic order in which the worker will be entitled to the full reward for his labour and there will be no exploitation of one class by another' and the Communist Party of India urged all workers to join its ranks to fight 'for the complete abolition of slavery, the caste system and inequality in all forms (social, cultural, etc.)'.[79] Drawn by these currents, Ambedkar formed the Independent Labour Party in 1936 to 'advance the welfare of the labouring classes', to draw links between dalit struggles and the struggles of the rest of the working-class.[80] In 1926, the communists and socialists organized the sweepers' union and forged a strike in Batala (Punjab). Drawing from the Calcutta sweepers strike in 1928 (at which communists such as Muzaffar Ahmed played a role), the Punjab sweepers formed the Safai Mazdur Sangh (SMS) the following year. The leaders of this union included communists (Guramdas 'Alam'), Congressmen (O.P. Gill, Chunni Lal Thapar, Balmukund, Santram, Mohtan Singh) and socialists (Master Kabul Singh, Devi Krishan and Balbir Singh Chowdhury). The

---

[77]Vijay Prashad, 'Between Economism and Emancipation', pp. 6–9.

[78]Ratan Lal Balmiki, Balmiki Colony, New Delhi, 20 March 1993; Ram Krishen Bhajni, Qila Kadam Sharif, Delhi, 23–24 February 1994.

[79]*Leader*, 22 March 1931; Asim Kumar Chaudhuri, *Socialist Movement in India* (Calcutta: Progressive, 1980), p. 20; B.T. Ranadive, *Caste, Class and Property Relations* (Calcutta: National Book Agency, 1982), p. 7.

[80]Zelliot, 'Dr. Ambedkar ', pp. 246–9.

1937 sanitation workers' strike in Kabul was led by the communists and socialists (Alaf Din, Fazal Din, Joginder Lal Jain and Meher Chand Ahuja) and the sweepers' rising in the North-West Frontier under Abdurrahim Popalzai was strongly influenced by them.[81] It was because of these people that both the colonial state and pro-business elements within the Congress called upon the unions to 'weed out of its organization mischief makers' who go about 'preaching the gospel of strike' (in the 1929 words of a right-wing unionist).[82]

In June–July 1939, the Jalandhar municipality's sanitation workers (through the SMS) went out on strike. Processions and civil disobedience filled the streets and sweepers from surrounding areas visited the city to observe the struggle. Some men among the marchers struck themselves with blades, both to demonstrate their own physical strength and their durability to their overseers. Dalit neighbourhoods remained empty and, O.P. Gill remembers, people had to lock their homes for the first time in popular memory (as no neighbours remained to tend to the homes). As the garbage trucks left the depots, eight leaders, who came from among the rank and file, lay in front of the trucks. The police stood ready and the local Congress leaders came to plead with the dalit leaders. O.P. Gill is still a loyal Congressman, but he was as ready as his friends who remember those days, to say that it was the Congress who sold their struggles out for a pittance. The 'Gandhi of the Doab', Pandit Mull Raj, who was the president of the provincial Congress entered the negotiations without any authority from the sweepers. The municipality and such nationalists formed an arbitration committee, but its only recommendation was that the sweepers return to work. There was no attempt to break the sweepers by offering them a provisional hike in wages (often reduced after the strike by the arbitration body) and acceptance of other small demands, for the Congress and the municipality sought to crush the sweepers with a small wage rise and with the incorporation of the unions into the institutional framework of the municipality.[83] In other words, the union

[81]'Chunni Lal Thapar ka Ludhiana mein shraddhanjali', *Jago, Jagte Raho,* April 1978; K.L. Johar, *Unsung Torch Bearers. Punjab Congress Socialists in Freedom Struggle* (New Delhi: Harman, 1991), p. 66; Abduljalil Popalzai, *Achut, khakrob Mufti-yi Islam ki qiyadat mein* (Lahore: al-Mahmud Academy, 1994).

[82]B.T. Ranadive, *The Independence Struggle and After* (New Delhi: National Book Centre, 1988), p. 61.

[83]O.P. Gill, Rolu Ram and other veterans, Jalandhar, 3–6 April 1993.

was to be a municipal organ to discipline the workers as well as for the Congress to mobilize bodies rather than as an organ of class struggle.

In 1947, Mohinder Singh noted that the municipalities and the Congress 'would rather tolerate, nay sympathize with attempts to raise wages than go the whole hog and abolish caste distinctions'.[84] Indeed, the Harijan Sevak Sangh agreed that 'in the work of economic uplift, trade unions can play an important part', but not in other work.[85] The unions, further, were asked to make periodic requests to the municipalities rather than to organize workers towards a strike or any such action. The Harijan Sevak Sangh was particular that such organizations must 'compel local bodies' by entreaty to produce reforms 'conducive to the well-being of the community', but they must not allow the workers to strike.[86] Concern and outrage was the idiom for this activism, but not demonstrations and a withdrawal of labour power. In 1937, when the Congress took power in some provinces, a senior Gandhian pleaded that 'when industrial labour is crying for sickness, insurance and holidays with pay, the sweeper does not even get a few hours on Sunday off'. He begged the government to act on the sweepers' behalf, but he did not ask the sweepers to engage in a satyagraha against a recalcitrant government.[87]

The Gandhian fear of the epidemic of strikes emerges with clarity in the 1940s. In 1946, the sweepers of Bombay, Srinagar, Multan, Delhi, Lahore and a host of other towns put down their dustpans and brooms in anticipation of a better world. The sweepers' militancy disturbed Gandhi who noted that 'there are certain matters in which strikes would be wrong. Sweepers' grievances come in this category'. If sweepers did not do their work, the cities' refuse accumulated and bred disease, so that sweepers must be enjoined to work for health reasons. But beyond that, Gandhi noted that he was opposed to the 'coercive methods' (that is, strikes) employed by the sweepers, since 'coercion cannot but result in the end in chaos'. To undercut the sweepers, Gandhi urged city-dwellers and the military to 'learn the art of cleaning their own and the city's drains, so that if a similar occasion arises they are not nonplussed

[84]Mohinder Singh, *The Depressed Classes: Their Economic and Social Condition* (Bombay: Hind Kitab, 1947), p. 103.

[85]Jairamdas, *Bhangi Ksht Mukti*, p. 7.

[86]Harijan Sevak Sangh, *Annual Report* (Delhi: Harijan Sevak Sangh, 1936–7), p. 16.

[87]Thakkar, 'Plight of the Sweepers'.

and can render the necessary temporary services'. That is, non-dalits must know how to do sanitation work for emergencies ('a similiar occasion'), but in all other times the dalits must do this work. To make the dalits happy, the non-dalits must 'stretch out the hand of fellowship to the Bhangis', to see that they get justice without resorting to a demand.[88] In terms of this 'hand of fellowship', a Gandhian noted that 'the Communist Party has successfully organized sweepers' unions and helped them to secure their rights through *hartals* [strikes], etc. But the Harijan Sevak Sangh's activities are confined mostly to welfare work. It cannot, therefore, successfully compete with the Communists for popularity among the Harijans. Don't you think that in view of this, the Harijan Sevak Sangh ought to alter its policy and method of work?'[89] 'We must be guided in our policy by our sense of right', Gandhi responded, 'not by the lure of winning cheap popularity. If the Harijan Sevak Sangh is convinced that it is working on the right line, it will keep on it, regardless of what others might or might not do'. The Harijan Sevak Sangh's unions, he argued, do not enter politics, but they pursue the betterment of the 'social or economic position of the Harijans'.[90] 'The Bhangis may not go on strike for lack of these amenities', Gandhi argued, 'but it is up to all citizens to raise their voice on behalf of them'.[91] Rather than strike, the sweepers might inform the municipality and the town that they will stop work as a 'temporary measure in expectation of relief' and hope that the message itself will result in benevolent action from above.[92] A strike, Malkani argued, leads to 'more and more cash which goes down the drain in drink' and this creates a tension between the sweepers and the rest of the town. Instead, he, like Gandhi, called for a 'sensible type of strike', a notification for better treatment without any animosity.[93] Most of the 1946 strikes achieved only one sop, higher wages, validating the bourgeois view of the workers' struggle as a strictly economic fight and not as a broad-based political struggle for power.[94]

[88]*Harijan*, 21 April 1946.
[89]*Harijan*, 21 July 1946.
[90]Ibid.
[91]*Harijan*, 12 May 1946.
[92]Ibid.
[93]Malkani, *Rambles*, pp. 225–6.
[94]*Hindustan Times*, 13, 22 and 25 April 1946 for the results of some strikes and Sarkar, *A Critique*, pp. 138–9 on bourgeois economism.

In 1946, a sanitation workers' union in Ballia (UP) informed the Congress that it was to go on strike on the issues of lack of medical care, maternal leave, leave to bury relatives, rising cost of living, wage increases, fixed pay days, rest time, statutory duties of overseers, roll-call at the Town Hall and not at the overseer's house, and finally, 'if we be human, let us be treated as such'. The Congress noted that 'a strike, especially a strike of sweepers, is a serious matter. It is to be considered carefully in all its aspects before it is undertaken. You will do well to meet responsible Congress workers in your district before you take any extreme step. All possible avenues of peaceful settlement should be explored before you have recourse to direct action'.[95] The quiet voice of democracy can be heard in the plea to be treated as human, but the Congress and the Harijan Sevak Sangh were unable to allow this voice to lead itself and to allow the antagonistic side of dalit liberation to emerge full-blown. During this period, no other agency (Ambedkar, the socialists, the communists) had the kind of organizational strength of the Congress and of the Harijan Sevak Sangh. The activism of the latter, however, did not develop the political demands of the Mehtars. Instead, they rendered the Mehtars demands into the institutional form of a charity organization, one that was wedded to 'uplift' of a few rather than to revolutionary change for all. The Harijan Sevak Sangh acted less like a union and more like a community development organization and its activists used the muscle of the Congress to draw many of the nascent union formations into its ideological and institutional orbit. When power was transferred in 1947, the sweepers' union collaborated with the municipality which was considered stable by them.[96] Paradoxically, in their desire to be treated as humans, the sweepers found solace in the institutions which sought to retain their monopoly over sanitation work. Though the struggle continued, Hindu militancy, which promised them freedom to the detriment of Muslims, seemed more attractive than liberation.

[95] All-India Congress Committee Papers, G-25 (KW-1), 1940–6, TL 1332, NMML.

[96] Harish C. Doshi, 'A Comparative Analysis of Occupational Changes among Two Scheduled Castes', *Emerging Sociology*, vol. 3 (1981), pp. 99–100.

6

Citizens

The promulgation of the new Indian republic derailed the dynamic set in motion by the militant Hindus and their confreres within the Balmiki community. The Constitution of the Indian Republic (1950) is known amongst many dalits as 'Dr Ambedkar's Constitition', a tribute both to the man who guided the text as well as to the kind of hopes enshrined in it. While the militant Hindu agenda did not disappear from the lives of the Balmikis, it was certainly curtailed by the onrush of state construction, particularly by the closely held desire amongst Balmikis for their emancipation as a result of benevolent state action. When this deliverance did not come and when the Balmikis felt the sharp edge of state violence in 1957, the opportunity to build upon the contradictions of Balmiki life given to the nationalist movement collapsed. There was a moment from 1950 to 1957 when the progressive movement within the republic's capital attempted to forge a historical bloc with the dalits as a constitutive element and such a bloc may perhaps have renewed the links across communities towards the creation of a new progressive will. This was not to be, partly due to the impact of state violence, but also due to the reduction of the dreams of the dalits by a bureaucracy that used every means to legally trounce those aspirations. This final chapter will take us from 1946 (when Gandhi went and lived among the Balmikis of Delhi) to 1957 (when the police opened fire on the Balmikis in that very locality). Within this decade we can see both the tremendous hopes of state and national construction as well as the intimations of failure.

GANDHI AMONGST THE DALITS

The historiography and mythography of bourgeois Indian nationalism squarely locates Gandhi in the midst of dalit history. A brief tour of any dalit neighbourhood will reveal statues of Gandhi, plaques which commemorate his visits and other such memorabilia which recognizes his role in making dalit freedom a part of the national movement. These relics of Gandhiana come without the social visions and designs which Gandhi developed and which have since been elaborated in critical ways. In 1949, Pyarelal warned his fellow Gandhians not to use their funds to museumize Gandhi, but to use the money to reconstruct society in a Gandhian manner. Before erecting another statue, Pyarelal wrote, Gandhians must 'tidy up the Harijan Quarters in Bhangi Niwas and elsewhere and introduce in them the minimum standard of sanitation and cleanliness and comfort that Gandhi had envisaged and to the realization of which he had mortgaged his future hopes'.[1] Despite Pyarelal's best efforts, Gandhi has been relegated to a statuary figure rather than offered as a theoretician and activist for socio-economic justice.

In 1946, Gandhi wanted to do more than simply make statements about untouchability and to visit dalits on occasion. His two decades long activism for dalit rights was severely criticized that year by B.R. Ambedkar (*What Congress and Gandhi have Done to the Untouchables*), by J.E. Sanjana (in the pages of the Gujarati newspaper, *Rast Rahbar*, and in his *Caste and Outcaste*) and by sweepers' unions. When Gandhi wistfully spoke of being reborn a sweeper, Sanjana pointed out that he 'can easily and promptly [be "reborn"] in this very life by going and living among, say, Bhangis—who do admit outsiders into their caste—and becoming one of them, instead of generously wishing to do so in the next problematic incarnation'.[2] Well aware of Sanjana's writings (he was read regularly at Sevagram), on 31 March 1946 Gandhi owned up to his hypocrisy and said that it was his 'duty' to live amongst the dalits.[3] To live amongst the dalits was not to be a personal or idiosyncratic act, but an act of penance and hope for all Hindus, since 'I have of late been saying that the Hindus have to become *atishudras*, not merely in name, but in thought, word and deed. For that token scavenging is not enough. I have, therefore, decided that I must go and actually live among Harijans in Harijan quarters'.[4] In

[1]*Harijan*, 8 May 1949.

[2]Sanjana, *Caste and Outcaste*, pp. 188–90.

[3]Brijkrishan Chandiwala, *Gandhiji ki Dilli Diary tatha Dilli ki Swatantrata Sangram* (Delhi: Gandhi Smarak Nidhi, 1970), vol. 2, p. 279.

[4]*Harijan*, 14 April 1946 and G.D. Birla, *Kuch Dekha, Kuch Suna* (New Delhi: Sasta Sahitya Mandal, 1966), p. 79.

1941, Gandhi advocated individual civil disobedience as a mode of satyagraha and his 1946 action was perhaps his boldest political gesture as an individual satyagrahi. This gesture has been emphasized historiographically for its boldness, but without an exploration of its limits. For the Balmikis, Gandhi came to them to 'make things easier for us'. Gandhi is a hero whose heroism is made richer by their accent on his limitations. 'Gandhi has killed our caste', radical Balmikis said in the early 1990s, a statement which refers to the Balmiki tendency to work within the system of power rather than in opposition to the established state of privileges.[5] That the Balmikis do not act as an antagonistic political force is explained by recourse not to a limitation in Balmiki culture, but to the structural forces set in place by the state (whose mast-head is Gandhi).

In the 1930s, Gandhi visited a number of dalit colonies in Delhi and he found conditions of life in them to be abhorent. In 1937, he described the Delhi colonies as 'the worst of any I had seen' and he urged the tax payers to wake up and 'make their city fathers realize their duty'.[6] Brijkrishen Chandiwala and G.D. Birla decided to locate Gandhi in the most recent colony which is today located on Mandir Marg. Eight hundred people lived in hundred rooms and shared two water taps and thirteen ramshackle latrines. The tenements looked like 'minature Black Holes', with as many as ten people sharing a room. 'How could they possibly live there with decency God alone knew', wrote Pyarelal. Shortly before Gandhi moved into the colony, volunteers from the Swayam Sevak Dal, from Shriram's Delhi Cotton Mills, from the Congress and from the DMC tried to improve the horrendous living conditions. They repaired the latrines, put the taps in working order and erected huts, tents and *shamianas* to give the colony 'an appearance of a camp'.[7] The temporary structures housed reception rooms, a secretariat, a guest suite, a field kitchen and an eating shed. 'How devastatingly representative of our mud-hut civilization and categorically different from the massive stone-built Imperial Secretariat and Viceregal Palace of Imperial Rulers', Aruna Asaf Ali wrote, 'but to

[5]Sunheri Devi, Seelampur, 22 February 1992 and Rakesh Milind, Balmiki Colony, New Delhi, 1993.

[6]*Harijan*, 5 May 1946; Chandiwala, *Gandhiji*, vol. 2, pp. 297–8; Rajnikant Varma, *Ek Zindagi: Gandhi ke Nama* (Udaipur: Tahsina Prakashan, 1984).

[7]Brijkrishan Chandiwala, *Bapu ke Charanonmein* (Delhi: Navajivan, 1949), p. 64.

a foreigner this camp is just a phoney H.Q. of a revolutionary organization about to take responsibility for the state'.[8] To Mountbatten's
press attaché this was one of Gandhi's 'great symbolic acts'.[9] By 1946,
no one assumed that the organization which was going to take charge
of the state would rule from mud huts. Gandhi had already become the
symbol for the future regime.

Gandhi insisted that the improvements to the colony be permanent,
since, as Pyarelal wrote, if they are only temporary 'the whole thing
will become a farce'.[10] He himself stayed in two rooms beside the
Valmiki temple which stood about 50 meters from the tenements. His
was a political gesture, not an instance of the glorification of poverty,
for he openly declared that the actual homes of the dalits appeared
worse than the worst prison cell he had experienced in India and South
Africa. At his first prayer meeting in the colony on 31 March 1946,
Gandhi said that he prayed that the 'day should come when he would
be able to stay in the houses of the Harijans themselves and partake of
the food they would serve'.[11] As of now, he could not 'live in the filth
in which they lived'. Gandhi, like Nehru, was scrupulously historicist
in his account of the squalor in dalit hamlets. 'The fault was not theirs,
but of those who had reduced them to that state'.[12] Gandhi referred to
the NDMC which paid little heed to the Balmikis' demands and
troubles. His camp was a symbolic gesture to turn the state's glance
towards the poor and to economic justice. Civil society was also asked
to do its job, for Gandhi urged volunteers to go to dalit hamlets 'not as
their patrons or teachers but as their true servants' in order to 'reach
their hearts and transform the look of things'.[13] Gandhi's presence in
the colony enabled him to reach out to the dalits as well as to use his
proximity to pressure the government.

[8]Aruna Asaf Ali, *Fragments from the Past* (New Delhi: Patriot, 1989), pp.
74–5.

[9]Alan Campbell-Johnson, *Mission with Mountbatten* (London: R. Hale,
1951), pp. 144–7.

[10]Pyarelal to Birla, 27 March 1946, *Bapu: A Unique Association*. Ed. G.D.
Birla (Bombay: Bharatiya Vidya Bhawan, 1977), vol. 4, p. 394; *Harijan*, 5 May
and 23 June 1946.

[11]Chandiwala, *Gandhiji*, vol. 2, p. 281; *Hindustan Times*, 28 April 1946.

[12]*Harijan*, 5 May and 23 June 1946; Chandiwala, *Bapu*, p. 67.

[13]*Harijan*, 5 May 1946; Chandiwala, *Gandhiji*, vol. 2, p. 298.

Portrait of Bhoop Singh

For dalits, Gandhi's stay enabled them to experience the barriers which separate them from their caste Hindu leadership. The most apparent barrier was inter-dining, for when some Balmikis invited Gandhi to eat with them on 3 April, he demurred, saying that 'it would be better if the money they wanted to spend on entertaining him were spent on educating a Harijan child'. 'You can offer me goat's milk', he said, 'but I will pay for it. If you are keen that I should take food prepared by you, you can come here and cook my food for me'. He denied Balmikis the right to offer hospitality and transformed their offers to a discussion of useless expenditure on 'vices' (such as wine, gambling and prostitution). 'I shall consider my stay among you amply rewarded if you give up these vices'.[14] Balmiki elders recount tales of Gandhi's hypocrisy, but only with a sense of uneasiness. When a dalit gave Gandhi nuts, he fed them to his goat, saying that he would eat them later, in the goat's milk. Most of Gandhi's food, nuts and grains, came from Birla House; he did not take these from the dalits. Radical Balmikis took refuge in Ambedkarism which openly confronted Gandhi on these issues. When Gandhi moved into the colony, radical

[14]*Harijan*, 5 April 1946; Chandiwala, *Gandhiji*, vol. 2, p. 280.

Balmikis protested his arrival. Gandhi, characteristically, empathized with their anger and their 'pent up resentment'. 'They have a right to be impatient', he said, and he asked Hindus to 'share with the Harijan their disabilities and to deny ourselves the privileges which the latter cannot share'.[15] This is precisely what he did. For the radical Balmikis, this was short of nothing.

Gandhi's presence in the colony is sufficient for bourgeois historiography. In text and guide books, in fiction and documentaries, the tale of Gandhi and the Bhangi Colony celebrates his compassion. In 1953, Rattan Lal Balmiki urged the NDMC to hold meetings in the Balmiki localities to commemorate the sojourn.[16] The contradictions of the sojourn (which Gandhi realized immediately) did not outlive his subsequent assassination and nor did it outlive the ideological investment the bourgeois–landlord state had in using Gandhi's ideals and biography as a justification for its own illiberal policies. In 1948, Khub Ram Jajoria (Advisory Council of the Chief Commissioner of Delhi) proposed that the city form a Harijan Welfare Board to work for socio-economic justice. The city accepted the spirit, but feared the costs so that nothing came of it.[17] Activism from above withdrew in the next decade under cover of Gandhi's sacrifices and his penance for the crime of untouchability.

FREEDOM DISINTOXICATED

Who knows how difficult
to nurture tyranny in one's stomach:
every limb to be scorched
and bones to be burnt.
I am the fruit of that time,
when on the tree of freedom
blossoms were falling.
Freedom was very near. . . .
Very far. . . .
My mother's womb was helpless

(Amrita Pritam, 'Majbur', 1947).[18]

---

[15]Chandiwala, *Gandhiji*, vol. 2, pp. 279–80; *Harijan*, 14 April 1946.
[16]*Hindustan Times*, 1 October 1953.
[17]DSA, DC Files, 1948, no. 67.
[18]Amrita Pritam, *Pratinidhi Kavitayeh* (Delhi: Rajpal, 1991), p. 66.

Fiction offers a potent witness to the trauma of the riots of partition, when the subcontinent was bathed in blood and when the ideals of nationalism were transformed into the rituals of bureaucratic management. In Noakhali, Gandhi struggled magnificently to produce humanity, but his individual prestige was not generalizable. In late 1947, Gandhi was unable to return to live with the dalits because his advisors feared for his life.[19] The state in Delhi was unable to protect tens of thousands of Muslims as the police either actively participated in the terror or remained paralyzed without morale.[20] The city was flooded with Punjabi refugees who came to seek shelter and refuge from the massacres. By January 1948, 'Delhi was like a dead city. The riot had just broken out and the Bhangi colony was full of refugees'.[21] The Balmiki colony, once congested, was now unbearable. Every available space was used for temporary huts and living conditions deteriorated. The NDMC allowed residents to utilize open land behind the colony which drew more desperate people to the area.[22]

The stress of the partition violence led the bureaucracy to complain of an intensified crisis of governability. To create stabilty and order as well as control over resources and people, the state equipped itself with extraordinary legal mechanisms such as the Essential Services Maintenance Ordinance (ESMO). ESMO, 'an ugly example of growing Indian fascism' (according to Jayaprakash Narayan),[23] allowed the state to revoke civil liberties from its subjects in an emergency situation. Such ordinances demonstrated a structural tendency towards undemocratic processes within the emerging Indian polity. The roots of this process can be located in the regime's assumption that social transformation 'was not to be achieved through a mass movement; it could be safely left to a large bureaucracy to supervise'.[24] The Congress, from the late

<hr />

[19]NAI, Home (Political), 5/6/46-Poll (I) and 5/44/46-Poll (I) and 5/7/47-Poll (I); Dharmendranath, *Dilli aur Azaadi* (Delhi: Hindi Akademi, 1990), chapter 16.

[20]Gyanendra Pandey, 'Partition and Independence in Delhi: 1947–48', *Economic and Political Weekly*, vol. 32, no. 36, 6–12 September 1997.

[21]*Harijan*, 18 January 1948.

[22]DSA, DC Files, 1948, no. 179 and 1948, no. 272.

[23]Sarvepalli Gopal, *Jawaharlal Nehru* (Cambridge: Harvard, 1979), vol. 2, p. 67.

[24]Sudipta Kaviraj, 'On the Crisis of Political Institutions in India', *Contributions to Indian Sociology*, vol. 18, no. 2 (1984), p. 231.

1930s, began to lose the ability to respond to the new tasks of the emerging epoch of political independence, as liberals such as Nehru began to rely increasingly upon the good graces of evolution and as conservatives such as Patel felt no need for much change to the polity.[25] First, the party saw itself as identical with the emerging bourgeois–landlord state. Second, the party/state appropriated the power to decide what constituted legitimate conflict which was to remain within established political forms and abjure any hope of transformation of the state's nature. Elections, in this view, became the primary form of dissent.[26] Mass protest did not sit well with the state, so the Congress changed from the party of popular militancy to ministerialism. The Congress demobilized its footsoldiers and told them not to make extraordinary demands on *their* state. Politics, for the state, gave way to resource allocation which was the task of the bureaucrat. Congress cadres moved from being activists to being patrons of the state's largesse. 'It is terrible to think', Nehru wrote to Krishna Menon in 1948, 'that we may be losing our values and sinking into the sordidness of opportunist politics'.[27] Third, the demobilization of the movement was made possible in strategic terms because the leadership believed in an evolutionary theory of national construction. Modernist forces in the leadership, such as Nehru, believed that the nation's historical mission would inevitably prevail over the politics of reaction and traditionalism. To keep the ideals of equality alive was sufficient. National construction through vigorous popular participation and activism was not to be the Indian road to development; that road was to be traversed by technocratic experts who would lead the bedraggled Indian people to a future freedom.

CONTRADICTIONS OF THE INDIAN STATE

In 1946, Kosambi pointed out that the èlite's 'moment of agony' would end with a retreat from the egalitarian promise of the freedom movement. At nation's dawn, the leadership side-stepped its egalitarian

---

[25]Sudipta Kaviraj, 'Indira Gandhi and Indian Politics', *Economic and Political Weekly*, 20–27 September 1986, p. 1698 and E.M.S. Namboodripad, *Nehru: Ideology and Practice* (New Delhi: National Book Centre, 1988), pp. 219–26.

[26]When the Congress central government dismissed the CPI state government in Kerala on 31 July 1959, it effectively revoked the ballot as the site of struggle at that moment.

[27]Gopal, *Jawaharlal Nehru*, vol. 2, p. 74.

contract even as it continued to make abstract pledges. The socialism of Nehru and the Planning Commission diverged dramatically from the tasks of the Congress ministries. There is no evidence, Kosambi wrote, 'that the Congress as constituted today is in the remotest danger of drifting (like its planning commission) towards socialism'.[28] The Indian state abandoned the designs of socialist construction (despite the statements at Avadhi in 1955) for a stategy of public investment uséd to finance high-risk sectors in order to pave the way for sheltered public enterprise. The crystallized ruling coalition (of landlords, kulaks, big bourgeoisie) was not to be threatened.

The bourgeois–landlord state did not discount the will of the dalits, for the state continued to cherish the abstractions of freedom (even if it relegated many of its tasks to the Directive Principles of State Policy). Equality is the Constitution's enunciated goal and not only does the Preamble resolve to secure to all of its citizens 'equality of status and opportunity', but article 17 abolished untouchabilty and made discrimination on its grounds cognizable. Formal equality, the state's managers realized, was often a shield to preservè extant inequalities. Therefore, the state began a far-sighted policy to *produce* equality of opportunity in order to draw the disenfranchised into the spoils of social wealth. Two judicial rulings offered the state with the ability to move in radical directions. In 1951, Justice Fazl Ali argued that equality did not mean that 'every law must have universal application for all persons who are not by nature, attainment or circumstances in the same position, and the varying needs of different classes or persons require separate treatment'.[29] In 1964, Justice Hegde took the argument one step further with his claim that 'advantages secured due to historical reasons cannot be considered a fundamental right guaranteed by the Constitution'.[30] Such profound and bold judgements offered the state the ability to *produce* equality, a task which it neither relished nor completed.

The Balmikis saw the state as an ambigious entity, at once pledged to produce equality *and* to preserve the established distribution of power and property. Eager for political legitimacy, the main political parties claimed to fight for socio-economic homogenization. Eager to retain its fragile coalition of landed and industrial èlites, the ruling

[28]D.D. Kosambi, 'The Bourgeoisie Comes of Age in India', *Exasperating Essays*, p. 16.

[29]*Charanjit Lal v. Union of India* (1951).

[30]*Viswanath v. State of Mysore* (1964).

coalition tended to shy away from activism of a structural variety. The Balmikis found themselves as clients of political patrons particularly after the patrons organized the disorganization of the Balmikis' political organs. Social service agencies withdrew in favour of temple organizations; militant unions lost their dynamism and accepted the leadership of the Congress' class collaborationist union, Indian National Trade Union Congress (INTUC). Balmikis began to accept the dominant sentiments of the regime, which the more radical among them named Brahmanism. Certainly Balmiki incorporation is fraught with conflict as dalits continue to struggle with contemporary forms of capital which challenge their own meagre gains won over the past five decades. The form of incorporation must be analysed as a case where the leading groups (Congressmen and their ideological and institutional kin) 'have the function of "domination" without that of "leadership": dictatorship without hegemony'.[31] What Gramsci implied by this contentious fragment is that the established leaders are more inclined to dominate rather than lead, where to lead means to build power among the subordinate so that they might radicalize the movement with their leadership. Without a radical transformation of the relations of power, the domination of the ruling coalition continues to be based on state violence. The regime developed a discourse of anti-untouchability within a few years of political independence which it saw as a sufficient response to the atrocities against dalits. When an act of violence occurs against dalits, the state immediately condemns the violence, but it does not challenge the conditions which produce the violence. The leadership produced an established anti-untouchability which is itself a shell of the emancipation of the dalits promised during the deliberations of the Constituent Assembly. Behind this established anti-untouchability lies the might of the state, which the dalits know will be wielded against any counter-untouchability action mounted by them. The regime developed four strategies to tackle the aspirations of the dalits which need to be analysed in detail.

Commercial Reason

Anti-Untouchabilty laws are frequently interpreted as a challenge to the barriers against equality for consumers in the market rather than against

---

[31]Antonio Gramsci, *Selections from Prison Notebooks* (New York: International Publishers, 1971), p. 106.

wide structural injustice. The Untouchability Offences Act (UOA) of 1955 outlawed discrimination on the grounds of untouchability with regard to access to sites of civil society (such as temples, shops, restaurants, educational institutions, neighbourhoods, conveyances, water sources, hospitals). UOA further protected dalits from wearing jewellery and other finery and it provided dalits with the right to conduct religious ceremonies, both ways to demonstrate status. Marc Galanter calculated that 64 per cent of the cases registered on the basis of this provision were for greater access to commercial establishments.[32] While the anti-untouchability legislation allowed dalits access to civil society, it did not provide dalits opportunities to be equal in the realm of production, a realm made inviolable by the commercial basis of law. Advantages secured due to historical reasons (such as property, capital and education) are not challenged by this interpretation. Compensation to dalits through the legislative action of reservations in governmental and educational establishments provided a number of dalits with the means to economic independence. Marc Galanter argues that the net result of the policies has been uneven, with a negligible section of the dalits moving into 'the modern class manning the organized sector'.[33] The bulk of the dalits have not benefited from these policies.

Labour Reason

As sanitation workers, the Balmikis are seen as essential to the state's apparatus and to the population's health. Since the bourgeois–landlord state continues the colonial state's predilection to see the Balmiki as an irreplaceable worker, the emancipation of the Balmiki has been suspended. ESMO illustrates the way in which the Balmiki is bonded to undervalued sanitation work and refuse removal. ESMO emerged during the Second World War as a means to prevent any disruption of the war economy. In 'normal times', Delhi's Deputy Commissioner wrote in 1943, state employees were allowed to leave service after due notice; during wartime, this was 'unreasonable' due to the 'grave urgency' of the moment. In Delhi, sanitation workers of the Badli

---

[32]Marc Galanter, 'The Abolition of Disabilities—Untouchability and the Law', *The Untouchables in Contemporary India.* Ed. J. Michael Mahar (Tucson: University of Arizona, 1972), p. 264.

[33]Marc Galanter, *Competing Equalities: Law and the Backward Classes in India* (Berkeley: University of California, 1984), pp. 541–6.

Dumping Ground tested ESMO in 1943; they were arrested and returned to their workplace. In 1947, the Industrial Disputes Act absorbed the ESMO provisions which the state used against sweepers during partition.[34] In 1965, the Supreme Court of India found that ESMO *did not* restrict the freedoms of speech, expression or association. In this respect, the Court argued that 'there is no fundamental right to strike'.[35] The state absorbed the undemocratic right to curtial fundamental rights and civil liberties if these infringed upon the delicate fabric of the ruling coalition at the same time as the state endowed dalits with enlightened social legislation.

Theocratic Reason

The state understood that social change cannot be its responsibility, but it must be shared by individuals whose consciousness must be altered. 'No amount of legislation will take us far', the state noted, 'unless the people themselves translate its provisions into action and the administrative machinery concerned with their implementation is fully conscious of their duty towards the Law, the Public and the Country'.[36] The state's hesitancy, however, did not come from a concern with an overemphasis on legislative action without corresponding social activism. Rather, the state argued that it is only *after* the consciousness of the people has been transformed that the state can act upon its progressive legislation. Certain 'people' became the touchstone for the state action: the Hindu orthodoxy, who had to first accept the liberal aspects of equality before the ruling clique risked social activism. This was called an attempt to win the consensus of the 'people', when in fact the limiting case of liberal law is the Hindu orthodoxy.

Contradictions within the regions of the bourgeois–landlord consensus allow us to see that despite the Indian state's reversal of colonial inaction with regard to untouchability, it inserted itself into civil society silently and cautiously. The Bombay Removal of Social Disabilities Act X made offences against dalits cognizable (this had much to do with the role of Ambedkar and the sustained radicalism of Maharashtrian dalits). In 1947, the Delhi administration considered its

[34]DSA, DC Files, 1950, no. 146; DSA, CC Files no. 46/2/43, Con. 1943 and 106/49-Con. 1949.

[35]*Radhey Shyam v. Postmaster General, Nagpur* (1965).

[36]*Report of the Commissioner of Scheduled Castes and Scheduled Tribes* (Delhi: GOI, 1952), p. 42.

implementation, but the government pleader, Bishamber Das, objected to this step. He wanted to use the UP Removal of Social Disabilities Act of XIV which did not hold offences against dalits to be cognizable (due in large part to the landlord–kulak domination of UP and the absence of a sustained radical movement amongst UP dalits), since 'Delhiwalas are more akin to the persons inhabiting UP and the Punjab'. The UP Act, Das urged, 'is a cautious advance in as much as it does not provide for compulsory access to shops by Harijans which may be opposed by the orthodox sections'. Further, 'it is expedient that these offences should be noncognisable otherwise there is a great chance of orthodox sections being harassed at the hands of the police on false complaints by Harijans'. Das won the day.[37]

Efficiency Reason

Within the first few years of the Indian state, nationalists began to apologize for its failure to provide an inflated notion of freedom. K.G. Mashruwala asked the Balmikis to empathize with the 'poor municipal bodies' whose budgets are scanty. Work conditions are important, but of equal (if not more) import was the administration and a 'decent building and a meeting hall'. The staff and Town Hall had to conform to 'modern standards', while manual labourers continued to be relegated to something less than modernity. 'So all talk about educating [sweepers] and properly housing them and giving them an equitable wage, etc., must be regarded at best as distant goals'.[38] In the short term, the poor had to find salvation in Gandhian shibboleths such as manual spinning and weaving. 'Let everyone who feels his present condition hopelessly bad, plod on with his present difficulties as best as he can, but let him side by side take to hand-spinning and hand-weaving'.[39]

To prolong the promise of equality as well as the implementation of the barest reforms, the state utilized a well-worn strategy, the establishment of fact-finding committees. In 1950, P.J. Solanki admitted that such commissions take time to do their research and to present their verdict and the government takes time to study such reports. Contentious reports 'will be pigeon-holed, with the result that the poor

[37]DSA, DC Files, 1948, no. 67.

[38]'Scavengers' Dilemma', *Harijan*, 10 April 1949.

[39]'Resuscitation', *Harijan*, 17 April 1949.

municipal workers will be reduced to a more and more miserable condition'.[40] After three years of deliberation, the B.N. Barve Scavengers' Living Conditions Enquiry Committee (1951) reported on Bombay province. This report was followed by the two Malkani reports, the Scavenging Conditions Enquiry Committee Report (1957–60) and the Committee on Customary Rights (1966). The National Commission on Labour (chaired by B.P. Pandya) published its report in 1969. Various states commissioned reports which closely followed the national pattern. The government endorsed these reports, but as Kanhayalal Balmiki pointed out in a bitter note of dissent to the 1966 Malkani Report, their decisions were not implemented. 'It is a stark fact', he wrote, 'that no serious consideration was given to the recommendations of these Committees nor could these be implemented'. There was no 'effective machinery', given that the government and the judiciary used these reports as toothless guiding principles. He hoped that *this* Report 'not meet the same fate as other Reports'.[41] Of course, it has. By why, 'of course'? The irreplaceability of the sweepers, as manual labour, and the parsimony of the municipalities towards its labourers left the sweepers in the unenviable position of being free without freedom.

To thwart radical action on the part of the Balmikis, the Congress and its kin attempted to disrupt the brief entry of communism into the lives of the Balmikis as well as to organize the Balmikis into class collaborationist unions. '*Sangarsh kyun karo, laddu lo*' (why bother with struggle, eat sweets—relax), the Congress said to the Balmikis.[42] State compensation provided the Balmikis with some avenues for socio-economic mobility, however the state's initiative was geared towards individuals and not towards structural change. Such individualism frustrated transformation and even stalwart Congressmen such as Jagjivan Ram complained that 'I thought there would be social revolution, but the only revolution is for political office [*kursi*]'.[43] 'When a sweeper finds permanent employment', Rattan Lal Balmiki

[40]P.J. Solanki, 'Government and Municipal Sweepers', *Harijan*, 5 March 1950.

[41]*Report of the Committee on Customary Rights to Scavenging* (Delhi: Department of Social Welfare, 1966).

[42]R.C. Sangar and Bhagmal 'Pagal', Jalandhar, 2–3 April 1993.

[43]Jagjivan Ram, *Bharat mein Jativad aur Harijan Samasyain* (Delhi: Rajpal, 1981), p. 89.

told me, 'he or she will say, *kam ho gaya* [the work is done]'.[44] Once a politician provides a sweeper with this small reward, both believe that the politician's job is complete. Reform led rapidly to reformism.

TWO PRINCIPLES OF DALIT LIBERATION

Democracy is always fought for in a language that is intelligible. To fight for political rights alone cannot satisfy the subordinate, for whom the democratic fight involves more than the right to vote. The bourgeoisie was satisfied with 'democracy' being rendered as suffrage and civil liberties; any wider interpretation had to include a criticism of the inequalities of property, of wealth, of dignity, and of destiny. Dalits, at certain moments, developed this antagonistic democratic agenda. Dalits battled for liberty which meant at least freedom from anarchic state violence as well as freedom to live in peace, health, and hope. Freedom was not seen as political liberty, but as the freedom of the will in the widest sense. A dalit communist in 1947 captures this instinct:

> *Listen brother Nihala, have you seen Freedom?*
> *No my friend, I have not tasted her nor seen her. . . .*
> *I heard from Jaggu that she has come upto Ambala,*
> *her back to the wall, her face to Birla.*
>
> (Guramdas 'Alam', 1947).[45]

1947, for the poet, simply meant the freedom of property and of exploitation. The freedom imagined by radical dalits came in another key: as freedom from property, from the filth of gain, from survival and the freedom to live in dignity. Such a vision of freedom will be analysed in the next section. This section will analyse two strategies of liberation whose principle is not the abolition of the notion of dalit, but liberation from the standpoint of dalit.

Territorial Independence

In 1942, Ambedkar formed the Scheduled Castes Federation (SCF) to organize dalits and to reach out to other oppressed elements in order to combat the Congress' claim to being the sole representative of the

---

[44]Rattan Lal Balmiki, New Delhi, 15 February 1992.

[45]Guramdas 'Alam', 'Azaadi', *Jo Mai Mar Gia* (Jalandhar: Alam Kutia, 1975), p. 39.

Indian peoples. The Left was, in the 1940s, busy with the People's War against fascism and with the formation of people's areas in various parts of the country (notably in Telengana, in Travancore, in Tebhaga and in Bihar); these tasks occupied the Communist Party of India (CPI) and the various socialist components (notably the Congress Socialist Party and the Praja Socialist Party). The liberals, who failed to organize among the masses, began to pin their hopes on the Congress, which they referred to as the party of national solidarity. In 1943, Ambedkar rued the demise of the Liberal Party, for 'to have popular Government run by a single Party is to let democracy become a mere form for despotism to play its part from behind it'. To ensure 'democratic processes, Ambedkar wished to confront the Congress with 'the possibility of its dethronement, of its being laid low, of its being superseded by a rival party'.[46] Failure to produce such a bloc moved Ambedkar to revisit an issue made popular amongst the dalits during the 1932 Poona Pact, the demand for separate electorates. This demand led the dalit movement towards a demand for territorial secessionism.

By 1940, the Congress and Muslim League leadership was unable to come to a negotiated settlement for power allocation in the future republic. Rather than continue discussion to create a formula for democratic processes, the League in 1940 simplified the question of political rights to territorial secessionism. 'If the British Government are really in earnest and sincere to secure the peace and happiness of the people of this Subcontinent', Jinnah said at Lahore, 'the only course open to us all is to allow the major nations separate homelands, by dividing Indian into "autonomous national states".'[47] Ambedkar defended the idea in his *Thoughts on Pakistan* (1940) and some dalits demanded a nation of *achhuts* (untouchables) alongside Pakistan called Achhutistan. 'The demand for Achhutistan is the demand for independ-

---

[46]B.R. Ambedkar, *Ranade, Gandhi and Jinnah* (Jalandhar: Bhim Patrika, 1945), pp. 57–8.

[47]'An Extract from the Presidential Address of M.A. Jinnah—Lahore, March 1940', *India's Partition*. Ed. M. Hasan (New Delhi: Oxford University Press, 1994), p. 55. In September 1942, the CPI accepted the notion of 'autonomous states' and argued that the 'slogan of Pakistan rests upon the democratic urge among the newly-awakened Muslim nationalities for self-determination'. G.M. Adhikari, *Pakistan and Indian National Unity* (London: Labour Monthly, 1943), p. 29. In 1946 this theory was rejected and the CPI argued that socio-economic contradictions will be best confronted within a 'common union'.

ence', wrote Besh Lal of the All-India Achhutistan Movement in November 1946; the SCF was known as the 'Pakistan of the Depressed Classes' and the Muslim League was seen briefly as the ally of the dalits.[48] An ally may provide assistance, but neither the League nor the Congress shared the vision of the dalits, which was to effectively share power rather than subjugate sections of the population. 'The cause of the Hindus and Muslims', Bhole argued in 1944, 'is not the cause of freedom; it is a struggle for power'. The dalits are 'struggling for liberty in this Indian turmoil. Their cause is the cause of freedom'.[49] The Achhutistan movement adopted the idea of secessionism, but it did so tactically. Therefore, it retained a strong critique of bourgeois-landlordism by its demand for an end to zamindari rights, for the distribution of land by extensive reforms, for the enactment of cognizable laws to grant socio-economic rights to dalits, for the formulation of a legislative arrangement whereby dalits would be guaranteed separate electorates, and finally, for a drive to educate dalits.[50] Secessionism, yes, but only as a tactic alongside a renewed committment to attain solutions to socio-economic contradictions.

Territorial secessionism was even more unclear in the context of the internal contradiction within the dalit community. In 1946, the Scheduled Castes' Uplift Union and the Ravidas Balmik Naujawan Sabha merged into the Delhi Scheduled Castes Welfare Association and thereby united the Balmiki and Chamar communities of Delhi. The group set up concrete tasks (such as an employment bureau) for itself and tried to found the basis for sustained unity. The next year, however, the Jatavs created the Jatav Sabha Conference in Delhi and threatened the unity of the year-old association. Furthermore the basis for unity was rather shallow since it relied upon the personality of Ambedkar, so that, after his death in 1956, the Balmikis of the Punjab SCF 'passed a resolution that they will dissolve the SCF and join the Congress en bloc'.[51] On 15 April 1951, radical dalits opened the Ambedkar Bhawan across the road from the Balmiki Colony, New Delhi. The complex was built to honour Ambedkar as well as to provide dalits with education.

[48] AICC files, G-19 (KW-1), 1946–48, NMML; R.R. Bhole, 'Untouchable India', *Asiatic Review*, vol. 39, no. 5 (July 1943), p. 292.

[49] R.R. Bhole, 'The Untouchables on the Move', *Asiatic Review*, vol. 40, no. 5 (April 1944). This assessment is also in Ambekdar, *Ranade*.

[50] AICC Files, G-25, 1940–41, NMML.

[51] L.R. Balley, Jalandhar, 1 April 1993.

The road which divides the Bhawan from the colony is a metaphor for the fissures between Ambedkarism and the Balmiki community. The divide is further illustrated in the pictures which the Chamars and Balmikis display on their walls: the former highlight Ambedkar, Jyotibai Phule and Raidas (alongside living leaders such as Ram Vilas Paswan, Kanshi Ram and V.P. Singh), while the latter opt for M.K. Gandhi, Indira Gandhi and Sanjay Gandhi (or Rajiv; but Sanjay because of his urban redevelopment programme during the National Emergency of 1975–77). Balmiki elders blame the dissolution of dalit unity at the feet of the Chamars who, they claim, began to mark the organizations with their stamp; Chamar elders blamed Balmikis for their lack of independence from the Congress bureaucracy. The resolution of this struggle turns upon the Balmikis' economic advancement. Without that prerequisite, the Balmikis appear at the negotiation table with less socio-economic power than the Chamars. Internal contradictions, such as these, prevented an easy call for territorial secessionism as well as prevented the national dalit leadership from the creation of a politics from the standpoint of dalithood. Such politics became possible after the Mandal commission (1990) imbroglio created the political space for the articulation of a national dalit politics, which had to confront its inner contradictions.

Cultural Parity

One evening in Jalandhar, when I asked him why he continued to refer to the Indian republic as Hindustan, Dravid Desraj smiled. It is, he said, the land of the Hindus. His 'people', he claims, are the original inhabitants of the subcontinent who are held captive by the 'Hindu Aryans'. Since the Balmikis must struggle with a Hindu state, Desraj argued, the Balmikis yield to what they experience as the dominant ethos.[52] Although Desraj's framework is not quite accurate (the state, after all, is a secular state despite the fact that the forces of Hindutva continue to exert relentless pressure to change its character), he is right to point to the assessment as the dominant mode by which Balmikis chose to accomodate themselves to what they regarded as the culture of the new nation. Assimilation, under the rule of the Hindus, was not seen as a failure, but as a compromise for the future.

[52]Dravid Desraj, Sukhdev Kalyan and Prem Valmiki, Jalandhar, 1–3 April 1993.

The forces of Hindutva, familiar to the Balmikis since the 1920s, re-entered their neighbourhoods in the 1940s to exert cultural domination and to create the basis of institutional hegemony. In 1944, the All-India Arya (Hindu) Dharm Seva Sangh of Sabzimandi circulated a zealous pamphlet among Delhi's dalits. The main theme of the pamphlet was the way in which some 'foreigners' (such as Scythians, Grecians, Iranians and Huns) converted to Hinduism when they came to 'Bharat' while others did not; the converted had every right to live in the country, while those who resisted conversion (such as the British and Muslims), it was argued, should be deported. If dalits did not display their loyalty to Hinduism, they would suffer death or deportation.[53] During the 1946–8 riots, dalits palpably experienced the character of the new nation. The RSS terror against Muslims and dalits was experienced as the assertion of Hindus who consolidated power in *their* country. The experience of Hindu assertion did not end with the riots of partition, for S.P. Mookerjee urged militant Hindus to 'cultivate close contacts with the labourers and Harijans' through the Bharatiya Jana Sangh, in order to consolidate and institutionalize their ideological strength.[54] Balmikis experienced the strong arm of Hindutva without the illusion of protection from the state; in order to secure protection, the general feeling among the Balmikis was to yield to the new ethos. The Balmikis depended upon their Hindu municipal officials for credit, jobs and for special treatment; for this, cultural Hinduization seemed an acceptable option, despite the loss of dignity. Balmikis altered their names as an indication of the process: Allah Rakha became Ram Rakha Mull (or Malhotra), Maula became Mool Raj, Ramzani became Ramji Lal, Allahwala became Lallu Ram, Khuda Baksh became Ram Baksh, Allah Ditta became Hari Dutt, Chiraj became Dharampal and women adopted the suffix Devi.[55]

After 1947, worship of Maharishi Valmiki became a way for the Balmikis to insert themselves into the Hindu community as Hindus (and not as dalits). One evening in 1993, as Delhi struggled with the decision of Hindutvawadis to hold a rally at Boat Club, Madan Lal Parcha told me of his pride in Valmiki. Hindus, he said, worship Ram

---

[53]*Bharat ki Janagana aur Hindu Jan Sankhya ki Loot* (Delhi: All-India Arya [Hindu] Dharma Seva Sangh), 1944.

[54]Deihi CID SB (noncurrent) records, 7th installment, no. 45, NMML.

[55]Roop Lal Shant, Jalandhar, 3 April 1993 and Faqir Chand, Delhi, 25 March 1993.

through Tulsidas' *Ramcaritmanasa*, a sixteenth-century text, and not through Valmiki's *Ramayana* of antiquity. 'We have always worshipped Maharishi Valmiki', he said to me without his own sense of a meaningful past, 'we are the real Hindus'.[56] Madan Lal did not mention the earlier and valuable traditions of Bala Shah which we shared on other occasions; at this point, it was important to contest the tradition from within its own logic which privileged antiquity. The Balmikis in the 1950s similarly challenged Hindus to accept them as Hindus. The first tactic was to insist that Valmiki's *Jayanti* (anniversary) be declared and celebrated as a national holiday. The government declared the holiday, but it disallowed processions. At Thaneshwar (Karnal), the festival was celebrated over two days with tableaux (*jhankis*), plays, kirtans, discourses and processions. In 1949, Ram Rakha Mull went to Ambedkar to ask him to intervene with the Delhi government regarding a procession. Despite Ambedkar's low opinion of the Balmiki's worship of Valmiki[57], he approached the authorities. The government allowed the Balmikis to use the Ram Lila route for their procession. Hindu groups, however, feared that the route might be polluted, but rather than reveal their own fears they pointed out that the Muslims who lived along the route might riot. That this was sufficient to alter the Ram Lila route itself was never raised. Undeterred, but shaken, the Balmikis went ahead with their programme.[58]

While jayantis are celebrated annually, the weekly propagation of the gospel of Maharishi Valmiki according to Ami Chand Pandit was the *satsang*, the singing of devotional songs in a group, a *kirtan mandal*. Sadhu Yodhnath's *bhajan mala* which accompanied the *Valmiki Prakash* aided the Balmikis as they praised their guru, and those songs can still be heard at the *aartis* in Valmiki temples (alongside the bhajans from Kabir and Nanak, testifying to the resilience of the heterogeneous traditions). All across north India, Balmikis join each other to share songs from various *gharanas* which bear within them old and resilient roots of the musical traditions which come from the saint-

[56]Madan Lal Parcha, Nabi Karim, Delhi, 25 February 1993.

[57]In the 1940s, Ambedkar told Bhagmal 'Pagal' that 'Valmiki is a one-man advertising agency for Ram Rajya'. Bhagmal 'Pagal', Jalandhar, 2 April 1993.

[58]Ram Krishen Saugwan, Kalan Masjid, Delhi, 21 March 1993; Bhagwan Das, *Valmiki Jayanti aur Bhangi Jati* (Jalandhar: Bhim Patrika, n.d.); *Hindustan Times*, 23 October 1953; Raj Kumar 'Hamdard', 'Adhikavi Maharishi Valmiki', *Jago, Jagte Raho*, 20 October 1978.

poets of the early modern era. The preaching of equality and humanity in these gharanas introduces an element of risk into the process of theocratic homogenization within an unequal socio-economic order. Necessarily the license given to homogeniety is much stronger than that carried by these egalitarian traditions, since both the state (tacitly) and elements in the ruling coalition (notably the aggressive forces of Hindutva) favour a subdued cultural homogeneity. Nonetheless, as Ram Ratan found in his research in the early 1950, egalitarianism retained some legitimacy although it seemed to be under constant threat.[59]

In the 1950s, the Punjab Balmiki Sabha along with the Brahman Sabha organized conferences to discuss the 'socio-economic problems of the sects they represented' and to pass a formal resolution.[60] The Balmiki leadership felt comfortable with the notion that their *sect* had problems like any other sect, rather than to argue that the roots of their problems stemmed from their dominance by the other sect which posed in these rare venues as its equal. Disillusioned Balmikis did not brook such casual illusions to the 'two sects' and they joined with Budh Sharan 'Hans' who asked his community, 'why are you being purchased at the hands of exploiters, taking their insults, you honourable ones?'[61] Unhappy with freedom under the hegemony of Hindus, even if to secure survival, radical Balmikis turned to alternative agendas for freedom such as trade unionism. The union provided Balmikis with a place to develop their antagonistic visions even though it was also prone to corporatism (the tendency to fight for higher wages through bureaucratic processes rather than to make the question of the wage a political battle).

DALIT STRUGGLES OF SOCIALIST LIBERATION

On 15 August 1953, the CPI asked the nation to observe Independence Day as Unemployment Day. Its political resolution in March argued that after 'six years of Congress rule, the country faces a situation as serious as ever in its history. The situation is a direct result of the

[59]Ram Ratan, *Socio-economic Studies of Bhangis of Delhi* (Delhi: University of Delhi, 1955).

[60]*Census of India*, 1961, vol. XIII, Punjab, Part VII-B, p. 55.

[61]Budh Sharan 'Hans', 'Safai Mazdur', *Jago, Jagte Raho* (20 November 1978).

policies of the Nehru government'.[62] In June 1953, the CPI joined with Balmiki unionists to host a conference for sweepers' unions at Sangrur (Punjab). The state needed to be put on notice and the fragile CPI-radical Balmiki alliance was prepared to do just that. In Delhi, on 29 October 1953, the Delhi Prantiya Valmiki Mazdur Sangh sent a thirty-day notice to the DMC of a hunger strike until death which would commence if its eleven demands were not met. When the DMC did not respond, six leaders began a hunger strike.[63]

The union launched processions and public meetings, while the DMC hired scabs from outside Delhi and utilized the police to tear into the united fabric of the dalits and the CPI. On 4 December, a meeting was held at Azad Park at which Amir Chand Nanda (CPI) urged the workers to adopt the red (communist) flag and avoid the tricolour (congress) flag. The Balmiki leadership endorsed the call and they began a march to Town Hall. A police official recorded the events:

> The tempo of the processionists was high and no sooner had they reached the Municipal Building, they forced their entry into the verandahs and started damaging the Municipal property and threw flower pots, etc. hither and thither. The processionists also made free use of bricks which in the best of excitement they brought from Azad Park and hurled them against the Police Force and the Municipal Employees.

The police arrested a number of people, notably the leadership. The protests continued undaunted, despite the fact that a number of sweepers lost their homes to arson fire, that the police continued to arrest the marchers and that dalit organizations loyal to the government began a disinformation campaign against the strikers (notably the Hindutva ensemble which included the Shri Balmiki Vir Dal). The DMC and the police complained of 'scenes of rowdyism' and the Hindutva groups blamed the CPI for 'instigating the sweepers to strike and to other acts of rowdyism'. For the bourgeois–landlord state and the Hindutva fragments, Gandhianism (in its positive incarnation) was seen as a benign style, a uniform, the protests of established politicians who sit on *dharna* (sitting protest) or conduct a *padyatra* (walking protest). Gandhianism, the politics of ethical justice and protest, which

[62]*Documents of the History of the Communist Party of India.* Ed. Mohit Sen (New Delhi: People's Publishing House, 1977), vol. 8, p. 220.

[63]What follows comes from four police files: Delhi CID SB (noncurrent) records, 9th installment, no. 324; 2nd installment, no. 14, 5th installment, no. 114 and 7th installment, no. 45, NMML.

was represented by the tactics of *ahimsa* (without violence) of a hunger strike, of processions, of the various non-violent methods was seen as 'rowdyism', as sedition, and as 'anti-national'. If the trade unionists were only Gandhians by terrible necessity, they were acting as Gandhians none the less. The bourgois–landlord state's violence demonstrated its gulf from popular nationalism.

Kanhayalal Balmiki, MP from Bulandshar and President of the All-India Mehtar Mazdur Sangh, the All-India Balmiki Mahasabha, the Delhi Provincial Municipal Workers' Sangh and the Balmiki Mandap Trust, took an active interest in the struggle as a mediator between the strikers and the DMC. The DMC president promised to look into the grievances, which ended the strike after Mr Balmiki pledged himself as guarantor of the DMC's word. The DMC did not move. On 23 March 1954, four sweepers began a hunger strike at Balmiki Colony. A dharna outside Mr Balmiki's home questioned his effectivity and his leadership. Mr Balmiki's political standing was saved by the assumption made by many of his less fortunate brethren that although he sat in parliament, he was still treated with disrespect; his failure to deliver his promises was forgiven as the fissures of caste reinforced his legitimacy at the same time as it questioned the good faith of the government. 'The assurances given by the President of the DMC [in December 1953] have never been fulfilled', Mr Balmiki wrote in a letter to Delhi's Deputy Commissioner, 'and all the more the sweepers and scavengers who participated in the strike were victimized in every possible way. I wholly and solely explained the whole position to the President DMC but, to my utter disappointment, the situation was never taken seriously'. As a 'silent spectator', Mr Balmiki detailed the threats from the DMC relayed to him by the sweepers. The sweepers have 'lost patience', he wrote, and yet, 'the DMC is still adamant to suppress the spirit of the workers who are fighting for their rights and demands for the last three years'. The struggle ended with nothing gained.

The Balmiki trade union leadership was not content with its battle for economic issues; indeed, the struggle was not just about wages, but also about dignity and the value of the labour of the Balmikis. In their neighbourhoods, the Balmikis fought for dignity, which often meant fighting their neighbours for space in crowded and congested areas abandoned by municipalities. The neighbours, in Delhi, happened to be Muslims. In 1955, Hamdard Stores (at Ajmere Gate) wanted to use a road which ran by its side. The store had never used the road before, but the desire was not unusual for an expanding enterprise in a congested city. The road abutted a temple to Valmiki. Ram Rakha Mull, a Balmiki leader, went on hunger strike at the temple, insisting that Hamdard retract its claim to the road. Hamdard specializes in Unani medicines and is owned and run by a Delhi Muslim family. In order to galvanize Hindu support within the DMC, Ram Rakha Mull placed a statue of Shiva on the road ánd refused to allow Muslims transit. Hamdard dropped their demand.[64] Such stories illustrate the ambiguity between protest and integration, between the Balmikis' demand for dignity as human and workers and dignity as Hindus.

Injustice along with deteriorating economic circumstances fuelled the fires of Delhi's sweepers. A study from the mid-1950s offers details of the sweepers' impoverishment. Ninety-two per cent of the sweepers were in serious debt whose cause was the poor wages and the inability of the sweepers to access credit at reasonable rates.[65] The municipal authorities knew of these conditions and the NDMC was in the midst of a rectification campaign with regard to its corrupt overseers (it sought to hire only those 'whose honesty can be relied upon').[66] Bombay sweepers went on strike in early 1957 to demand implementation of the Barve Report and Delhi sweepers, soon after, submitted demands (for medical facilities, gratuities, housing, revision of pay scales, representation on the NDMC, immediate removal of all supervisors) along with a strike notice. On 22 July 1957, two sweepers started a hunger strike after sufficient provision of notice to the NDMC (under section 22[1] of the Industrial Disputes Act of 1947).[67] By 30 July, ten sweepers from the union sat on a hunger strike in front of the NDMC office. Rattan Lal Balmiki, who represented the union at the negotiations, recounted the unsavory pressure politics used by the NDMC against the strikers, notably spreading confusion (such as Dayal's statement that the strike was illegal because of inadequate notice).[68]

---

[64]Kamla, Sadan Lal and Ram Krishen Saugwan, Kalan Masjid; Dharam Singh Pujari, Ajmere Gate, 21–28 March 1993.

[65]Charanjit Chanana, *An Enquiry into the Socio-economic Conditions of Sweepers Employed in NDMC, 1955–56* (New Delhi: Delhi School of Economics, 1956).

[66]*Hindustan Times*, 9 July 1957.

[67]First notice of the strike was given on 1 July 1957. *Lok Sabha Proceedings* (LSP), 1 August 1957, p. 6357; *Hindustan Times*, 30 July 1957.

[68]Rattan Lal Balmiki, New Delhi, 2 February 1992.

On 31 July, Nehru told Parliament that strikes 'in a public utility or public service affected the community directly and could not be judged from the same point of view as that of an industrial strike'. The sweepers strike was about to be joined by a strike of public sector employees and Nehru warned both that 'it is one thing to have [the right to strike] and another to exercise it irrespective of the consequences'.[69] The NDMC took two steps to avert the crisis. First, it intensified negotiations with the union. In the Lok Sabha, D.P. Karmarkar (Health Minister) promised the 'sympathetic consideration' of local authorities especially because the complaints came from essential workers. 'Some of the demands obviously cannot be granted', Nehru said after his Minister, 'they are outside our scope'.[70] Dayal, echoing Nehru and Karmarkar, told the union that the NDMC was not going to make unilateral decisions and that it did not have the finances to concede the list of demands.[71] The state fabricated a shell of sympathy without any mechanism to solve the crisis at hand. Karmarkar tried to flatter the sweepers with more vague promises, but the union was uninterested.[72] Second, the NDMC relied upon scabs to break the union's back. The *Hindustan Times* reported that 'the enthusiasm of the police to maintain a skeleton sanitary service in the teeth of opposition from the strikers ruined the chances of a settlement'.[73] Baru Ram recalled the jeers and jokes which he and his comrades suffered from the police as they escorted the conscripted sanitary staff in NDMC trucks. The police and the officials, in turn, began to trade insults with the congregated Balmikis.[74]

At 3:30 pm on 31 July 1957, one truck left the NDMC workshop which stands beside the Balmiki Colony. As a second truck tried to leave, the state inquiry argues that 700 strikers surrounded it and pelted the policemen with brickbats.[75] In 'self-defence', the police opened

---

[69]*Hindustan Times*, 1 August 1957. *Raja Kulkarni v. State of Bombay* (1951) and *Ram Krishnian v. President District Board, Nellore* (1952) fought against just this sort of argument.

[70]LSP, 31 July 1957, pp. 6170–1.

[71]*Hindustan Times*, 30 July 1957.

[72]Rattan Lal Balmiki, Balmiki Colony, New Delhi, 4 February 1992.

[73]*Hindustan Times*, 1 August 1957.

[74]Baru Ram and Khilati Ram, New Delhi, March 1992; Bhagwan Das, *Safai Karamchari Dewas, 31 July* (New Delhi, 1990).

[75]Ministry of Home Affairs, *Delhi Firing Inquiry Committee Report* (5/36/-Police I).

fire, stormed the colony, killed one man and injured an indeterminate number. A twelve-year-old boy was arrested along with the other Balmikis, taken to hospital in critical condition and then, handcuffed to his bed. The only 'facts' that stand without challenge are that when the second lorry left the workshop, some sort of disturbance took place, and then, the police opened fire and stormed the colony. MPs who visited the area found neither stones nor brickbats. Some Balmikis told me that they exchanged abusive slogans with the police which annoyed them and DSP Palta ordered a lathi charge. When the Balmikis resisted, someone ordered the police to fire. The animosity towards the state for bringing in the scabs, motivated the Balmikis militancy. 'We were only doing what we had learnt from Gandhi', Bimla Devi told me, 'we were seeking what was just by acting peacefully'. 'What else could we have done'? Baru Ram recalled, 'we had no means to fight, so why would we have tried to provoke the police. We simply wanted what was ours . . . our daily bread and justice'.[76] The shadow of Gandhi indeed hung over the entire proceedings: the hunger strikes, the nonviolent demonstrations, in sum satyagraha in action. The NDMC broke the rules by bringing in the scabs.

In the Lok Sabha, on 1 August, G.B. Pant (Home Minister and, ironically, head of the Hind Sweepers Sevak Samaj) drew on elaborate parliamentary rhetoric to absolve the government of responsibility for the fiasco. The government, he said, 'was sad and sorry'.[77] S.A. Dange (CPI), two days later, summed up the government's mood correctly as 'sympathy in words, no demands to be conceded'.[78] The government did not want to concede any demands, Pant noted, because 'larger interests have to be guarded'. Certain contexts 'compel us to adopt a method which may be altogether unpalatable and even detestable for the sake of guarding the health of large numbers'.[79] Sanitation is beyond democracy, an interest of state which cannot be held to the same standards as the protests for self-rule. That comparison was raised in the Lok Sabha, especially by the communists and socialists, and on the streets by people such as Baru Ram and Bimla Devi, for whom the state had fallen very low indeed. But it is precisely because of these

[76]Baru Ram, Bimla Devi, Rattan Lal Balmiki and others in February–March 1992.

[77]LSP, 1 August 1957.

[78]LSP, 3 August 1957.

[79]LSP, 1 August 1957, pp. 6376–7.

people, the leftists and the exploited that Pant said the bullets had to be fired. 'We realize that the class to which these people [the sweepers] belong have not had the benefit of education or even of refinement. They can be easily led away and their difficulties did not always receive that amount of sympathy and attention which one would very much wish should be given to them'.[80] The people are stupid, the Left are manipulators. However, the sweepers union had by 1957 purged its ranks of communists and it was run by people such as Rattan Lal Balmiki, who to this day has the greatest fear of anyone from the Left. In fact, his own class collaborationist union warned the rank and file, on 2 August, against 'being led by subversive elements into ways that may have led to breach of peace'.[81] The Delhi administration described the crowd as 'excited and determined' which could have done great damage to the police and to the petrol depot, so that the crowd deserved no quarter. The administration declared that 'in emergencies the law permitted the police to resort to firing in self-defence and to protect property'.[82] Who authorizes the police to fire?

The state, in lieu of a clear policy, encouraged the police to take a hardline with the sweepers. Local residents told the press that the 'policemen seemed to be acting in a spirit of revenge'.[83] Stories of police brutality abounded (a pregnant woman was dragged out of her room and kicked repeatedly; police also fired into homes). 'In a small way', said Sadhan Gupta (CPI) who visited the colony, 'it was a replica of Jallianwala Bagh'. It cannot be 'self-defence', he said, 'it is pure vendetta'.[84] The police did not only attack the residents of Balmiki Colony, but they independently cracked down on strikers at Kakanagar, Khan Market and Pharting Lane Cemetery. Sucheta Kriplani (Congress) pointed out that the firing was a 'legacy of British tradition; it is a hangover of British imperialism'.[85] 'It was our Jallianwallah Bagh', young Balmikis said to me in 1992, and indeed, it was. 'It happened in the age of the British', they said, and although their chronology was incorrect, they accurately recorded the event as an act of colonial domination. 'The trigger comes so easily to the fingers of our police',

[80]LSP, 1 August 1957, p. 6376.

[81]*Hindustan Times*, 3 August 1957.

[82]*Hindustan Times*, 1 August 1957.

[83]*Hindustan Times*, 1 August 1957.

[84]LSP, 1 August 1957, p. 6378 and 3 August 1957, p. 6867.

[85]LSP, 3 August 1957, p. 6332.

Sadhan Gupta declared, 'that we have lost even the sense or capacity of being appalled at firing when we hear of one'.[86] The police must be told that they are there to 'preserve peace no doubt', said Surendranath Dwivedy (Praja Socialist Party), 'but they have also a duty to protect and help members of the public'.[87] 'If the police started shooting bullets when we try to fight for our rights', Sadhan Gupta noted, 'it will be an evil day for our country'.[88] A folk song from Meerut offers us an analysis of the state from the standpoint of the dalits, which is close to that of these parliamentarians. 'Kaise hain meri anuyayi', asks a fictional Gandhi, 'maine gaddi jinko dilayi'.[89]

> How are my followers, for whom I achieved political power?
> Are they serving everyone, dying for the well-being
>   of the people?
> How are the bureaucrats, are they the same [as in British days]
>   or have they changed?

Badle bhi hai, ya vaise hai? The question of changelessness resonates in the context of the events of 1957.

The Constitution provided the Balmikis with the right to press for their uplift, even if through the increments of reform, at the same time as it legitimized the state's power. When the state undertook the task of repression to preserve the rule of the dominant classes, it violated the delicate resolution it had forged to dull social contradictions. The moral and intellectual leadership had to condemn the repression in order to retain some element of legitimacy. Further, the regime needed to 'manufacture appearances of accountability' through indifferent criminal prosecutions and commissions of inquiry which led nowhere.[90] In this case, the Delhi administration conducted its own inquiry, which absolved the officials. Nevertheless, an inquiry was conducted and the officials apologized for the 'misunderstandings' which led to violence.

Kanhayalal Balmiki told the Lok Sabha after the firing that 'we know that our backs are bent today, they are bent by the might of the

---

[86]LSP, 3 August 1957, p. 6866.

[87]LSP, 3 August 1957, p. 6875.

[88]LSP, 3 August 1957, p. 6871.

[89]The bhajan was written by Dukhayal and collected by Ved Prakash Vatuk, Thieves in the House (Varanasi: Viswavidyalaya Prakashan, 1969), p. 101.

[90]Upendra Baxi, Towards a Sociology of Law in India (Delhi: Satvahan, 1987), p. 131.

broom. We do not wish to bend in front of bullets. We want our backs to be straight and the conditions that endure today, we know how to fight them, and we do not fear them'.[91] That day, sweepers and their supporters demonstrated outside the Lok Sabha. They shouted slogans such as *Dalli Police ka Nash Ho* (destruction to the pimp police), for *dalli* (as *dalal*) meaning pimp, sounds much like *Dilli* for Delhi. The police are pimps of a regime which hides behind its excesses. Later that day, the dead Balmiki was burned at Nigambodh Ghat. Bhoop Singh had come to visit his sister and he joined the demonstrations in sympathy and anger. He paid the price for a community into which he had been born. The Balmiki community took out a funeral procession which was modelled after the funerals of national heroes in order to remind the nation of the special predicament of dalits. His portrait stands in Gandhi's room of 1946.

From 3 to 6 August 1957, the Lok Sabha debated the ESMO bill. Pant, on 5 August, stated ominously that labourers work 'because they are citizens of the country and they have the privilege to serve the people by rendering essential services'.[92] If work is duty, then A.K. Sen (Minister of Law) was correct to announce that 'the right to strike is not a fundamental right'.[93] The CPI disagreed. An economic contract cannot be seen to be spiritual nor moral; the entire edifice was neither spiritual nor moral, so why should workers view their role in spiritual and moral terms? When the system is immoral, why should workers be made to bear the burden of upholding morality at their own cost? 'To compel a man to accept a certain employment against his will is serfdom', said Dange (CPI), 'and serfdom is ruled out under the fundamental rights of the Constitution under article 19'.[94] 'I am afraid that a new type of fascism is emerging', Naushir Bharucha (CPI) pointed out, 'and this bureaucracy under the guise of maintaining essential services is showing its bare teeth and fangs against labour. I call this bill a break of faith with labour'.[95] The Leftist opposition failed to carry the day. ESMO was passed on 6 August 1957 by 226 votes to 51. Nehru, Shastri, Radha Raman, Jagjivan Ram and Kanhayalal Balmiki voted for the measure.

[91]LSP, 1 August 1957, p. 6382.
[92]LSP, 5 August 1957, p. 7032.
[93]LSP, 3 August 1957, pp. 6731–2.
[94]LSP, 3 August 1957, pp. 6736–7.
[95]LSP, 6 August 1957, p. 7265.

ESMO stands in direct opposition to the sentiments expressed by the Congress and the state after the firing in Balmiki Colony. Nehru, before a trip to Japan a few years later, wrote a firm and fond letter to Rattan Lal Balmiki and urged him to keep the struggle alive. Mr Balmiki is indulgent to Nehru, but he has no patience for Karmarkar (Health Minister) whom he calls '*Hath mar Hath*' (he who gives with one hand and takes with the other). This is his definition of democracy, to offer empty promises. If Gandhi were alive, Mr Balmiki said, 'our condition would not be as it is'. Instead of being popular in his own homeland, Gandhi is well-regarded by foreigners. The days of Gandhi are over and true Gandhians are now morose. In anger, he told me that the very capitalists (*sarmayadar*) who had supported the British took power in 1947 through the force of money and guns. In 1957, the will of Balmiki struggle was broken.[96]

Nehru, before his death, returned to a Gandhian resolution to the emancipation of sweepers. On 2 January 1964, he invited Delhi's sweepers to Ramlila Maidan.[97] Embarrassed by the regime's failure and unhappy that 'all Indians [are unable] to live decently and work honourably', Nehru offered the sweepers a bill of goods (milk, food, shelter, education, health care and dignity). 'This is our government', he said, 'and we have our own Constitution which provides for our worker comrades and that those who are considered "low" should receive special care and protection . . . It gives me great pain to see that although we achieved independence 16 years ago, during which we did much, started big industries, gave attention to agriculture and improved it, yet the weaker sections did not receive proper attention and they did not make sufficient progress'. 'Even though the nation has failed you', Nehru said, 'there is still hope', notably from technology and social ecology. With new latrines and sewage systems, the sweepers had the hope of being liberated from the conditions of their work. With clean homes and the abolition of harmful customs, the sweepers can 'do much in helping yourselves rise and along with you our nation'.[98] Nehru put the onus back on the dalits rather than address their demands.

Within the context of the bourgeois–landlord state, liberation was restricted to the formal pronouncements of equality along with some

[96]Rattan Lal Balmiki, February 1992.
[97]Malkani, *Clean People*, Appendix II.
[98]Ibid.

small gifts (which are both important means to further struggle, but hardly the ends of emancipation). For many Balmikis, the first decade of the state spelled the doom of the project of emancipation. Since then, three inadequate projects dominate the lives of Balmikis: a reliance upon the tired will of the Congress, the turn to Hindutva and a move into the arms of those who are driven solely by some primordial idea of dalitness. The state's inability to produce equality (whether by social engineering or social struggle or some combination of the two) created some measure of distrust amongst the Balmikis and destroyed their faith in its authority. Instead, they replaced that faith with the authority of faith, with the conviction that the militant Hindu agenda would work for them. In this sense, the activities of the young Balmikis within the Hindutva ensemble these days speaks of a protest against their exploitation, even though it is a protest which fails to fully grasp its horrid limitations. The presence of the communist parties in dalit localities (as is now so in both Karol Bagh and in the old city), in addition, shows us that the fight continues and it is far from over. The revival of Ambedkar within some elements of the community due to the assertion of the Lohiaite and Ambedkarist Social Democrats and to the events around the Mandal Commission (1990) offers some hope for a reconstruction of a radical agenda. Such an agenda will need to offer as its minimum postulate the need for a fusion between dalit politics and the politics of exploited and oppressed people in general. A recognition of the importance of the history of such attempted fusions will perhaps drive forward this necessary strategy.

Epilogue

One warm evening in Jalandhar, in the company of a number of veterans of the Ad-Dharm movement, Rolu Ram told me about the value of clichés. People hate them, he said, because they have been heard before. If there is no change in the·conditions represented in the cliché then the phrase bears repetition. The value of poetry, he continued, is its ability to take general sentiments and put them into wondrous phrases; his own special poet is Mohammed Iqbal, whose imaginative use of language invokes much appreciation among these Balmiki elders. Rolu Ram was not to recite Iqbal on this evening; he simply offered me a cliché, *unhan de andaron aje chhut chhat di badbu a rahi hai* (the stench of casteism arises from within them).[1] For the Balmikis, he said, the phrase is a cliché in the less well-known meaning of the word, a commonplace statement. When I asked, impertinently, why the community appeared so willing to make alliances with those who looked down upon them, the veterans smiled and told me that I should ask the youth. The elders were done with the travails of struggle.

   In Delhi, a few days before, I sat with a group of Balmiki elders at the Maharishi Shri Valmiki Mandir off Mandir Marg.[2] The evening prayer, the aarti, was over and a group of men and women sat in the vicinity of the temple talking about my ongoing research as well as of the problems of India. The Babri Masjid lay in ruins in Ayodhya, the flames of Behrampada and of Seelampur still smouldered and the right-wing political formations began to make energetic appeals to the Balmikis for support in their anti-Muslim, anti-poor project. Just a month prior, Sampradayikta Virodhi Andolan and the People's Movement for Secularism adopted the temple grounds for the start of a peaceful protest march which ended at Gandhi's *samadhi* (memorial). As we spoke, Rattan Lal Balmiki was in the midst of a dharna against the municipality; he wanted them to remove their workshop which blocked a view of the temple from the road. Again, the Balmiki Colony on Mandir Marg was at the centre of history. That March evening, young boys returned to a few more overs of cricket on the playing-field

[1]Rolu Ram, Jalandhar, 6 April 1993.
[2]Balmiki Colony, New Delhi, 28 March 1993.

and young girls turned to their household chores and their sewing classes which are conducted on the fringes of the temple. The conversation, disturbed only by the sounds of the young and of the animals who stood tethered beside us, turned to the future of the Balmiki community and to the problems of leadership. Babu Krishen took the floor and told a story of the sacrifice (*qurbani*) of leaders:

In the realm of a king, a priest put a mantra into the kingdom's only well. The mantra would make all those who drank from it mad. Only the king and his vizier [minister] knew of this and they hid in the palace. The subjects drank the water and went mad. In time, they gathered outside the palace shouting to the king: you are mad, come down you sister-fucker. The vizier asked the king, 'do you love yourself more or your people'. If you love yourself, lets run away from here. If you love your people, lets go and drink from the well and be mad like the rest. The king said, I am of the people—I must be mad with them. So they drank and joined the people.

After Babu Krishen, Maharaj Chena told a parable, with an altogether different meaning:

In a realm, there was famine. The king toured the region to see if he could do something. He came to a badly distressed village. The people all offered their stories. He said, choose a leader who will come to me to represent your case. The people began to bicker, one with the other. The king said, 'I'll go now; you choose a leader and send the leader to my darbar tomorrow'. The next day the entire village arrived and the king surmized that no leader had been chosen. He said, I have a tank of water into which I shall throw this ball. The person who gets it first will be the leader. One person ran towards the tank, an elder caught his foot, another caught his foot, another held his foot. . . .

The point was very clear and the discussion which ensued allowed the two parables to set its framework. At one end, the leaders must be good and at the other end, the people must be willing to put forward a leader whom they will support, and the people must be happy to see success amongst themselves and not tear down each other. What was most striking about the two stories was the premise of the king's benevolence. In both stories, the king acts justly, but the people are the ones who fail. These tales clarify the Balmikis' relationship with the state, for their social being is structured in direct subordination to the will of the state: as municipal employees, they are at the state's behest; as Scheduled Castes, they must beg the state for those offerings which are seen less as a right and more as charity; as those among the forgotten under class, they are at the mercy of those instruments of the state (such as the police and the petty bureaucracy) who put their very homes under threat. The memory of 1957 reminds the Balmikis that their own syndicalist actions are inefficient compared to the military might of the state. Given these parameters, the vast bulk of the Balmikis find themselves forced to act as if the state were considerate.

From 1957 until the present, the Balmikis made many attempts to reconstruct the forms of political protest forged during the period under review, but none of the struggles produced significant political projects. The 1950s put paid to even the faint glimmers of Balmiki initiative, as the community took shelter in the putative benevolence of the state and the Congress. The principal reason for this defensive attitude amongst the bulk of the organized Balmiki population came from the relentless campaigns against the various political forms developed from the 1920s onwards. Not only did the Congress combat the militancy of the safai karamchari trade unions, but the guardians of the established order also went after the Balmiki cultural and social groups as well as after the many political formations floated by B.R. Ambedkar and his followers. Balmiki politics came under the hegemony of the Congress and of the Hindutva factions from the 1950s and the Balmikis found themselves in a position of subservience to the petty satraps in the Congress organization and to the class of municipal administrators. In places such as Delhi, the alliance of the Hindus (many from Punjabi refugee trader communities) in the Congress and in the municipality faced the amorphous and defeated Balmikis with an immense sense of self-confidence and superiority. The dominant Balmiki attitude of servitude towards the state (in spite of the occasional sensibility of anger against the state's representatives) stems from this reliance for succour upon the state and its representatives.

In 1943, B.R. Ambedkar criticized the Harijan Sevak Sangh and the Congress for its distribution of 'petty gifts to petty untouchables', since this was 'buying, benumbing and drawing the claws of the opposition of the untouchables which [Gandhi] knows is the only force which will disrupt the caste system and will establish real democracy in India'.[3] Such a critique of purchased loyalty and of the degradation of community dignity recalls the struggles of the dalits to forge their own destiny, one thwarted by the many circumstances detailed in this book. Half a century ago, Ambedkar offered a slogan which is not heard much these days, *Bhangi Jharoo Choro* (Bhangi, Leave the Broom). He believed that the first step toward liberation was to be a permanent and collec-

---

[3]B.R. Ambedkar, 'Mr Gandhi and the Emancipation of the Untouchables (1943)', *Writings and Speeches*, vol. 9, p. 431.

tive withdrawal of dalits from menial occupations. Ambedkar consistently argued that we should abolish the idea of dalithood, being careful not to obliterate in the process the creative cultures produced by dalits. An abolition of dalithood cannot occur if we continue to rely upon those structures that keep the dalits in place. The end to dalithood cannot be enacted through the law only, but it has to be struggled for as part of the class struggle which continues to define our modern world. If our present is to be bearable, we are under a moral obligation to join in that dream to construct a nation in which each member feels the 'longing to belong' and the capacity to enact that desire.[4]

[4]B.R. Ambedkar, 'The Triumph of Brahmanism: Regicide or the Birth of the Counter-Revolution', *Writings and Speeches*, vol. 3, p. 309.

Glossary

akharas	gymnasiums
ashraf	respectable classes
dalaos	trash depots
Dalits (lit. oppressed)	untouchables
dalitudhar	uplift of dalits
gotra	filial form of caste
jamadar	overseer-jobber
jati	experiential form of caste
kabaari	recyclable trash
kursinamas	genealogies
mohallas	neighbourhoods
pirs	saints
qaum	community
rais	èlite
razil	working classes
safai karamcharis	sanitation workers
satyagraha	action on the basis of truth
varna	vedic/textual form of caste
varnavyavastha	organization of four varnas

Archival Sources

MANUSCRIPT SOURCES: OFFICIAL

Delhi State Archives, New Delhi.

Miscellaneous files of records for the period 1857-1912

Proceedings of the Chief Commissioner, 1912-30 (notably in the Departments of Home, Education, Local Self-Government, Revenue and Agriculture, and Military)

Files of the Deputy Commissioner's Office

Delhi Municipal Corporation, Records Department, Town Hall, Delhi.

Delhi Municipal Proceedings, 1879 onwards

National Archives of India, New Delhi.

Government of India, Home Department Proceedings (in the following branches: Census, Education, Judicial, Medical, Military, Municipalities, Police, Political, Public ['Delhi'], Sanitary)

Government of India, Education Department Proceedings (in the following branches: Municipalites and Sanitary)

Government of India, Revenue and Agriculture Department Proceedings (in the following branches: Agriculture, Famine and Land Revenue)

Report on Vernacular Newspapers (also called Selections from Vernacular Newspapers) for Northwest Provinces & Oudh and Punjab

Nehru Memorial Museum and Library, New Delhi

Delhi Central Intelligence Department Proceedings, Special Branch Papers

MANUSCRIPT SOURCES: UNOFFICIAL

All-India Congress Committee, papers (NMML)

Balmiki, Rattan Lal, papers, miscelleny and photo album (Courtesy, Shri R.L. Balmiki, Balmiki Colony, New Delhi)

Bhole, R.R., papers (NMML)

Chandiwala, Brij Krishen, papers (NMML)

Gandhi, M.K., papers (Gandhi Memorial Museum, Delhi)

Harijan Sevak Sangh, papers (Harijan Sevak Sangh, Kingsway Camp, Delhi)

Malkani, N.R., papers (NMML)

Nehru, Jawaharlal, papers (NMML)

Oral History Transcripts (NMML: Chhabil Das, Ganpat Rai, Guru Dutt, Jugal Kishore Khanna, Lala Feroze Chand, Mohan Lal, Murli Dhar Taneja, Padma Kant Malaviya and Santram)

Pandit, Nanak Chand, papers (NMML)

Rai, Ganpat, papers (NMML)

Sapru, T.B., papers (National Library, Calcutta)

United Society for the Propagation of the Gospel (NMML)

Index